When Government Fails

When Government Fails

The Orange County Bankruptcy

Mark Baldassare

UNIVERSITY OF CALIFORNIA PRESS
Berkeley · Los Angeles · London

A joint publication with the
Public Policy Institute of California

University of California Press
Berkeley and Los Angeles, California

University of California Press, Ltd.
London, England

© 1998 by
The Regents of the University of California

Library of Congress Cataloging-in-Publication Data
Baldassare, Mark.
   When government fails : the Orange County
bankruptcy / Mark Baldassare.
      p.   cm.
   Includes bibliographical references and index.
   ISBN 0-520-21485-4 (alk. paper). —
ISBN 0-520-21486-2 (pbk. : alk. paper)
   1. Investment of public funds—California—
Orange County. 2. Derivative securities. 3. Debts,
Public—California—Orange County. 4. Municipal
bankruptcy—California—Orange County.
5. Citron, Robert L.   I. Title.
HJ3835.C3B35   1998
336.794'96—dc21   9732806
                                                CIP

Printed in the United States of America

9 8 7 6 5 4 3 2 1

The paper used in this publication meets the minimum requirements of American National Standard
for Information Sciences—Permanence of Paper for
Printed Library Materials, ANSI Z39.48-1984.

Compositor: Publication Services, Inc.
Text: 10/13 Sabon
Display: Sabon
Printer and Binder: Haddon Crafstmen, Inc.

We have perfected the reverse repo procedure to new levels. . . . The downside risk is very minimal.

Bob Citron, before the Orange County
bankruptcy in December 1994

Contents

List of Tables

Foreword

It is rare for a local government to declare bankruptcy, and even rarer for a government that is one of the fastest growing, richest counties in America. *When Government Fails: The Orange County Bankruptcy* by Mark Baldassare is a compelling account of how voters' fiscal conservatism and the pressure for high-quality public services came into conflict. This story is being played out in numerous local governments throughout California and, increasingly, throughout America. As California legislators and administrators at the city and county levels struggle with severe restrictions on their ability to raise local revenues, recently tightened by the passage of Proposition 218, the temptation to search for "creative solutions" will only intensify. Orange County's creative solution was dramatic, short-lived, and risky—a gamble with the taxpayers' money and trust. Like most gambles with the public trust, it did not pay off.

Mark Baldassare joined the Public Policy Institute of California (PPIC) as a visiting fellow with a commitment to analyze what had happened in Orange County and to place that experience in the broader context of changing local government in California. He is uniquely positioned to carry out such a study, given his many years as a recognized scholar on suburban America and his thorough knowledge of Orange County gained from his experience as director of the highly regarded Orange County Annual Survey. Dr. Baldassare's identification of the importance of the bankruptcy for the future of local government finance in California makes the study a natural complement to the evolving research agenda of PPIC.

When PPIC was launched in mid-1994, state and local governance was the subject most frequently cited as worthy of immediate attention. This analysis of the Orange County bankruptcy is especially satisfying in that it meets three of our initial criteria for establishing a research agenda. First, the topic is of *long-term significance*, but the findings are also *timely* and *relevant* to the ongoing debate. Second, a whole chapter is devoted to *practical recommendations* of immediate use at the county and state levels. And third, PPIC was able to support someone who had *substantial knowledge* of the subject before embarking on the project. This represented both an efficient use of PPIC resources and an opportunity for a scholar to take on a subject that might otherwise not have been his highest priority.

This book represents one of many studies now under way at PPIC addressing the financial future of state and local government in California. Much has been written about the implications of the fiscal limitation movement, but the documentation and analysis needed to provide an understanding of what is happening are still rather thin. PPIC was created by its cofounders, Roger Heyns and William Hewlett, for the specific purpose of providing the numbers, analysis, and talent needed to improve our knowledge of issues such as the one addressed in this book—the management of local government in an atmosphere of long-term fiscal retrenchment. *When Government Fails* is PPIC's first major contribution to an improved understanding of public finance in California. We trust that its findings and recommendations will be a well-received and constructive contribution.

David W. Lyon
President and CEO
Public Policy Institute of California

Acknowledgments

The writing of a book about the Orange County bankruptcy was not an easy task, even for an urban scholar who was an eyewitness to this shocking event. This project would never have been possible without financial support, research assistance, and encouragement from a variety of people and institutions.

I was a visiting scholar at the Public Policy Institute of California in San Francisco while writing this book. The institute provided me with partial funding for a sabbatical from teaching, an office and library, and administrative support. I am very grateful to David Lyon, the president, for his belief in the importance of this project and for all of his words of encouragement along the way. I benefited from the many experts on the state's population, governance, and the economy on site. The research fellows and staff members who helped me in various ways included Mike Teitz, John Ellwood, Paul Lewis, Hans Johnson, Michael Dardia, Ed Feasel, Fred Silva, Andy Grose, Joanne Spetz, Michael Shires, and Mary Sprague. I received valuable comments about the book during a roundtable discussion that was held at the Public Policy Institute of California on March 7, 1997. The roundtable participants included Ray Watson, Richard Robinson, Rudy Nothenberg, David Brodsly, David Lyon, Fred Silva, Mike Teitz, Andy Isserman, Paul Lewis, and Michael Shires. I benefited from reviews of the manuscript by Terry Clark, Sherry Bebitch Jeffe, Cheryl Katz, Max Neiman, Jack Peltason, Joyce Peterson, Kim Rueben, and Seymour Sachs. I appreciate the careful reading and editing of the copy-edited manuscript by Arabella Cureton.

I was also fortunate to have an affiliation at the Institute of Urban and Regional Development at U.C. Berkeley during my sabbatical year. This gave me opportunities to meet and discuss ideas for my book with urban scholars such as Claude Fischer, Don Foley, Judith Innes, Alan Jacobs, Marty Wachs, and Melvin Webber.

I also wish to thank Marc Levin and the staff at the Institute of Governmental Studies Library at the University of California at Berkeley. They provided me with a steady stream of books, government reports, articles, and news clips on the bankruptcy.

I also want to acknowledge the helpful advice of Terry Clark, who is the director of the Fiscal Austerity and Urban Innovation Project at the University of Chicago. I had a number of conversations with Terry while working on this project. He provided me with his earlier papers and shared his ideas. His writings have influenced my thoughts about the governance issues that are evident in the Orange County bankruptcy, especially the role of New Fiscal Populists and state fiscal austerity.

The University of California at Irvine allowed me to take a nine-month sabbatical leave from my duties as chair of the Department of Urban and Regional Planning. I am grateful to Dan Stokols for his continuing support of my research endeavors and to several department colleagues. Chancellor Laurel Wilkening and Executive Vice Chancellor Sidney Golub also delivered encouraging words on this project. I received library and research assistance from Christine Maher and Mandy Krawitz in our department staff.

I could not have written this book without the background information from the U.C. Irvine Orange County Annual Survey. I am appreciative of the financial support that I received from the University of California at Irvine and the many local corporations, foundations, and government agencies that helped to fund this study. The Orange County Annual Survey is a random telephone survey of 1,000 households that I have directed each year since 1982. This ongoing project on political, social, and economic trends has played a major role in my developing knowledge and ideas about the Orange County region and U.S. suburban regions in general. Shortly after I arrived in Orange County in 1981, it became obvious to me that Orange County was a trend-setting suburb and that my time and energy as an urban scholar should be directed toward monitoring the trends in public opinion, demographics, and governance in this region. I had no idea that the books, papers, and reports from this project would one day make a major contribution to understanding the worst municipal bankruptcy in modern U.S. history.

Many of the local government officials, business leaders, and heads of nonprofit organizations that I met in the course of conducting the Orange County Annual Survey also played significant roles at various stages in the Orange County financial crisis. I talked to many of these community leaders on a regular basis during the crisis and interviewed some in the summer of 1996, after the county exited from bankruptcy. Much useful information and many interesting insights were offered in their behind-the-scenes accounts. They took a great deal of time off from their busy schedules to talk to me and gather documents that could contribute knowledge for this book. The primary motivation for most of these individuals was to pass along to others what they had learned from the financial crisis. I thank these local leaders for transferring the trust they had in me as a local public opinion expert to the very different domain of an independent scholar writing a book about a delicate and controversial local issue.

Several people close to the bankruptcy were so kind as to offer their files, notes, news clips, press releases, and reports. These include Bob Haskell, Paul Brady, Vicki Matthews, Tom Matthews, Nina Nghia Vo Nguyen, Kathleen Freed, Ernie Schneider, Mike Ruane, Gary Hunt, Jan Mittermeir, John Moorlach, Stan Oftelie, Roger Stanton, Brad Gates, Dan Young, Janet Huston, Gary Hausdorfer, Hank Adler, and Peter Case. I also received useful information from Dr. Sherry Bebitch Jeffe of the Claremont Graduate University about the state's role in the Orange County bankruptcy.

The *Los Angeles Times* Orange County edition commissioned several public opinion polls that I conducted during the Orange County financial crisis. These news surveys provide a record of public opinion from December 1994 to November 1996 that is integral to this book. I wish to thank Carol Stogsdill, senior editor, for allowing me to conduct these polls. Martin Baron, the Orange County editor, provided many good ideas about survey questions and gave me considerable freedom in the survey design. Marty Baron also loaned me all of the transcripts from the Orange County grand jury investigation of the financial crisis, which are an important source of information about the causes and initial responses to the bankruptcy. I also wish to thank Bill Nottingham, Lenny Bernstein, Eric Bailey, Dan Morain, Shelby Grad, Michael Wagner, and Renee Lynch of the *Los Angeles Times* for sharing their detailed knowledge and sources about several elements of the bankruptcy.

I also received assistance from the *Orange County Register.* Michael Fried provided me with demographic trends during the financial crisis. Elliott Blair Smith shared with me some of the knowledge he had gained in covering the bankruptcy.

I would like to thank Cheryl Katz for her assistance at every stage of this project. We collaborated on the data collection and statistical analysis of the Orange County Annual Survey and the Times Orange County Poll. Cheryl also provided some library research for relevant books and journal articles and a search for newspaper articles on the bankruptcy. She also offered suggestions on how to conduct the in-depth interviews, was a good listener throughout the project, and provided honest feedback and advice after reading the manuscript. Our children, Benjamin and Daniel, motivated me with their curiosity about all of the time I was devoting to writing and to my daily progress. I hope they will someday read this book and find lessons for life in these pages.

Mark Baldassare
San Francisco
November 1997

CHAPTER I

Introduction

Roots of the Bankruptcy

Orange County, California, became the largest municipality in U.S. history to declare bankruptcy when it filed for Chapter 9 protection at 4:52 P.M. on December 6, 1994. Municipal bankruptcies are rare events that generally occur only in rural places. Large cities had always sidestepped bankruptcies when their state governments came to the rescue. On that date in December 1994, the fifth most populous county in the United States, a suburban region with two and a half million residents, began an odyssey that may well rewrite the books on local fiscal crises in the United States.

This Southern California county, in between Los Angeles and San Diego, is best known as the home of Disneyland and the rich and famous who live in its million-dollar "Gold Coast" homes. It is also the unofficial capital of Republican politics, claiming Richard Nixon as a native son and electing a string of outspoken conservatives to Congress. A municipal bankruptcy was a shocking turn of events for a county with a national reputation for its affluent residents and conservative politicians.

When Government Fails provides a comprehensive analysis of the Orange County bankruptcy. This introductory chapter presents a framework for understanding the unique nature and outcome of this financial crisis. The chapters that follow delve into the underlying causes of the fiscal catastrophe. We then follow the dramatic story from the events that led up to the bankruptcy, through the local officials' response to the fiscal emergency and the road to recovery, to the local government reforms implemented in response to the crisis. This book also discusses the larger lessons to be learned from the mistakes made in Orange County and offers policy recommendations for state and local governments to avoid future fiscal catastrophes.

WHAT HAPPENED?

The Orange County government backed into a massive financial crisis in a most unusual manner. County Treasurer Bob Citron was in charge of the Orange County Investment Pool. By 1994 he had gathered about $7.6 billion in deposits from the county government and nearly 200 local public agencies. Citron had a track record of providing high-interest income to his local government investors. He boasted, "We have perfected the reverse repo procedure to new levels." He did this by borrowing money and investing it in derivatives, inverse floaters, and long-term bonds that paid high yields. Then he borrowed more money with the borrowed money. By 1994 the size of the county pool had ballooned to $20.6 billion as he borrowed $2 for every $1 on deposit. He was on a desperate mission in which he took more risks to raise more interest income for local governments that had recently seen their tax allocations cut by the state. The Federal Reserve Board kept raising interest rates throughout 1994. Bob Citron kept buying securities on the hunch that the Fed would lower rates at the end of the year.

In the spring of 1994 the challenger in the county treasurer's race issued warnings that the county pool had suffered massive losses and did not have the cash to pay back the massive short-term loans to the Wall Street firms. No one listened. Citron won reelection and kept betting on lower interest rates throughout the summer months. The Board of Supervisors and other county officials did not stop him until it was too late. By November 1994 county officials found out that he had lost about $1.64 billion in government funds through these risky investments. The county did not have the cash on hand to withstand a run on the money by the Wall Street lenders and local government depositors. County officials went into panic mode in early December. They urged and sought their treasurer's resignation. They unsuccessfully tried to sell off the risky securities. The banks that had lent Citron the money threatened to seize the securities from the county pool that they held as collateral. The county government declared bankruptcy after the first bank took this action. Their hope that the bankruptcy filing would halt other fund seizures by the Wall Street lenders proved to be misguided. The bankruptcy, however, did stop the fund withdrawals by the local government depositors. The county government, twenty-nine of thirty-one Orange County cities, all of the school districts, and most of the transportation, water, and sanitation agencies had large sums of money on deposit. Their $7.6 billion in government funds were now frozen.

The days after the bankruptcy declaration in Orange County were filled with chaos and confusion. The county supervisors were seeking a way to keep the county government functioning. They were also trying to limit the financial meltdown of the county pool, which had a real possibility of experiencing further massive losses if interest rates rose again. Officials from the schools, cities, and special districts were trying to assess the damage that would be done to their local operations by the bankruptcy. Their feelings of betrayal and distrust toward the county officials who held their money were growing. The public was venting its anger and frustration toward local elected officials, whom they blamed for allowing such an irresponsible use of taxpayer money. There were threats of a state takeover and the temporary appointment of a state trustee if the fiscal crisis in Orange County grew worse. But there was no signal that the state government would provide a bailout for this struggling county.

The Orange County fiscal crisis had many twists and turns from the dark days in December 1994 to the emergence from bankruptcy eighteen months later, in June 1996. The county's credit rating immediately fell to "junk status," and the Wall Street firms continued to sell off the billions of dollars in securities they held as collateral for the county's borrowing. A former state treasurer, Tom Hayes, was called in to manage the county pool. By late January Hayes had sold off the risky securities and established the pool loss at $1.64 billion. He set up a mechanism allowing the local governments to withdraw some of their funds from the pool on an emergency basis. In December the Board of Supervisors appointed the county sheriff and two other county officials to a crisis team to keep the county government working. They made sure that the county programs had the funding they needed and recommended a first round of budget cuts. A local financial executive, Bill Popejoy, was appointed to the new position of chief executive officer of the county government in early February. He set in motion the severe staff and budget cuts that were needed to balance the budget and made a sweeping housecleaning of the county officials who were tainted by the fiscal collapse. Three local business leaders headed up a negotiating team that arranged a settlement between the county government and the cities, schools, and special districts on how to divide the remaining county pool funds. Local governments could get most of their deposits right away, with promises to get the rest back at a later date, if they agreed not to sue the county government. This settlement plan was approved by all parties.

By March 1995 the Board of Supervisors reluctantly placed a proposal for a half-cent sales tax increase on the ballot as part of the financial recovery plan for Orange County. They had run out of other ideas to pay for the mounting debts of their bankrupt county government. A worse financial crisis seemed imminent, since there were $1 billion in bonds coming due in the summer months and no way to borrow this money. Local voters overwhelmingly defeated the sales tax increase on June 27, 1995, after a campaign that saw local elected officials distance themselves from this county ballot measure. This would create a mad scramble for another recovery plan. The governor refused to bail out the county and threatened a state takeover. The bond investors agreed to roll over the county's debts for another year in exchange for more interest earnings.

After a few false starts, a recovery plan was shaped by the county government in August 1995. They would divert tax funds from other county agencies to the general fund so they could borrow the money to pay bondholders and vendors. The local governments who lost money in the county pool agreed to wait for the county to win the lawsuits they had filed against Wall Street firms to be paid back in full. The state legislature passed the bills that were needed to divert the current tax dollars to a recovery fund, and the governor signed the bills in October 1995. The county presented its recovery plan to the U.S. bankruptcy court in December 1995, a year after its Chapter 9 filing. In June 1996 the county government sold the $880 million in bonds it needed to pay off its debts. The Orange County bankruptcy officially ended on June 12, 1996.

The bankruptcy is over, yet this is far from a happy ending for Orange County. The county government had to take on a crushing level of long-term debt to resolve its fiscal problems. Orange County's bonds are still rated as speculative, meaning that the county pays a higher cost for borrowing. The local governments are still about $850 million short because of the funds they are still owed from the county pool. All of this limits the abilities of the local governments to respond to current needs and plan for the future. Most hurt are the county's poor, whose services were cut during the bankruptcy and have not been fully restored. The only hope for financial recovery is if the county wins the billions of dollars in lawsuits filed against the Wall Street firms that did business with the county treasurer. That hope remains a dream as of this writing.

WHY DOES IT MATTER?

The Orange County bankruptcy is worthy of careful consideration for several reasons. First, this is the biggest municipal bankruptcy in U.S. history. Previous bankruptcies involved relatively small sums of money and took place mostly in rural locales. Never before had a local government in a large municipality taken the step of declaring bankruptcy. Nor were the amounts previously lost close to $1.64 billion.

This fiscal crisis in local government was also like no other. The bankruptcy was in a growing suburban county rather than a declining central city. It was precipitated by a risky investment strategy instead of a shortage of taxes and too much spending. The fiscal crisis had serious implications for a large number of local governments, not just one municipal government. The county government was forced to redirect existing tax dollars rather than turning to the state for a bailout. Orange County was able to exit bankruptcy in eighteen months, whereas fiscal crises usually take years to resolve.

The Orange County bankruptcy also merits scrutiny because the same problems could be repeated in other municipalities throughout the United States. Orange County is not the only municipality where local officials are searching for creative ways to increase their revenues in order to provide more public services. Many local governments are operating under tight fiscal conditions. Elected officials in numerous locales are faced with voters' demands for more public services and their unwillingness to pay higher taxes. Other local governments also have structures that allow public officials to operate with great autonomy and little fiscal oversight. It is thus important to identify the lessons to be learned from the Orange County experience.

This book seeks to fill a large void in the knowledge about the Orange County bankruptcy. There has been a blizzard of news stories about this event, but the emphasis of the media inquiries has generally been narrow. The few scholarly works on the subject to date tend to focus on the investment and finance issues surrounding the bankruptcy (see Jorion, 1995; Kearns, 1995; Petersen, 1995; Flickinger and McManus, 1996; Johnson and Mikesell, 1996; Chapman, 1996; Johnston, 1996; Lewis, 1996; Jump, 1996). So far the Orange County fiscal crisis has not generated the amount and variety of scholarly research seen following fiscal crises in big cities (see Clark, 1976; Sinnreich, 1980; McClelland and Magdovitz, 1981; Benjamin and Brecher, 1988; Liebschutz, 1991; Fuchs, 1992) or when Proposition 13 passed in California (see Sears and Citrin, 1982; Kaufman and Rosen, 1981; Laffer and Seymour, 1979; O'Sullivan, Sexton, and Sheffrin, 1995; Schwadron and Richter, 1984; Adams, 1984; Lo, 1990). Yet the size, nature, and relevance of the Orange County fiscal crisis point to the fact that an objective and comprehensive analysis of this event is needed. This book is written with the goal of providing a detailed account of the bankruptcy and its implications for a broad audience of policymakers, academic scholars, politicians, and concerned citizens.

SHOCK VALUE

The Orange County financial crisis was a surprising event for many people. The residents of Orange County, the local news media, and local elected officials were astonished to learn that their county government had declared bankruptcy. So were the sophisticated Wall Street investors, state leaders, federal officials, academics, and public policy experts. This fiscal disaster was unlike any that had been previously seen or even considered. Many observers began to wonder if this unexpected crisis could be repeated elsewhere. This book considers some of the special qualities of the Orange County bankruptcy, each of which offers an important reason to study this extraordinary event carefully.

At the outset, it is important to note that municipal bankruptcies are very uncommon events. The *New York Times* headline on December 7, 1994, "In Rare Move, California County Files for Bankruptcy Protection" (*New York Times,* 1994a), speaks to the shock value generated by a bankruptcy court filing. Although businesses and individuals commonly rely on the bankruptcy courts to sort out their financial troubles, this is not the case for local governments. The Chapter 9 bankruptcy filing was created for municipalities during the Great Depression. However, there had been only 491 municipal bankruptcies in the United States between 1937 and 1994. Since 1980 there had been 120 municipal bankruptcy filings. To place this number in perspective, there were an average of 16,000 U.S. corporate bankruptcies per year in the 1980s (California Debt Advisory Commission, 1995, pp. 49–50; *New York Times,* 1994a).

Although municipal bankruptcies are rare, a Chapter 9 filing by a large local government was unprecedented prior to the Orange County case. Before December 1994 most municipal bankruptcies involved small cities and small special districts in rural places. In 1991 Bridgeport, Connecticut, became one of the larger places to file for Chapter 9 protection, but the court ultimately disallowed the bankruptcy and ruled that they were able to pay their bills. Large cities such as New York, Philadelphia, Cleveland, and Washington have been on the brink of financial disaster, but in every one of these cases a bankruptcy filing was avoided (California Debt Advisory Commission, 1995, pp. 49–50; *New York Times,* 1994a). Financial markets had grown to accept the fact that municipal bonds were safe. Even the large and troubled local governments ended up paying their debts and escaping bankruptcy. The Orange County event thus redefined the expected outcome of municipal fiscal stress.

The Orange County financial crisis was on a scale never seen before. The county government had a budget of over $3.7 billion and had about 18,000 employees. The Orange County Investment Pool that was frozen by the bankruptcy filing was a $20 billion fund that had lost about $1.6 billion. The county government defaulted on over $100 million in bonds within days of the bankruptcy. It found itself in real danger of defaulting on over $1 billion in short-term debt within a few months. Previous bankruptcies had typically involved relatively small amounts of money.[1] For instance, the 362 filings between 1937 and 1994 amounted to a total debt for those municipalities of only about $217 million. Other estimates place the average default per municipal bankruptcy at $2 million throughout the 1970s (California Debt Advisory Commission, 1995, pp. 49–50; *New York Times,* 1994a). The Orange County case was the first instance in which there were large sums of money in a municipal bankruptcy.

Moreover, the cause of the Orange County financial crisis represented a new scenario for local fiscal problems. In sum, the county treasurer had invested local government funds in risky ways that resulted in the loss of large amounts of public money. Local fiscal stress usually occurs because a large central city is caught in a situation of rising expenditures, such as growing health care and welfare rolls, and declin-

1. The biggest previous bankruptcy involved the Washington Public Power Supply System. The issue here was the inability to pay back $2 billion in tax-exempt bonds for the construction of nuclear power plants (*New York Times,* 1994a).

ing tax revenues, resulting, for example, from middle-class residents and businesses moving out of the central city. At some point the lenders lose confidence in the central city's ability to pay its mounting debts. The investment firms did not stop lending funds to Orange County because the local tax and spending environment had changed. Orange County had one of the highest credit ratings of any county government in California up to a few months before the bankruptcy filing. The Orange County debts were the result of a leveraging of county funds to buy risky securities to create more interest income. A municipality with no outward signs of fiscal stress had brought problems upon itself.

In the past when large cities were near bankruptcy, their state governments always came to their aid. For instance, the state government would extend the city credit or provide state backing for the local government bonds when the financial markets became nervous about the municipality's ability to pay its debts. One reason state governments would act to avoid a local fiscal calamity is because they did not want to place a large number of residents at risk of losing their police and fire protection, schools, and other essential services. Another reason is that a municipal bankruptcy could have ripple effects on other local governments and even on the state's ability to borrow money. A financial adviser to state and local governments said about the Orange County financial crisis, "In every other major credit crisis in government in the last 25 years, states have taken a lead role. . . . There is an implied moral obligation of states to help their municipalities" (*New York Times*, 1995a). However, the California state government did not intervene to enable Orange County to avoid a bankruptcy filing. Nor did the state government offer to lend money or back local bond offerings to end the bankruptcy. There were many reasons for this inaction, including the fiscal austerity of California's government in the 1990s. Still, the limited role of the state in this case is a major departure from the ways that large municipal fiscal crises were handled in the past.

The fact that the Orange County financial crisis occurred in a suburban region is another special quality of this event. Large cities are generally the local government entities that get into big financial troubles. Moreover, most municipal bankruptcy filings involve tiny local governments in rural areas. The suburban regions are supposed to have fiscally responsible local governments, with their middle-class residents providing a dependable revenue source. There is simply no precedent for a suburban county government encountering a serious fiscal crisis. It turns out that the suburban context of the Orange County bankruptcy had a role in generating the fiscal problems and limited the ability to have an effective early response to the crisis.

Another important attribute of the Orange County financial crisis is that it struck so many local government entities at once. In previous instances, such as in New York or Cleveland, one large city was faced with a serious fiscal problem. Once again, the fact that the Orange County event occurred in a suburban metropolitan region added a new twist. This county has almost 200 local government entities, including the county government, thirty-one cities, the regional transportation agency, the local school districts, local water agencies, sanitation districts, and many small local special districts. Almost every local government in Orange County had money on deposit in the county pool. When the Orange County Investment Pool went into a tailspin, causing the county government to declare bankruptcy, the funds of all of the local governments were also frozen. The basic public services in Orange County are provided by this large, diverse, and decentralized group of local governments and public agencies. This suburban system of delivering local services is so decentralized that it created a great deal of uncertainty about how residents would be affected by the Orange County bankruptcy. Later on, finding a solution to the fiscal crisis would be complicated by the fact that so many local government leaders would have to agree on a recovery plan.

In the past, voters in local elections had not usually been asked how they would like to resolve their fiscal crisis. All of this was to change with the Orange County bankruptcy. In places such as New York or Cleveland, local taxes and fees would be raised, and local budgets would be cut, as the city officials and state government saw fit. Nearly two decades earlier California voters had placed restrictions on their local governments' abilities to raise taxes. If a tax increase were needed for Orange County to repay its debts and emerge from bankruptcy, this would have to be approved by the local voters. The fact that the local voters had veto power over recovery plans was an unprecedented situation. This realization about post–Proposition 13 California shook to the foundations the relations between California municipalities, bond investors, and Wall Street firms. County government was forced into creative financing of the debt when the Orange County voters refused to go along with their county leaders' tax plans. The state allowed them to divert current tax funds.

The Orange County plan for full recovery is also a distinctive element of this event. When the voters said no to new taxes, the county government changed its strategy from raising taxes to suing its way out of the financial crisis. Orange County has filed lawsuits worth billions of dollars against many private firms that had financial dealings with the county government. These include the companies that sold the risky securities for the county pool and those that audited the county's finances and rated the county's bond offerings. The complete recovery of the financial losses suffered by the county government, cities, local schools, and special districts will require that the local governments all receive large sums of money from these lawsuits. This has clearly set a new precedent. There has never before been a financial recovery plan devised by local governments that places such emphasis on winning lawsuits.

The quick resolution of the Orange County bankruptcy is another special attribute of this local fiscal crisis. The county government had a recovery plan in the courts a year after it declared itself bankrupt, having reached an agreement with all units of local government in Orange County. Within a year and a half, the county government went to the financial markets again to borrow money to pay off its debts, which allowed it to emerge from bankruptcy. When the financial mess surfaced in December 1994, everyone assumed that it would be with the county for years. This perception was based on the corporate world of bankruptcies, in which claims and counterclaims can take many years to unravel. This view was shared by those who knew about the financial disasters in big cities—for instance, the fact that it was more than half a decade before New York could borrow money on its own again. That the bankruptcy had such a short life is one of the most astonishing facts in this unusual episode of municipal finance history. It is also somewhat deceiving. There will be a legacy of the Orange County fiscal crisis for many years, namely, tight county budgets, large debt payments to recover from the bankruptcy, and service cuts for the poor. The future is highly dependent on the county's winning its lawsuits to recover the financial damages.

The Orange County bankruptcy, because of all the special qualities that have been mentioned, generated much confusion when the financial emergency occurred. It was difficult to ascertain the causes and predict the local impacts. There was a great deal of uncertainty among the local leaders and state officials about how to respond to the immediate problem. It was hard to conceive of a blueprint for recovery from a large municipal bankruptcy. There was a lot of concern about the long-term consequences not only for this region, but also for the state and national municipal bond market.

THE NEW YORK MODEL

For more than twenty years New York City has offered the most dramatic example of a large municipality on the brink of financial meltdown. As a result, our thinking about the causes of and responses to urban fiscal strain have in many ways been conditioned by the New York crisis. Since the New York crisis has become the dominant model for understanding fiscal problems in big cities, I examine this event and contrast it with the Orange County bankruptcy. From a review of the details of the New York model, it becomes clear that the Orange County bankruptcy is different in many respects.

In 1975 New York City was borrowing money with short-term loans to pay for its day-to-day expenses and employee salaries. When these loans came due, they were repaid by borrowing more money in short-term loans. Eventually the banks refused to lend more money without an outside guarantee of payment and better fiscal management. The state of New York intervened by creating agencies that guaranteed the city's loans and imposed tighter fiscal controls on city government. The federal government initially balked at a financial bailout but ultimately loaned the city $2 billion (Clark, 1994b). New York City was unable to enter the credit markets on its own again until the early 1980s.

Over the years many have reached the conclusion that New York City's problems were caused by demographic and economic changes. For instance, the migration of about one million poor blacks and Puerto Ricans to the city had raised the city's expenditures for schools and public assistance. At the same time, manufacturing jobs and the white middle class were fleeing to the suburbs, which depleted the city's tax revenues. Other scholars claim that the public employee unions and attempts to manage political and social conflicts had resulted in severe overspending (Shefter, 1985).

When other large cities had serious financial problems, they resembled the New York experience. These included the cities of Cleveland, Chicago, and Philadelphia. When these problems arose, demographic changes and economic decline were again cited as causes. The serious gaps between increased spending for the poor and the declining tax revenues from the middle class were also noted. In Orange County the problem was a loss of funds from risky investments rather than demographic and economic changes.

When other big cities faced fiscal problems, they followed New York's lead and turned to the state government for help. An official from Moody's Investors Service notes, "While states are not on the hook to secure local debt issues, other states have nevertheless stepped up in cases of adversity. New York State was quite active with respect to New York City's recovery after its 1975 default, the State of Ohio was directly involved following the 1978 default by Cleveland, and the creation of the Chicago School Finance Authority and the Philadelphia Intergovernmental Authority represents significant state responses to local fiscal crises" (Senate Special Committee on Local Government Investments, 1995d, p. 40). The state offered no such aid to Orange County.

Moreover, New York and other big cities faced long-term borrowing problems. The same official from Moody's noted, "New York City did not borrow on its behalf for six years after default and Cleveland for five years. Philadelphia lost market access for three years due to serious fiscal difficulties and it never defaulted" (Senate Special Committee on Local Government Investments, 1995d, p. 43). By contrast, Orange County returned to the credit market to repay its debts within eighteen months. The bankruptcy attorney for the county government said, "The conclusion of the Chapter 9 case by the end of the year . . . in terms of the history of comparable corporate cases would constitute light speed" (Senate Special Committee on Local Government Investments, 1995e, p. 18).

In the New York crisis and those facing the other big cities, Chapter 9 filings were always avoided because of state actions. When Orange County declared bankruptcy, the investment firms struggled to comprehend the meaning of this radical change. An official from Standard & Poor's noted, "Through bankruptcy filing, county officials sent the message that they did not necessarily intend to repay all the county's obligations. . . . Bankruptcy and default would probably become more common for local officials" (Senate Special Committee on Local Government Investments, 1995d, pp. 47, 49). An official from the Franklin Resources investment firm added, "The phrase 'full faith and credit' really does mean something to the individuals and firms that create the markets. . . . The benefits that state and local governments derive from it are based on a tradition and bond of trust between the lender and the borrower" (Senate Special Committee on Local Government Investments, 1995d, p. 18).

The Orange County crisis does not fit the New York City model. This was not a problem created by demographic and economic changes, out-of-control spending, or a large drop in tax revenues. It was not solved by state aid. An official from Moody's Investors Service observed, "In the case of New York City, they had borrowed six billion more than they had. . . . I would distinguish New York City from Orange County in the sense that . . . Orange County had the ability to pay. The perception was never that New York City had the ability to pay" (Senate Special Committee on Local Government Investments, 1995e, pp. 32–34). In sum, we need to look elsewhere than New York to understand the causes of and solutions to the Orange County crisis.

THE ROGUE TRADER

To understand the causes, events, and implications of the bankruptcy, it is essential to realize how far back the roots of the crisis go. This will dispel some of the myths about the causes and identify the conditions that both enabled and complicated the crisis, the recovery, and Orange County's future prosperity.

The genesis for the Orange County bankruptcy dates back more than fifteen years. In 1978 the state's voters passed Proposition 13, which imposed strict limits on property tax increases and the abilities of local governments to raise taxes. These actions had a crippling effect on county governments, which relied heavily on property taxes as a revenue source. Counties survived only because of a state bailout. After the passage of Proposition 13 county governments were in a frantic search for new nontax revenues, since their property taxes were cut and their voters would not pass tax increases. The state passed a series of bills that deregulated the investments of county treasurers. This would allow local governments to make more money with the funds they had on deposit. They gave county treasurers, such as Bob Citron, permission to borrow money and invest in risky securities. In Orange County local officials became accustomed to living off the interest income of the county pool. They relied on Bob Citron to solve their fiscal problems. His actions led the county and local governments into deep trouble.

The first myth to dispel is that this fiscal tragedy was solely the result of this "rogue trader" named Bob Citron. This belief led some observers early on to conclude that the Orange County crisis has little relevance to other places. This is a dangerous point of view that avoids a more thorough analysis of the structural context of the financial crisis. It prevents us from learning anything from Orange County's mistakes.

In fact, Bob Citron was the catalyst of the Orange County financial crisis. His risky investments put the county in jeopardy. However, the county treasurer's actions took place because certain conditions were present to an extreme degree in Orange County during the early 1990s. Other municipalities and suburban regions today share the qualities that were present in Orange County. The problem could thus be repeated elsewhere, if a catalyst and the same conditions exist.

We have all heard about rogue traders who have wreaked havoc on the financial institutions they represent. These are usually stories about individuals working within private firms. For instance, a few years ago Nick Leeson brought down the Barings Bank of London through his risky investments in the Singapore financial market (Leeson, 1996; Fay, 1996). In the case of Orange County, it was a public official named Bob Citron who was involved in financial wrongdoing. The only lesson to be learned from focusing solely on the rogue trader theory of the Orange County crisis is that greedy people commit illegal acts, which are ultimately uncovered and then punished. I do not intend to minimize the importance of Bob Citron and his actions. Certainly, the huge losses and county bankruptcy would not have occurred without him. The fact is, however, that his actions occurred within a particular institutional setting. Although his risky activities may have represented an inappropriate use of public funds, they were legal according to the state's laws. There was no evidence that Bob Citron was personally profiting from the securities transactions. The Orange County treasurer did commit crimes, but they involved the misappropriation of profits and losses from local governments to the county fund, rather than the risky investments that led to the fiscal meltdown.

By dispelling the myth that the "rogue trader" was the only reason for the fiscal collapse, we focus on the fact that the individual's actions that led to the bankruptcy did not occur in a vacuum. The county treasurer's position was a virtual fiefdom of unchecked powers within the politically fragmented structure of county government. The state government had loosened the restrictions on investments and reporting to such an extent that Bob Citron was allowed to engage in excessive leveraging and the purchase of derivatives. State leaders created this lax environment in response to the financial burdens that the state and local governments faced after Proposition 13. In addition, many local elected leaders approved of his "high risk, high yield" strategy. The interest income from the county investment pool gave the county, cities, and special districts a needed source of revenues. Local elected officials placed pressures on the county treasurer to increase the interest income because the voters placed pressures on them by following a fiscal agenda that included their reluctance to approve new taxes. The state government also provided the motivation to increase the amount of interest income when it began appropriating a larger share of the property tax funds from local governments in the 1990s. In this book I argue that several factors help to explain why the risky actions of Bob Citron were allowed and even encouraged to take place against a backdrop of increasingly dire warnings that his actions would lead to a financial disaster for local governments.

THE REAL ORANGE COUNTY

Another myth that I seek to discredit is that Orange County is an atypical place that has no bearing on the rest of America. A common conclusion drawn from this perspective is that the financial crisis might offer lessons for those in Orange County, but not for anyone else. Thus the dangerous idea is born that bankruptcy is an irrelevant event.

Orange County is often described as a wealthy white suburb. This has led to the belief that this government bankruptcy was a case of rich people gambling and not wanting to pay their debts. Their personal wealth would insulate Orange County residents from any real consequences of the huge losses of local government funds.

Orange County's population is, in fact, more typical than its national image. Most Americans live in suburban regions that are similar in many respects to Orange County. The vast majority of Orange County's 2.5 million residents are not wealthy; they are people who are solidly in the middle class. Many have invested their life savings in owning a home and are financially struggling to pay their monthly bills. They moved to suburbs that were supposed to provide good schools, nice neighborhoods, public libraries, and police protection. The county can no longer be described as racially homogeneous and white. After a large foreign immigration in the 1980s and 1990s, Hispanics and Asians make up about a third of the population. There are large numbers of residents living in poverty. The newly arrived depend heavily on the health care and social services that are provided by the county government. A county bankruptcy would have serious consequences for these groups.

Orange County's politics are often viewed as being far to the right. This is largely a result of its strongly Republican voting patterns and the election of several outspoken conservative legislators. The fact that the local residents did not support a tax increase for the bankruptcy recovery was thus dismissed by some political observers as a response by extremists that would not be repeated elsewhere. This is another reason given as to why the Orange County crisis should be viewed as out of the mainstream.

However, the average Orange County resident is not a political extremist. The vast majority of residents there describe themselves as moderate to somewhat conservative in political orientation. Their policy preferences show a pattern of conservatism on fiscal issues and liberalism on social issues. They oppose welfare spending, favor tax cuts, and do not want the government to interfere in the private decisions of its residents. They are distrustful of elected officials and especially doubtful of their fiscal management skills. Orange County voters have supported tax increases when they thought they were needed, and they have opposed new taxes when they thought the money would not be put to good use. Orange County voters reflect the political ideas and distrust of government leaders expressed by many middle-class residents throughout the United States today.

When we accept the fact that the Orange County crisis happened in mainstream America, and is not solely the fault of a rogue trader, the need to fully explore the bankruptcy takes on a greater sense of urgency. The ultimate purpose of this book then becomes an effort to understand the elements of the financial crisis that have relevance for other U.S. cities and suburban regions. Our attention turns to the conditions that led up to the bankruptcy. Only through a detailed understanding and analysis of each of the conditions that led to this unexpected financial crisis can we identify the specific lessons that can be learned from the Orange County bankruptcy.

THREE CONDITIONS
THAT ENABLED THE BANKRUPTCY

Three factors are at the heart of the Orange County financial crisis: the political fragmentation in local government, voter distrust of local government officials, and the condition of fiscal austerity in the state government. These are not unique factors; each can be found in many U.S. locales. What is different is that they were all present, and in strong degrees, in Orange County during 1994.

TABLE 1-1   THREE CONDITIONS PRESENT
IN ORANGE COUNTY

Political fragmentation	Lack of a central political authority
	Many local governments
	Overlapping jurisdictions and decentralized services
	Elected officials who are locally oriented
Voter distrust	Opposition to most tax increases
	Belief that government wastes a lot of money
	Maintenance of spending for middle-class services favored
	Cuts in spending for welfare programs favored
State fiscal austerity	State expenses exceed tax revenues
	State programs shifted to local governments
	Local governments pay larger share of state programs
	Local government funds shifted to state budget

It is the strength of their collective presence that explains why the bankruptcy took place in Orange County. Some observers may differ in the importance placed on the respective effects of political fragmentation, voter distrust, and state fiscal austerity. I would argue that a comprehensive understanding of the financial crisis requires a deep understanding of the interplay of all three factors (see Table 1-1).

POLITICAL FRAGMENTATION

The political fragmentation of local government is widely viewed as an important condition for suburban regions such as Orange County. These sprawling areas are typically made up of dozens of local municipal governments, a county government, regional single-purpose agencies, local school districts, and local special districts. These local governments often have overlapping geographic boundaries and jurisdictions. Political fragmentation refers to the fact that numerous local governments within suburban regions are pursuing their own separate policies (Baldassare, 1992). These local efforts are largely uncoordinated and, at times, directly compete with one another.

The significance of political fragmentation in suburban regions is underscored by the fact that these vast geographic areas outside of big cities are now where most Americans live and work. In 1960 one in three U.S. residents lived in the suburban regions outside of central cities. By 1970 there were 84 million Americans living in the suburbs, which was more than in either the central cities or rural areas (U.S. Bureau of the Census, 1951, 1961, 1977, 1987). By 1980 the suburbs had rapidly expanded as a workplace, and there were 100 million suburban residents (Palen, 1992, 1995; Pisarki, 1987). Nearly half of all Americans lived in suburban regions by 1990, for a total of 115 million residents. Many large states now have a majority of their populations living in suburban regions, including California (Palen, 1992, 1995). Because of their size, suburbs now play a leading role in defining public policy.[2] For instance, the suburban vote has been the deciding factor in recent presidential elections (Schneider, 1991).

The political fragmentation of local government has been blamed for a host of metropolitan problems. These include fiscal strain in central cities, as the white middle-class tax base has moved from the cities to the suburbs, and the racial and economic segregation of central cities and suburbs (Bollens, 1986; Kasarda, 1978; Logan and Schneider, 1982; Schlay and Rossi, 1981; Weiher, 1991). There is also an increasing recognition that suburban problems can be traced to political fragmentation. Examples include traffic congestion, air pollution, sprawling land use patterns, a lack of affordable housing, and inefficient delivery of local public services (Burnell and Burnell, 1989; Danielson, 1976; Dolan, 1990; Dowall, 1984; Lewis, Paul, 1996; Logan and Schneider, 1981; Neiman, 1980; Schneider and Logan, 1981, 1982). Some scholars believe that political fragmentation in the suburbs is an intentional policy effort that, despite its local and regional costs, provides a structure allowing white, suburban, affluent homeowners to use local zoning and municipal boundaries to avoid the higher tax burdens for health and welfare services for the poor in the central cities (Miller, 1981; Peterson, 1981). Some political scientists and economists, however, point to the benefits of having political fragmentation in the suburban region. They say that having many small governments provides local residents with a wide variety of choices for receiving local public services (Ostrom and Parks, 1973; Ostrom, 1983; Stein, 1990; Tiebout, 1956).

Although there is some dispute over the actual benefits and costs of political fragmentation, there is no argument that this is a highly visible and persistent phenomenon in the suburbs. There has been a great deal of opposition to local government consolidations and the forma-

2. Teitz (1996) also discusses the impact of metropolitan growth and suburbanization on urban planning.

tion of suburban regional governments. The pervasive nature of fragmentation in the political structure is rooted in the "local orientation" of suburban governments. Public opinion surveys and community studies have noted for some time that suburban residents tend to distrust large urban government bureaucracies, favor smaller communities, show a preference for decentralized public services, and have a strong desire to maintain local home rule (see Baldassare, 1986; Fischer, 1984; Michelson, 1976; Popenoe, 1985). To some extent, this is probably a result of the previously held preferences of suburban residents who moved out of big cities. Local elected officials in the suburbs have generally supported the locally oriented preferences of residents, both because this pleases their constituents and because it has allowed them to keep their political powers intact. Regional governments are thus unusual, since suburban residents have generally defeated ballot measures for central city–suburban consolidations and have also shown opposition to suburban government mergers (Campbell and Dollenmeyer, 1976; Zimmer, 1976; Baldassare, 1989). The regional governments that exist are often the single-function agencies that are dedicated to transportation, water, or environmental quality (Baldassare et al., 1996; Bollens, 1997; Saltzstein, 1996; DiMento and Graymer, 1991).[3]

Local governments in suburban regions such as Orange County have faced many challenges as they have undergone a process of "urbanization."[4] The movement of people and jobs to the suburbs has resulted in more traffic congestion, noise, pollution, and overcrowding of public facilities. Many suburban residents have complained about too much development (Baldassare, 1986) and have reacted with a NIMBY ("not in my back yard") mentality that is increasing segregation and inequality (Logan and Schneider, 1981, 1982). At the same time, there has been a rapid increase in the minority population as a result of black migration from the central cities and foreign immigration from Latin America and Asia (Farley and Frey, 1994; Frey, 1993, 1994; Stahura, 1986). The growing social diversity has had many consequences for local governments, including the need for more schools, health and welfare programs, and increasing worries about the effects of immigration and racial change by suburban residents (Baldassare, 1996).

3. There are regional governments in place, such as in Minneapolis and Miami. See Paul Lewis (1996) for a discussion of regional government in the Portland area.
4. The urbanization of the suburbs is a topic that has been discussed since the 1970s (see Masotti and Hadden, 1973, 1974).

The structure of local governance has made it difficult for U.S. suburban regions to cope with the challenges such as growth and ethnic
change that they are now confronting. Notably, political fragmentation
has resulted in an inadequate response to regional problems such as
traffic congestion, air pollution, open space preservation, infrastructure
improvements, affordable housing, and growth management. These regional issues cannot be managed through the separate efforts of local
governments.

Orange County is a classic example of political fragmentation in a
suburban region. In fact, there are layers upon layers of political fragmentation in the local government structure. Within the county government, the members of the Board of Supervisors focused their
attention on the local districts that elected them. The lack of a central
authority before the bankruptcy allowed the county treasurer to act in
a semi-autonomous fashion. Outside of county government, the cities
operated in ways that were fairly independent of the county government, and with little regard for one another. The school districts, regional single-purpose agencies, and local special districts engaged in
delivering their services with little consideration for the county and city
authorities. This political fragmentation of a suburban region poses serious constraints on local governance that were made obvious by the
fiscal crisis. There was a lack of communication about fiscal decisions
before the bankruptcy, difficulties in coordinating a local government
response to the fiscal emergency, and more barriers to overcome when
cooperation was needed to reach consensus on a fiscal recovery plan.[5]

Orange County is also a reflection of the problems faced by suburban
regions as they have become the dominant form of community throughout the United States. The suburbs have been transformed by rapid population growth and foreign immigration. Their local officials have a
pressing need for infrastructure improvements and more funding for
public schools, health, and welfare. The fragmented nature of local government has meant that they are slow to respond to these needs. The unwillingness of the voters to raise taxes has limited the options for
developing home-grown solutions. This is the suburban context that has
become dominant in the 1990s, a time in which Orange County's elected
leaders turned to their county treasurer for extra income.

5. Other discussions of suburban political fragmentation, local government compe-
tition, and Orange County governance issues can be found in Teaford (1997); Schneider,
Teske, and Mintron (1995); Kling, Olin, and Poster (1991); Schneider (1989); Logan and
Molotch (1987); and Jackson (1985).

VOTER DISTRUST

Another critical condition is the influence of voter distrust in local government. Politics and elections in the suburbs have been dominated by voters who are reluctant, more often than not, to have their local taxes raised (see Baldassare, 1986, 1989). This tendency among local voters goes well beyond the base of the strictly Republican or conservative voters who want to cut taxes and government spending. The antitax sentiment is found across political parties and left and right political ideologies. Its base of support is the middle-class, young, and well-educated residents in suburban regions. This voter group now exerts a strong influence on local politics throughout the United States (Clark and Ferguson, 1983; Clark and Inglehart, 1997).

Many studies have pointed out that the citizens' revolt against taxes should not be confused with a desire to reduce local government spending. The voters who support state tax limitations are simply voting against high taxes, but they want current levels of spending to be maintained or increased for public services (Citrin, 1979; Ladd and Wilson, 1982; Courant, Gramlich, and Rubinfeld, 1979, 1980). Only with respect to welfare and other government services for the poor are middle-class voters willing to accept less government spending. Otherwise, these voters expect to receive the same level of services even after their taxes are reduced. In general, there seems to be little connection between the voters' preference to maintain or increase spending for local services and their lack of willingness to pay higher taxes.

These antitax attitudes may seem unreasonable, if not irrational, without consideration of the political perceptions underlying these views. This new political movement emerged at a time when the public was expressing less confidence in public officials and institutions (Lipset and Schneider, 1983). Many of the antitax voters believe that most public bureaucracies, including their local governments, are inefficient and waste the money that is paid to them in taxes (Clark and Ferguson, 1983). These voters thus have feelings of distrust toward local elected officials—in particular, a low regard for their handling of spending, taxes, and budgets. For this reason, suburban voters can feel justified in demanding lower taxes while asking their local leaders to maintain current spending levels and provide high-quality services.

Suburban voters have sought to elect local government officials who share their tax and spending views. The elected officials tend to follow what they perceive as the local electorate's preferences on fiscal issues, and this usually makes them highly reluctant to increase local taxes (Baldassare, 1986). Local elected officials often face a serious dilemma while trying to meet the demands of the suburban public. They must devise a fiscal strategy that allows them to maintain or decrease taxes, and also maintain or increase spending for local services. At the same time, the middle-class residents of the suburbs can hold very high expectations for the quality of local services they receive, such as schools, fire and police protection, roads, parks, and recreation.

Only in rare circumstances can voter distrust be overcome and a local tax increase pass. Suburban residents have supported tax increases for local services that they consider to be deficient. They are more likely to favor a tax increase, for instance, for improving schools, police protection, or roads (Baldassare, 1989). However, middle-class voters would be highly unlikely to support a tax increase for general spending purposes or for health and welfare services for the poor. When they do support a tax increase, they require that the funds be "earmarked" specifically for the services they think need improving. This is because they do not trust their local government officials to make the right decisions with unrestricted new taxes.

The emergence of widespread voter distrust has elevated the role of citizens' preferences in local politics. The local leaders who are elected by a distrustful electorate tend to follow the policy preferences of their constituents rather than going to their party leaders or special interest groups for advice. These politicians are more likely to follow the public's views in making policy choices. The voters have also demanded the power to approve tax increases at the ballot box in California and other states. Thus, the voters' opinions on fiscal issues can and do set local tax and spending policies.

Local elected officials in many suburban regions have learned the hard way that, when they are forced to turn inward to solve their problems, their voters are not very accepting of tax increases. Suburban middle-class residents are generally unwilling to have their taxes raised for most purposes. The locally elected leaders are expected by voters to maintain or decrease tax levels at the same time they are providing high-quality services at an adequate level for their residents. Suburban regions are thus often lacking in the fiscal resources they need to provide services, even though the population is often dominated by middle-class residents who are able to pay more taxes.

"New Fiscal Populists" are the new breed of local elected officials flourishing under the conditions of voter distrust. Their existence helps us to understand how Orange County and other seemingly well-off municipalities can fall into a fiscal crisis. Previous researchers have tended to focus on the ability of localities to generate tax revenues, as measured by the economic base of the city, and the ability to pay off debt, as measured by the ratings and prices in the municipal bond market. Orange County showed relative strength in the economic domain. It also had an excellent credit rating only months before the bankruptcy. The role of local government leaders is the important, missing ingredient in determining why fiscal problems can emerge in some places and not others, and can be more or less persistent over time.

Terry Clark is credited with redefining urban fiscal stress in big city and suburban settings (Clark, 1978, 1994b; Clark and Ferguson, 1983; Clark et al., 1992). Clark (1983, p. 175) has described how local officials operate in four different "political cultures" that explain their fiscal management approaches. New Deal Democrats reflect liberal views on fiscal issues and social issues, tending to favor more spending for public services, even if it means higher taxes and greater debts. Ethnic Politicians also support this liberal fiscal approach, as exemplified by strong support for health and welfare spending, though they tend to have conservative views on social issues. New Deal Republicans have conservative views on both social issues and fiscal issues, reflecting a preference for lower government taxes and spending, even if this means cuts in a wide range of public services. The New Fiscal Populists are those who express a combination of fiscal conservatism and liberalism on social issues. They want to reduce government costs and taxes if possible. However, they prefer to do so without reducing middle-class services, although they are not opposed to cuts in health and welfare spending. New Fiscal Populists also seek to control spending and maintain middle-class services by improving productivity and management. When the local government in Orange County sought to maintain the current level of services without raising local taxes, by employing a more "productive" use of the cash in the county pool in the form of generating more interest income, it fit the mold of New Fiscal Populism.

The New Fiscal Populist leaders have been elected because their policy views are in tune with those of a large number of middle-class voters who distrust their governments (Clark, 1983, 1994a). Most Americans today have negative views about welfare spending, favor lower taxes, support lower government spending, and believe that their governments are wasteful with tax moneys and are inefficient bureaucracies. At the same time, many have liberal views on personal liberties,

such as favoring personal choice for abortions and opposing government censorship. They also tend to support stricter environmental regulations and local growth controls. The trait of liberalism on social
issues and conservatism on fiscal issues is present in Orange County.

The New Fiscal Populist leaders are found in specific types of communities. This is because the fiscally conservative voters tend to be
highly educated, higher-income residents in high-technology occupa-
tions. Fiscal conservatives are also present in communities with
younger and middle-aged populations and fewer nonwhites and poor
residents (Clark and Ferguson, 1983; Clark and Inglehart, 1997). This
pattern reflects a new political movement that is based on issues coali-
tions that cut across political parties, special interest groups, and ideologies. The New Fiscal Populists have sometimes been described as
"yuppie" politicians because of these characteristics (Clark, 1994c), yet
they could just as accurately be described as "suburban" politicians.
Orange County shares many of the demographic and political characteristics that are present in the communities where the New Fiscal
Populist leaders are found.

Citizens' preferences thus play a major role in determining the policies of New Fiscal Populists (Clark and Ferguson, 1981, 1983;
Hoffman and Clark, 1979). These leaders have made a promise to the
voters that there will be no new taxes. So they seek to contain or lower
taxes, and contain or reduce overall government spending, while maintaining or increasing the level of middle-class services. In order to maintain or increase services without raising taxes, they seek to improve
staff productivity, improve fiscal management of existing tax dollars,
and selectively adopt low-visibility revenue raising devices. In Orange
County, New Fiscal Populist leaders were in the position of having to
maintain services without increasing taxes when they faced cuts in state
revenues. This is a major reason that they wanted more interest income
from the county pool.

The rise of New Fiscal Populists provides a framework for understanding the Orange County financial crisis. It places the focus on the
style of fiscal management by the local leaders, the political pressures
that were exerted by distrustful voters, and the inability to adapt to the
changing fiscal environment brought about by state and federal actions.
In true fashion, the political culture was neither Republican nor
Democrat. The local leaders, including Republicans on the Orange
County Board of Supervisors and a Democrat in the county treasurer's
office, won support from both parties. The local leaders were praised

for their innovative approach to raising revenues by increasing interest income. The Orange County financial crisis can thus be viewed as the failure of these New Fiscal Populist leaders to adapt to changing fiscal conditions.

Orange County is a suburban region with local politics that are dominated by voter distrust. Most Democratic, Republican, and independent voters hold antitax views. They have elected city and county government officials who share their desire to reduce the tax burden. The local leaders face pressures from the voters to find the revenues to maintain or increase services without raising taxes. This may have led to the reliance on the interest income that was generated by taking risks with the county pool. Later on, a new tax to pay for the recovery would face strong opposition from the voters and local officials, thus limiting the solutions to the Orange County financial crisis.

STATE FISCAL AUSTERITY

A third important dimension is the impact of fiscal austerity on suburban governments. In earlier eras generous state and federal spending on highways made possible the massive migration to the suburbs (Baldassare, 1986, 1992). The 1980s and 1990s have been decades in which the federal government, faced with large budget deficits, has fewer financial resources to aid the state and local governments. Federal and state funding has become severely limited at a time in which suburban regions have grown in size and social complexity. In California the state's budget pressures have meant that there are inadequate outside revenues to fund public infrastructure projects and local public services. The condition of fiscal austerity at higher levels places great pressures on suburban governments, as in Orange County, to find additional funds for services. This can influence their decisions on seeking new revenues and their search for solutions when a local fiscal crisis occurs.

California has limited resources to share with the counties and other local governments because of voter-imposed rules on balancing the state budget and limiting tax increases. In this case, voter distrust has added to fiscal austerity. To make matters worse, the state government has faced growing expenses and declining revenues in the 1990s as a result of a serious economic recession and rapid population growth from foreign immigration. State officials claimed that many of the services mandated by the federal government were not fully funded. The state's fiscal austerity was so severe that property tax funds were taken from the local governments to reduce the state budget deficit.

When the Orange County bankruptcy struck, some argued that this county's troubles could be traced to state and local government relations. The *New York Times* (1995a) announced in a headline that the Orange County event reflected "a bankruptcy peculiar to California," and the story went on to say that this was part of the legacy of the state's Proposition 13. But others insisted that the county government brought on all of its own fiscal problems through foolish investments. Public opinions polls show that the voters blame their county leaders rather than the tax revolt. I trace the impact of the state's fiscal austerity, some of it created by state tax limitations, on local government finance. There are several ways in which Proposition 13 and the national tax revolt had direct and indirect effects on the Orange County bankruptcy.

In June 1978 a California citizen initiative called Proposition 13 offered all homeowners a substantial savings on their property taxes. The state's voters approved this measure by a two-to-one margin, beginning the national "middle-class tax revolt" (Sears and Citrin, 1982). The effects that tax-limiting measures have on state and local governments are often a matter of controversy. Some policy experts have talked about the negative consequences of Proposition 13. Yet the state's voters have steadfastly held by their support for this measure. In fact, California voters have extended its powers at the ballot box. Most recently, state voters passed Proposition 218 in November 1996 and extended the limitations on local tax increases. Orange County voters passed Proposition 218 by a wide margin despite their funding shortage after the bankruptcy.

When Proposition 13 became part of the state constitution, it imposed strict limits on property tax revenues. This had the immediate effect of cutting property tax receipts for local governments throughout the state (Kaufman and Rosen, 1981, pp. xv, xvi). The citizens' initiative also imposed limits on the abilities of state and local governments to raise new taxes. Local governments such as counties, cities, school districts, and special districts could not increase taxes without approval of the local electorate. The voting requirement made it more difficult to replace the property tax losses. Bob Citron was one of the county treasurers calling for the loosening of investment practices after Proposition 13 passed, so that county governments could increase their interest income.

The Orange County bankruptcy was the first urban fiscal crisis in which a recovery plan would require the voters' approval. This was not the case, for instance, in New York, Cleveland, or Philadelphia. This fact was noted, and it raised alarms on Wall Street. An official from Moody's Investors Service observed, "They have a fiscal emergency. There seems to be no measure either at the county's level or at the state level to give them special powers in a fiscal emergency to overcome the restrictions they're dealing with" (Senate Special Committee on Local Government Investments, 1995d, p. 52).

Another unintended and equally dramatic effect of the tax revolt was to increase the dependency of county governments on the state government. State intervention was needed because of the dramatic drop in local property tax funds. The year before Proposition 13 passed, the county governments received $3.01 billion in property taxes, or 34 percent of their general revenues. By 1981–1982, their property tax revenues had decreased to $2.37 billion, or 22 percent of general county revenues. This was a serious blow to a growing region like Orange County.

State and local government relations were also redefined after Proposition 13. Between the 1977–1978 and 1981–1982 fiscal years, state aid to the county governments increased from $2.09 billion to $3.58 billion (Misczynski, 1984, pp. 24–25). The state government assumed all of the costs of some county programs, and it partially funded other county programs. The state also took charge of redistributing local property tax revenues. A complex formula was used to reallocate local property taxes to the counties for their general county funds (Schwadron and Richter, 1984; Misczynski, 1984). Thus, local governments have lost much of their budgetary flexibility. They rely heavily on the state for revenues, since property taxes are diminished and they cannot usually raise local taxes. Fred Silva, former state legislative aide, observed that since Proposition 13 passed, "Major changes in economic conditions that affect state revenue will have an immediate effect on local services. . . . Service levels for school districts, county health services, and most general local government services are now dictated annually by a political system far removed from the day-to-day service decisions and needs of local communities" (*California State Library Foundation Bulletin,* 1988, p. 5). Orange County's elected officials have always complained that the state did not give them their fair share of property taxes.

The complex relations between state and local funding that were pieced together over a decade were severely tested during the 1990s. The state government no longer had a surplus of funds to pay for local government services. In fact, the state budget had a huge deficit. The state took back billions of dollars in property tax funds that it had previously committed to counties, cities, and special districts. The local governments had very few options to make up for these lost revenues. Several of the smaller counties were close to fiscal collapse after these cutbacks (*New York Times,* 1995a). Los Angeles County was more than a billion dollars in the red. In Orange County the treasurer took on a great deal more risk in the county pool in order to generate more interest income. To some extent, this episode of state fiscal austerity, which led to a reduction in local government funding, was what brought on the Orange County fiscal crisis.

The Orange County bankruptcy exposed the new realities of state and local government relations. The county government could no longer turn to the state for help. The county could not raise tax revenues on its own, since the state rules called for voter approval. The county was not able to make large spending cuts, since most categories of expenses were now dictated by the state government. An official from Moody's Investors Service spoke of "the growing belief that the structural underpinnings of local government finance here in California is fragile and fairly unforgiving. The post–Proposition 13 limits give Orange County few options to deal with a fiscal emergency" (Senate Special Committee on Local Government Investments, 1995d, p. 38).

Proposition 13 is but one example of a trend in which fiscally strained federal and state governments have pushed responsibilities to the local government level. In their study of a wide range of urban policy issues, Steinberg, Lyon, and Vaiana (1992, p. 2) conclude, "Through a series of deliberate federal and state policy decisions over the last three decades, local governments, especially the governments of cities and urban counties, have been forced to assume increasing responsibility for meeting these rising demands—but their financial capacity has not grown correspondingly."

Orange County is clearly a suburban region that has experienced the impact of state government fiscal austerity. In the early 1990s the state government reduced the allocation of property tax revenues for the county, cities, and special districts. This was perhaps the event that led to the search for other revenues, in the form of interest income from risky investments in the county pool, to compensate for these losses.

The state's budget problems removed the possibility of any form of a bailout as a response to the local fiscal crisis, or any kind of state financial assistance as part of the financial recovery. The state's fiscal austerity constrained the kinds of local government reform that were instituted after the bankruptcy. For instance, they changed the rules for local government investing instead of returning the property tax funds to local governments.

STAGES OF THE FISCAL CRISIS

Political fragmentation, voter distrust, and state fiscal austerity were key factors not only at the outset of the Orange County fiscal crisis. They were important during the various stages of the bankruptcy and are still in evidence today. This notion is the guiding principle of the book. Table 1-2 identifies these three conditions and some of the ways in which they are critical to understanding why the financial crisis occurred, how the local government responded to the crisis, the kinds of policy solutions that were put forward, and the local government reforms that were implemented.

For instance, the fiscal problems in Orange County can be traced to the political fragmentation that allowed a lack of oversight of the Orange County treasurer. Voter distrust put pressures on elected officials to provide more services without raising taxes. As for state fiscal austerity, the fact that the state government was taking back property tax revenues from cities and county governments put enormous demands on local elected officials to find new revenues in the months before the financial crisis.

The response to the fiscal emergency in Orange County included the creation of a chief executive officer to provide central authority in county government. This was done to overcome the political fragmentation of the county government. Because of the belief by distrusting voters that the crisis could be resolved by cutting waste in government, the bankruptcy caused more anger than angst. State fiscal austerity explained the lack of intervention in the financial markets by the state government at a time when Orange County was in great need of outside help.

The fiscal recovery plan was based on raiding funds for the regional infrastructure while maintaining local services. This is because elected officials in this politically fragmented area valued local programs over regional needs. Voter distrust ruled out the possibility of a tax increase

TABLE I-2   THREE CONDITIONS AND THE STAGES OF THE ORANGE COUNTY BANKRUPTCY

	Political Fragmentation	Voter Distrust	State Fiscal Austerity
Fiscal problems in Orange County	Lack of treasurer oversight Lack of fiscal accountability Local vs. regional emphasis by local elected officials	Public pressure to find ways to pay for more services with the same or less in taxes	Limited state funds for local governments State takes back local tax revenues
Responses to fiscal emergency	Create county CEO and operations management team County business leaders mediate local government negotiations	More voter anger than fear Public believes the problem can be solved by cutting waste	No state intervention State offers expertise and threatens a takeover
Fiscal recovery plans	Pay debts by diverting county taxes from regional infra-structure funds Preserve local public services Local governments mostly paid back	No new taxes Cut services for poor Maintain services for middle-class taxpayers Lawsuits to replace lost revenues	Allow county government to divert county taxes
Local government reforms	Oversight of county treasurer Restrictions on county investments CEO to improve fiscal accounting Little county government restructuring Reject regional government and consolidation	Term limits for local officials More tax limits for local governments Reject charter in order to elect vs. appoint treasurer	Tighten local government fiscal regulations Avoid state and local fiscal reform

being approved by local residents. Fiscal austerity determined a limited role for state government, specifically, approving state legislation that allowed Orange County to divert county tax funds to pay its debts.

The local government reforms after the crisis took on an unusual form because of the three conditions. The desire to maintain the status quo of political fragmentation meant that reforms were restricted to improving fiscal oversight of the county treasurer without drastically changing the structure of local government. Distrustful voters did approve term limits for local elected officials and further tax limits, but not a charter amendment that would have changed the treasurer from an elected to an appointed position. State legislation was passed that tightened the regulations on county treasurers, but, because of state fiscal austerity, the reforms stopped short of addressing the state and local finance issues that are at the root of Orange County's fiscal problems.

In this book I provide evidence from many different sources that three factors are at the root of the bankruptcy and all of the events that followed. Bob Citron could not have operated as he did without their presence, yet his actions were what allowed these three conditions to have such serious consequences. The facts presented later in the book, for all of the stages of the crisis, offer compelling reasons to believe that the Orange County bankruptcy does have relevance to other large cities and suburban regions. The political fragmentation of local government, voter distrust, and state fiscal austerity can be found in many places.

THE APPROACH

The research for this book is based on the comprehensive case study approach. I rely on several sources of data to describe and analyze the Orange County bankruptcy. I reviewed local government reports and statistics, including city and county budgets, internal memos and reports, information on the county investment pool, local elections, census data, and government organization charts. I also examined the volumes of Orange County grand jury testimony on the fiscal crisis. I analyzed information from the state government, including budgets, bills, and demographic and economic trends that have impacts on state funding for Orange County and other local governments. As part of this research, I read the reports and investigations of various state agencies and the legislature on the Orange County bankruptcy. I report the results of a large number of public opinion surveys that I conducted before, during, and after the bankruptcy. These polls help to explain the voters' distrust and policy preferences. I also conducted in-depth interviews with local officials from county government, cities, schools, and special districts and local business leaders. I have used their firsthand knowledge to better understand the events during the financial crisis. The data I have gathered through this research are supplemented with background information from newspaper reports. They provide a time line, quotes and information from key public officials, and other important details about the bankruptcy that cannot be found elsewhere. All of this research has been done with the purpose of uncovering the factors at work at various stages of the crisis and determining the implications of the Orange County financial crisis for public policy.

SUMMARY OF CHAPTERS

This book is divided into nine chapters. This introductory chapter discusses the roots of the bankruptcy. Chapter 2 looks at the social, economic, political, and structural conditions that were present in Orange County right before the fiscal crisis. Chapter 3 details the California context in which the Orange County government was operating. The next four chapters provide a comprehensive analysis of the events in 1994 leading up to the bankruptcy, the local governments' responses to the fiscal emergency, the recovery plan that allowed the county government to emerge from bankruptcy, and the local government reforms that were implemented as a result of the financial crisis. Throughout these four chapters the emphasis is on how the political fragmentation present in this suburban region, the voter distrust of local government officials, and the fiscal austerity of state government contribute to understanding all of the phases of this financial crisis. The final chapters discuss the larger lessons to be learned from the bankruptcy and offer specific policy recommendations for state and local actions to avoid future problems such as those experienced by Orange County.

CHAPTER 2

The Orange County Setting

Orange County is a place that is widely known but largely misunderstood. Many see it as vastly different from other U.S. communities. In fact, Orange County has a lot in common with many other regions, though admittedly this was more true in the years leading up to the bankruptcy. By focusing on the facts surrounding Orange County, we can better understand why the fiscal crisis happened in this place and the reasons it can happen in other locales throughout the nation.

Orange County, California, has a variety of images in the national media. It is best known as the home of Disneyland, the self-proclaimed "Happiest Place on Earth." Then there is the "Gold Coast" of Newport Beach, where boat rides take tourists near the million-dollar homes of Hollywood's rich and famous. A few miles inland is Irvine, offering a middle-class suburban paradise equipped with greenbelts, swimming pools, tennis courts, and artificial lakes in what is the largest and best-known example of a comprehensively planned community in the United States. Those who travel to Orange County arrive at the John Wayne Airport, where they are greeted by a giant statue of the famous cowboy star who once called Orange County his home. In many ways, the Orange County that people are familiar with is larger than life.

Conservative politics also have a large role in the public's image of Orange County. It is the birthplace of Richard Nixon, the location of his presidential library, and the place where cheering supporters welcomed back the former president after Watergate disgraced him. The county's voters gave another Republican from California, Ronald Reagan, two landslide victories in the 1980s. In an earlier time, Orange County had gained notoriety as a headquarters for the John Birch Society and its radical-right philosophy of fierce anti-communism and conspiracy theories. Today, Rev. Lou Sheldon has made Orange County known as a headquarters for Christian political activists. On the national stage, former U.S. Congressman Bob Dornan's speeches have helped to extend the image of Orange County as a breeding ground for ultra-conservative ideas.

Now the Orange County that is admired by some and criticized by others also has a fiscal image. Along with its reputation as fantasyland, home of the rich and famous, suburban paradise, and right-wing haven, it is now in the record books for having the largest municipal bankruptcy in U.S. history.

RAPID GROWTH AND SOCIAL DIVERSITY

Local governments in Orange County were affected by several demographic trends in the early 1990s. They were confronted with one of the largest and fastest-growing populations in the United States. A large foreign immigration was also changing the age, race, and ethnic composition. These trends placed fiscal pressures on local governments by challenging them to provide both more and different services. Local officials responded by seeking more interest income from the county treasurer.

Orange County has a short but dynamic history. It is a geographic area of 790 square miles located on the California coast to the south of Los Angeles and to the north of San Diego. It was incorporated by the state legislature in 1889, when it became separate from Los Angeles. At the time, Orange County had fewer than 20,000 residents. In the not so distant past, then, this was an agricultural county with large ranches and farms. As recently as 1950 Orange County had fewer than a quarter million residents.

Disneyland opened its doors in the early 1950s, and with that the era of rapid suburban development was to begin. The county gained about 2 million residents between 1940 and 1990, and 1 million of these arrived between 1970 and 1990 (see Table 2-1). Within four decades Orange County's land was transformed from rural-agricultural to residential-suburban to a commercial-industrial-residential form of urban-

TABLE 2-1   ORANGE COUNTY
POPULATION GROWTH

Decade	Total Population
1990	2,410,556
1980	1,932,709
1970	1,422,372
1960	703,925
1950	216,224
1940	130,760
1930	118,674
1920	61,375
1910	34,436
1900	19,696

SOURCE: California Department of Finance (1996a).

ized region. In the mid-1990s the county population was about 2.5 million residents.

As of 1992 Orange County was the fifth most populous county in the United States. Only Los Angeles, Cook (i.e., Chicago area), Harris (i.e., Houston area), and San Diego counties are more heavily populated (see Table 2-2). Orange County ranked seventh in terms of population increase, with a gain of 551,868 residents between 1980 and 1992. In previous times, the source of growth was migration from the eastern United States. The recent growth of the county, however, is the result of foreign immigration from Asia and Latin America.

By 1990 Orange County had some of the largest concentrations of Hispanics and Asians in the United States. Orange County ranked fourth in Asian population, with nearly a quarter million Asian residents, many of Vietnamese descent. To place these numbers in perspective, Orange County had more Asian residents than San Francisco. Orange County ranked sixth in Hispanic population, with over a half million residents and more Hispanics than the Bronx. Most Hispanics in Dade County are of Cuban heritage, so, as indicated in Table 2-2, Orange County has the fifth largest population of Mexican heritage.

The trend of racial and ethnic change is evident when we compare the 1980 and 1990 censuses (see Table 2-3). The percentage of the Orange County population that is white and non-Hispanic declined from 78 percent to 65 percent. This group includes 1.55 million residents. Meanwhile, the percentage who are Hispanic increased from 15 to 23 percent, and the percentage of Asians doubled from 5 to 10 percent. The

TABLE 2-2   ORANGE COUNTY
RANKING IN POPULATION

U.S. Counties with the Largest Populations, 1992

1. Los Angeles, CA	9,053,645
2. Cook, IL	5,139,341
3. Harris, TX	2,971,755
4. San Diego, CA	2,601,055
5. Orange, CA	**2,484,789**

U.S. Counties with the Largest Asian Populations, 1990

1. Los Angeles, CA	954,485
2. Honolulu, HI	526,459
3. Santa Clara, CA	261,466
4. Orange, CA	**249,192**
5. San Francisco, CA	210,876

U.S. Counties with the Largest Hispanic Populations, 1990

1. Los Angeles, CA	3,351,242
2. Dade, FL	953,407
3. Cook, IL	694,194
4. Harris, TX	644,935
5. Bexar, TX	589,180
6. Orange, CA	**564,828**

SOURCE: U.S. Bureau of the Census (1994).

TABLE 2-3   ORANGE COUNTY'S RACIAL
AND ETHNIC COMPOSITION

	1980	1990
White and non-Hispanic	78%	65%
Hispanic	15	23
Asian	5	10
Black	2	2

SOURCE: U.S. Bureau of the Census (1994).

black population remained stable, and relatively small, at 2 percent. The ethnic and racial shifts that are taking place in Orange County's population are explained by the different rates of growth and migration within each group. The white and non-Hispanic population grew by only 3 percent in the 1980s. In contrast, the Hispanic population grew by 97 percent, the Asian population by 177 percent, and the black population by 60 percent.

The census figures indicate that the Asian and Hispanic populations are largely composed of immigrants. Orange County has been a major site for foreign immigration since the 1980s. One in four county residents is foreign born, compared with one in twelve U.S. residents. As a result, Orange County ranks seventeenth in foreign-born population among all U.S. counties. Sixty-four percent of the growth of the minority population in Orange County between 1980 and 1990 can be directly attributed to foreign immigration. As of the 1990 U.S. census, 78 percent of the Asians and 48 percent of the Hispanics in Orange County were foreign born (see Baldassare, 1996). Also indicative of the large immigrant population that has recently arrived is the fact that one in three Orange County households in 1990 had a language other than English spoken at home. For the most part, these households were speaking Spanish, although some were speaking Asian languages. In the United States as a whole, only about one in seven households speak languages other than English at home.

In the period between 1990 and 1994, there is every indication that the trends of rapid population growth and racial and ethnic change were taking place. Overall, the population increased by about 170,000 residents. Most of the growth was driven by foreign immigration, as indicated by estimates of nearly 100,000 legal immigrants entering Orange County in the early 1990s (California Department of Finance, 1995). Between 1990 and 1994, it is estimated that the white and non-Hispanic population increased by only about 10,000, while the Hispanic population increased by over 100,000 and Asians increased by about 50,000. These most recent estimates of race and ethnicity place the white and non-Hispanic population at 61 percent, the Hispanic population at 26 percent, the Asian population at 11 percent, and the black population at 2 percent (California Department of Finance, 1996b).

ECONOMIC RECESSION

In the 1980s Orange County was a "job machine," creating 377,000 new jobs. Employment grew at a faster rate than population (Baldassare and Wilson, 1995). By 1990 Orange County's employment reached 1.3 million. Eight in ten employed residents were commuting to jobs inside the county, and more than 90 percent were commuting to work by automobile. New transportation infrastructure failed to keep pace with job growth. Many residents complained about their commutes and the state of the county's freeways. As a result, public opinion surveys consistently found that traffic was rated as the biggest county problem in the 1980s (Baldassare and Katz, 1994).

The Orange County economy slowed measurably beginning in 1990. The severe recession in Southern California was taking its toll. The sources included a decline in the aerospace and defense industries, downsizing of large companies, and a sharp decrease in housing prices and home construction. Between 1991 and 1993 Orange County's economy shed 57,000 jobs. A weak recovery began in 1994 as the county gained back 11,400 jobs. Overall, though, the early 1990s was a period in which the Orange County economy was in a period of downturn (E & Y Kenneth Leventhal, 1996).

As an indication of the widespread nature of local job losses, 36 percent of Orange County residents in a 1994 survey said they were worried that they or someone in their family would experience job loss in the next year. Fewer than three in ten residents described the Orange County economy as being in excellent or good shape. Less than half expected the local economy to improve within two years (Baldassare and Katz, 1994).

Income growth also came to a halt in Orange County during the early 1990s. Between 1980 and 1990 the median household income in Orange County had increased in constant 1990 dollars by about 25 percent, while the nationwide increase was only about 6 percent (Baldassare and Wilson, 1995). The median household income stood at $49,000 in 1990 and dropped by 4 percent to $47,000 in 1994. Even though inflation was low during these years, the typical Orange County household was losing ground as many saw their incomes stagnate or decline (see Appendix B, Table B-1).

The economic recession and lack of income growth had a significant impact on consumer confidence. The number of residents who said their finances were better off than they were the year before declined from 50 percent in 1989 to 35 percent in 1993. The number who expected to be better off next year decreased from 56 percent in 1989 to 41 percent in 1993. Orange County's consumer confidence was higher compared with the United States as a whole in the 1980s, but lower in 1992 and 1993 (Baldassare and Katz, 1993).

The housing market was adding to the economic malaise. In Orange County in the early 1990s, homeowners accounted for six in ten households. They were hearing about a steep decline in the value of local homes. Between 1980 and 1990 the median home value in Orange County increased by 52 percent in constant 1990 dollars. The median home value in the United States increased by 14 percent in constant

1990 dollars (Baldassare and Wilson, 1995). The average or mean price of a single-family home in Orange County rose from $99,000 in 1980 to $257,000 in 1990. But when employment growth and household income growth stopped, so did the rise in home prices. Between 1990 and 1994, the average home price dropped by $41,000, from $257,000 to $216,000 (*Orange County Register*, 1996a). To many county residents, these lower home prices meant that their single largest investment was losing money. Clearly shaken, only 12 percent described owning an Orange County home as an "excellent" investment in a 1994 survey (Baldassare and Katz, 1994).

In the years leading up to the 1994 bankruptcy, economic trends were placing new fiscal pressures on Orange County governments. Business slowdowns and employment declines resulted in less tax revenue and more demands for public services from the unemployed. The lack of income growth reduced consumer spending, which led to lower sales tax receipts. The decline in housing costs meant that local governments could no longer rely on yearly increases in property tax dollars. In fact, a prolonged decline in housing prices meant that property tax collections would fall.

MIDDLE-CLASS RESIDENTS

One of the misperceptions about Orange County is its reputation of being a very affluent suburban region. This popular belief is based partly on the national media focus on the more "glitzy" beach areas. In general, the county's wealth has been overstated. The high housing costs work to counteract the higher-than-average incomes. The overall income picture has also changed as a result of the rapid growth of the lower-income immigrant population in the 1980s. The county's economy also cooled off in the early 1990s. The local recession sent jobs, incomes, and housing values into a decline.

Compared with the nation on four of the social and economic indicators that typically reflect high social status, Orange County does not emerge as a highly affluent suburban region. As of 1990, 60 percent of households own their homes in Orange County, less than the 64 percent rate of home ownership in the nation. Twenty-eight percent of the adult population are college graduates, which is not that much higher than the 20 percent recorded for the nation. The median household income in Orange County is about $46,000, which is about 50 percent higher than the $30,000 average for the nation. But this higher income must be

TABLE 2-4   ORANGE COUNTY'S RANKING IN
SOCIAL AND ECONOMIC STATUS

Indicator	Orange County	United States
Percent of owner-occupied housing units, 1990	60.1	64.2
Percent of adults with a bachelor's degree, 1990	27.8	20.3
Median household income, 1989	$45,922	$30,056
Median housing value, 1990	$252,700	$79,100

SOURCE: U.S. Bureau of the Census (1994).

weighed against a median housing value over $250,000, which is more than three times the $79,000 average for the nation in 1990 (see Table 2-4). Orange County does not rank among the top twenty-five counties in terms of home ownership, college graduates, or median household income. It does, however, rank eleventh in median housing value.

Most Orange County residents do not consider themselves to be highly affluent. When asked to describe their social class, 55 percent of Orange County adults say they are in the middle class, one in four say they are in the upper or upper middle class, and 18 percent describe themselves as lower or lower middle class. Over time, the percentage of those who describe themselves as middle class has been fairly stable.

When asked about their household incomes, half of the residents say they have just enough money to pay their bills and obligations. This is similar to national statistics. One in six say they do not have enough to make ends meet, while one in three report that they have enough so that they can save money and buy extras (see Appendix B, Table B-2).

Financial worries are also common among Orange County residents. Six in ten say they worry about money very often or fairly often, while four in ten say they do not often worry about money. These financial worries are tied to housing costs. Again, residents are paying some of the highest housing costs in the nation, and this seems for many to nullify their higher household incomes (Baldassare and Katz, 1992, 1996).[1]

___

1. When asked about their personal finances, 17 percent of Orange County residents described themselves as very satisfied, 50 percent as somewhat satisfied, and 33 percent as dissatisfied. Once again, most residents are thus moderately satisfied with their personal finances. As further evidence of declining economic fortunes, the percentage saying that they were dissatisfied had increased by fifteen points since 1982 (Baldassare and Katz, 1992).

TABLE 2-5   ORANGE COUNTY POPULATION
BELOW THE POVERTY LINE

	Population	Percent of Total Population
1990	200,860	8.3
1980	138,585	7.2

SOURCE: County of Orange (1993).

The foreign immigration has also contributed to the lower social status. There has been a growth in the lower-income population in Orange County. As of 1990 there were more than 200,000 residents living below the poverty level. This amounts to about 8 percent of the total county population. Between 1980 and 1990, the size of the population living in poverty grew by more than 62,000. The poverty population grew at a rate of about 45 percent for the decade (see Table 2-5).

Thus, it is inaccurate to describe Orange County as a wealthy county that went bankrupt. It is a remarkably average U.S. suburban region, except for its high housing costs. Orange County is a suburban region that is predominantly middle class. Most of its residents have modest means and are struggling to pay their monthly housing bills. The recession in the 1990s shook their confidence. It is thus not surprising that residents would express concerns about raising taxes and would welcome efforts by the county treasurer to find nontax revenue sources to pay for middle-class services.

FISCAL CONSERVATISM AND VOTER DISTRUST

How conservative is Orange County? Once again, the national stereotype is exaggerated. Voter registration records, election results, and public opinion surveys can be used to draw an accurate profile of the county that has become synonymous with political conservatism in modern-day America. In fact, it is not that extreme.

Before the bankruptcy struck, in November 1994, voter records indicate that Orange County was 52 percent Republican and 35 percent Democrat. Thirteen percent were registered as independents or belonged to other parties. There were nearly 650,000 Republicans, compared with 428,000 Democrats and about 164,000 independents and other party members, among the 1.2 million registered voters (see Table 2-6). Voter registration figures were similar in the 1996 election.

TABLE 2-6   ORANGE COUNTY'S
POLITICAL PARTY AFFILIATION, 1994

	Registration	Percent
Republican	648,996	52
Democrat	428,038	35
Independent/other party	163,744	13
Total	1,240,778	

SOURCE: Secretary of State (1994).

Since the 1970s, as Orange County has been rapidly growing,
Republicans, independents, and other party members have been sur-
passing the Democrats in terms of growth (Secretary of State, 1972,
1994, 1996).

Republican candidates for president in the 1980s enjoyed overwhelming support that went well beyond their party's 52 percent registration in Orange County. Ronald Reagan won by 68 percent to 23 percent in 1980 and by 75 percent to 24 percent in 1984. George Bush
won by 68 percent to 31 percent in 1988. Democrats, independents,
and other party members were also attracted to the Republican tickets
in these presidential elections.

The landslide of support for Republican presidential candidates in
Orange County ended in 1992. George Bush received only 43 percent
of the vote, compared with 32 percent for Bill Clinton and 24 percent
for Ross Perot. Again, in 1996, overwhelming support for the
Republican ticket failed to materialize. Bob Dole received only 51 percent of the vote, compared with 38 percent for Bill Clinton and 8 percent for Ross Perot (Secretary of State, 1980, 1984, 1988, 1992,
1996). These trends suggest that for Republican candidates to do very
well in Orange County, they have to reach out beyond the Republican
Party's base and attract significant numbers of Democrats and independents to their causes. It was possible for them to find common
ground in political orientation and policy preferences across parties in
Orange County. The national Republican candidates who did well,
such as Ronald Reagan, appealed to the popular themes of tax cuts
and voter distrust.

Republicans running for elected office in Orange County have done
very well in recent decades. They did so by articulating the popular
views of fiscal conservatism, that is, maintaining middle-class services
without raising taxes. All of the U.S. Congress members, state legislators

in the assembly and the senate, and members of the Board of Supervisors were Republicans as of November 1994.[2] In fact, the only Democrat holding countywide elected office at that time was Orange County Treasurer/Tax Collector Bob Citron. He was a local politician who was promising to give Orange County voters more revenues to pay for more services without new taxes.

The political orientation of Orange County residents is not nearly as monolithically conservative as one might expect. When asked to describe their political orientation, six in ten adult residents place themselves in the middle-of-the-road to somewhat conservative categories. Only one in six in the 1994 survey claimed to be very conservative in terms of politics. There are sizable blocks of moderate to somewhat conservative voters in both political parties. Nearly half of the Democrats and two out of three Republicans describe themselves in these terms. Only 5 percent of Democrats and one in four Republicans say they are very conservative (see Appendix B, Table B-3).

The results from public opinion surveys indicate that many Orange County voters are "fiscal conservatives" (Clark and Ferguson, 1983). That is, they tend to be conservative on fiscal issues and liberal on social issues. There is a large element of voter distrust at the root of their political attitudes. In a fall 1994 survey for the Los Angeles Times Orange County edition, three in four residents agreed that "when something is run by the government it is usually inefficient and wasteful." Eight in ten voters agreed that "poor people have become too dependent on government assistance programs." Two in three voters said that "the federal government controls too much of our daily lives." The Republicans and Democrats agree on these issues.

But there are also signs of liberal perspectives on nonfiscal issues. Three in four local voters agree that "there needs to be stricter laws and regulations to protect the environment." On the high-profile social issue of abortion, a 1992 survey found that 66 percent oppose "a law that would prohibit abortion in most cases," with only 29 percent in favor and 5 percent undecided (see Appendix C, Table C-1). The strong support for giving the individual a choice on abortion and other social issues has been a consistent finding in public opinion surveys in Orange

2. The Republican domination in Orange County elections is so well known that the defeat of Republican Congressman Bob Dornan by Democrat Loretta Sanchez in the fall of 1996 was national news. In actuality, Bob Dornan had been elected in an Orange County district that has been predominantly Democratic in registration since 1984.

County. This trend is found among Democrats, Republicans, and others (Baldassare, 1984; Baldassare and Katz, 1986; Times Orange County Poll, 1989, 1996a).

There are also consistent signs of conservatism on fiscal issues across party lines in Orange County. Seventy-four percent said that "many people who are currently on welfare are not really eligible" (Baldassare, 1985). Fewer than half agreed that "the government should guarantee every citizen enough to eat and a place to sleep" (Times Orange County Poll, 1994b). Sixty-eight percent said they "think the current welfare system changes things for the worse by making able-bodied people too dependent on government aid." Sixty-eight percent were in favor of cutting off all welfare benefits to people who have not found a job or become self-sufficient after two years. Nearly half said they wanted welfare programs to help low-income families to be either reduced or eliminated, while one in seven wanted them increased (Times Orange County Poll, 1995a).

Orange County's voting record on state and local initiatives confirms the findings of the public opinion surveys. The voters at the polls are fiscal conservatives. But even on this conservative litmus test, there is not complete consistency. There were times when local voters actually supported state and local tax increases in the 1990s.

Orange County voters overwhelmingly supported Proposition 13 when it was on the state ballot in 1978. Seventy percent voted for the citizens' initiative to limit property taxes. Proposition 4 won by an even larger margin in the special election in 1979. The Gann initiative to limit local and state government spending was supported by 82 percent of the voters in this low-turnout special election (see Table 2-7). There is no question about the county's staunch support for statewide tax and spending limits.

The record in Orange County shows that voters have been selective in their support for local tax increases. A measure to increase the Orange County sales tax by one-half cent for transportation programs won by a 55 percent to 45 percent margin in November 1990. This was after a one-cent sales tax increase for transportation failed by a wide margin in 1984 and a half-cent sales tax increase lost by a narrow margin in a special election in 1989. This local tax increase had the advantage of dedicating new funds to transportation systems. For years residents had said that traffic was the top county problem. The measure finally passed when the sales tax increase was reduced from one cent to one-half cent and mention was made about how the money would be

TABLE 2-7   ORANGE COUNTY VOTING IN
THE 1970S: STATE INITIATIVES TO LIMIT
TAXES AND SPENDING

Proposition 13: Tax Limitations		
Yes	404,878	70.3%
No	171,274	29.7

66.3% voter turnout in June 1978

Proposition 4: Spending Limitations		
Yes	247,437	81.6%
No	55,803	18.4

35% voter turnout in November 1979

SOURCE: Secretary of State (1978, 1979).

spent. The ballot measure included the establishment of a citizens' advisory committee to oversee the use of the tax money.

Orange County voters, however, overwhelmingly turned down another sales tax increase in May 1991. Only 26 percent supported a measure that would have increased the local sales tax by one-half cent to pay for more jails and courts, while 74 percent opposed it (Secretary of State, 1990; Orange County Registrar of Voters, 1991).

Orange County voters had a split ballot on tax and spending issues in November 1993. Fifty-two percent supported a half-cent state sales tax increase dedicated to spending on public safety. This tax increase passed at a time when concerns about crime were at a high point in the county. At the same time, 76 percent voted against a measure that would have allowed local school taxes to pass with a majority vote instead of a two-thirds vote as required by Proposition 13 (Secretary of State, 1993).[3]

The political climate in Orange County has the overall effect of making local elected officials reluctant to raise taxes. Local voters are fiscal conservatives who are distrustful of government. They will support tax increases only if they know that the money will be directed toward what they define as a major need. The reduction of local services is unpopular,

3. As a further sign that the county is liberal on social issues even while it is conservative on fiscal issues, a majority of Orange County voters supported Proposition 215, which legalized marijuana use for medicinal purposes (Secretary of State, 1996).

since many voters believe that funding can come from cutting waste in government. In the 1990s local elected leaders were inclined to look for other local revenues to meet growing needs in the midst of declining state support. Democrat Bob Citron's investment policies offered Republican elected officials a promising option, that is, raising interest revenues to maintain or increase local services.

THE WEAK STRUCTURE OF COUNTY GOVERNMENT

Orange County provides a classic example of the weak structure of local government in a suburban region. The profile is one of political fragmentation and locally oriented leaders in county government. These are the structural factors that led to a lack of oversight of the county treasurer before the fiscal crisis. Figure 2-1 outlines the basic structure of county government in fall 1994. Orange County is a "general law" county; thus, state laws largely determine its structure. At the top are the five members of the Board of Supervisors, who are elected within local districts to serve four-year terms. At the time of the bankruptcy, they were Tom Riley, Jim Silva, Roger Stanton, Gaddi Vasquez, and Harriet Wieder. There is a county administrative officer who is appointed by the Board of Supervisors. At the time, this was Ernie Schneider. The organization chart then divides county government functions into five branches. The General Government and Services Agency has four departments that are headed by countywide elected officials, including the assessor, auditor-controller, county clerk/recorder, and treasurer/tax collector. Five agency heads are appointees of the board. The branch of Public Protection includes the district attorney and sheriff/coroner's offices, which are headed by countywide elected officials; these were Mike Capizzi and Brad Gates. The municipal courts' and superior court's judges are elected by district, and six other departments in this branch are headed by appointees of the board. The Health Services, Community and Social Services, and Environmental Resources agencies each include numerous departments. Most of these departments are headed by appointees of the board, except for the public administrator/public guardian.

There are several weaknesses at the top of this organizational structure. Most important is the fact that the Board of Supervisors does not actually represent the county. Instead, the five supervisors are elected by district. The supervisors are thus oriented toward the

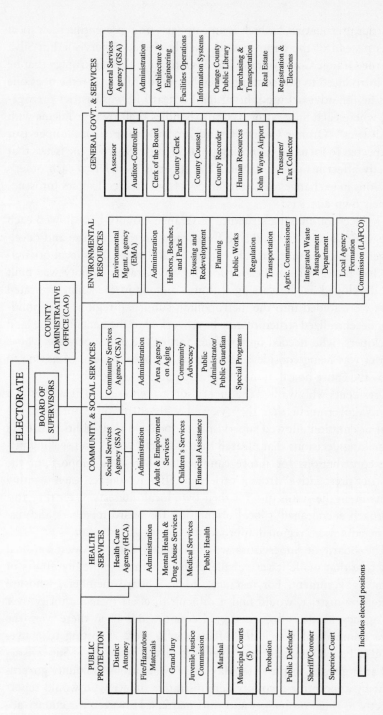

Figure 2-1. Structure of County Government in Orange County, December 1994. Source: County of Orange (1994).

"district prerogative," which is an emphasis on representing their local areas instead of the entire county. Newly elected supervisor Jim Silva told the Orange County grand jury investigating the bankruptcy that he was introduced to this concept when he ran for office. "I remember one term he [an advisor] used, first time I'd heard it, was district prerogative, where each Supervisor basically handles their own problems with the district" (Orange County Grand Jury, 1995a, p. 17). A supervisor is expected to focus on exercising political authority over the issues that directly affect his or her district. The supervisors defer to each other's decisions in exchange for future support from their colleagues for issues in their own districts.

The decision-making structure in Orange County has allowed each supervisor to take the lead role for decades in the land use and development decisions that affect his or her local district. This local orientation has had great significance for the way Orange County was built and developed as the vast agricultural regions in the unincorporated areas were folded into the metropolitan suburban region. This politically decentralized structure may have worked to the benefit of the land developers, who needed only the support of the one supervisor whose district was being considered for zoning changes, instead of having to lobby the entire board. It may have also had the support of city officials and residents who wanted the supervisors to represent their wishes in a county government that they viewed with suspicion. Moreover, the local orientation allowed supervisors to focus on their political careers by making decisions that pleased their district's voters and seeking private contributions for future campaigns. There was support for the "district prerogative" from a variety of different sources, each wanting to maintain the status quo for their own local interests. Over time this approach encouraged a local orientation for board members and discouraged a more regional approach to county government.

The Board of Supervisors was also faced with an organizational structure that made it very challenging to manage the daily affairs of county government. For instance, the five board members, who are elected by district, would find it difficult to exert their authority over the agency heads, who are elected countywide. Then there were the large numbers of nonelected officials who were reporting to a five-member board instead of one chief executive. The Board of Supervisors had attempted to improve the day-to-day operations of county government by appointing a county administrative officer who would report directly to them on budget and staff matters. However, the county administrative officer had no authority over the heads of any county agencies. Ernie Schneider, the chief administrative officer and previously the director of the Environmental Management Agency, said of this arrangement, "When I interviewed for the C.A.O. job, I told the Board that this was a dysfunctional organization the way it was set up" (Orange County Grand Jury, 1995b, p. 101). Schneider called the current structure a "disaster waiting to happen" and argued at that time "that you can't have 30 separate department heads reporting individually to the Board" (Orange County Grand Jury, 1995b, p. 104). He sent a memo to the Board of Supervisors in January 1990 outlining his plan to have all nonelected agency heads report through the CEO to the Board of Supervisors. In February 1993 he requested to the Board of Supervisors that his position be upgraded to chief executive officer. The Board ignored his requests in both cases, and at times they were openly hostile to the CEO proposal. One of the board members had actually argued in a 1990 memo that the Board of Supervisors is the "plural" chief executive officer for the county.

Even the CEO concept would not have addressed the politically sensitive issue of gaining more authority and control over the day-to-day operations of agency heads who are countywide elected officials. Treasurer/Tax Collector Bob Citron is a perfect example of a county official who was elected to represent a broader constituency than was any supervisor elected by district. Again, Supervisor Jim Silva's first exposure to the system of county government provides some useful insights into the lack of power that county supervisors had over the countywide elected officials. Silva recalls his first meeting with Treasurer Bob Citron. While on the campaign trail, Silva said, "I asked him about the investment pool and he basically said he's doing a very good job. He has a very good track record, and if I didn't believe him, that I could read his press clippings. And he turned around and walked away from me" (Orange County Grand Jury, 1995a, p. 31). The novice to county government was taken aback by the rude nature of this encounter and said, "I introduced myself as Jim Silva. I'm a candidate for the Board of Supervisors, and I thought right there he would want to talk with me because if I would be elected, I'd be working with him" (Orange County Grand Jury, 1995a, p. 31). The candidate for supervisor perceived that the county treasurer should have treated him with greater respect, or at least more curiosity, since he was a potential member of the Board of Supervisors. But the treasurer's role had autonomy and independence from the Board of Supervisors because it is an elected countywide office. The supervisors were not that relevant to the daily affairs of Treasurer Bob Citron.

In addition to the structural problems, there are other circumstances that resulted in a weak Board of Supervisors at the time of the financial disaster. Two of the five members, Tom Riley and Harriet Wieder, were retiring at the end of December. Both of these county officials had served for many years. Two new members would be joining the board in the middle of the bankruptcy. Riley was also chair of the board in 1994, and a new chair would be named to that position in January 1995. The changes in board personnel and leadership added to the chaos and confusion during the crisis.

ORANGE COUNTY'S SIMILARITIES WITH OTHER COUNTY GOVERNMENTS

It is important to note that the structure of county government in Orange County, with all of its obvious shortcomings, is not at all exceptional. There are fifty-eight counties in California. Every county has a Board of Supervisors, with its members elected to serve four-year terms. All but San Francisco, which has eleven board members, elects five members to its Board of Supervisors. Fifty-five of the fifty-eight counties elect their board members by district. The exceptions are San Francisco, San Mateo, and Tehama, which had at-large county elections in the fall of 1994. Fifty-four of the fifty-eight counties elect their treasurers. Only Los Angeles, Sacramento, Santa Clara, and Glenn counties have treasurers that are appointed to the county government. Forty-seven of the fifty-eight counties have an appointed county administrative officer. Five counties have more powerful officials, such as a county manager, CEO, or county mayor. Five counties are in rural areas and do not have full-time administrators (California State Association of Counties, 1996).

The similarities between Orange County and other counties in the state are partly derived from the fact that forty-five of the fifty-eight counties are "general law" counties and only thirteen have their own charters. Orange County, however, is one of the few populous California counties that does not have its own charter. Alameda, Fresno, Los Angeles, Sacramento, San Bernardino, San Diego, San Francisco, San Mateo, and Santa Clara counties all have their own charters. It is important to point out that a charter government does not necessarily mean a more accountable political structure. Most of the charter counties still have the structure of county government described here as dysfunctional in Orange County, including local district elections for five board members, a county administrative officer with little authority, and a treasurer who is elected countywide.

There are also many similarities between the structure of county government in Orange County and what is found elsewhere in the nation. Based on a survey of 3,044 U.S. counties, eight in ten have an elected board of supervisors. Half have their board members serving four-year terms. About one-third have five-member boards and hold district elections. Nine in ten elect the county treasurer. By contrast, few counties have people in positions that would improve the oversight and management of county departments. One in six say they have a full-time county administrative officer. One in twenty elect a county mayor (Koehler, 1983).

MANY LOCAL GOVERNMENTS

County government is just one element of the fragmented political structure of local government in Orange County. There are also many cities, school districts, single-purpose regional agencies, and local special districts involved in local governance. Orange County has thirty-one municipal governments, each with its own mayor, city council members, and city budgets to provide local public services (see Figure 2-2). This is a highly diverse group of cities in terms of size and population composition. No city comes close to representing a central city for this suburban region. The largest places are Santa Ana and Anaheim, each with fewer than 300,000 residents. In 1990 seven cities had populations of over 100,000, ten cities had populations of more than 50,000 and less than 100,000, nine cities had populations of fewer than 50,000 and more than 25,000, and five cities had fewer than 25,000 residents. Only about 6 percent of the population lived in the unincorporated areas served by the county government.

In addition to the thirty-one Orange County cities and county government, other key elements define the local government structure. The Orange County Transportation Authority is a massive single-function agency with its own budget, sales tax, and appointed board of directors. There are twenty-seven local school districts, which each have their own elected governing boards, bond financing, and budgets (State Controller, 1992a). There are 126 special districts that deliver water,

Figure 2-2.   Orange County Cities. Source: Center for Demographic
Research (1996).

sanitation, and other public services in certain areas, with their own
budgets, financing, and elected officials (State Controller, 1992b). A full
portrait of the politically fragmented government within this suburban
region would thus include at least 186 local government entities. This
explains how nearly 200 public agencies could have invested their
money with Citron.

The ways in which local governments in Orange County responded to the political fragmentation they faced is also important. In county government the supervisors followed the "district prerogative," which focused on their local areas. In the cities the elected leaders were also locally oriented. Most cities were members of the Orange County Division of the League of California Cities, but that was a voluntary association that did not involve much in the way of city-to-city cooperation. Typically, cities were competing for business and commerce centers within their borders. As a rule, the cities were hostile toward the county government because of land use conflicts.

A telling story from the Orange County grand jury testimony involves, again, Jim Silva. He describes the questions he asked about the $40 million that the City of Huntington Beach had in the county investment pool while he was a member of its city council. The city treasurer said, "The County Investment Pool had X number of million dollars on deposit so that if the city did need their money back, they could get the money back" (Orange County Grand Jury, 1995a, p. 27). Silva reported on that statement, "So with that I felt pretty secure because it seemed like there was several hundred million dollars on reserve that would be used to pay the City back if they needed that money" (Orange County Grand Jury, 1995a, p. 28). But he failed to consider the fact that about 180 other cities, local school districts, and local special districts may have been given similar assurances, and that the combined investments of these local governments could not be covered by the county pool's deposits on hand. Nor did the Huntington Beach officials check with their counterparts in other Orange County cities to see if they had raised similar concerns with the county treasurer about the liquidity of the county investment pool.

The grand jury testimony provides a good example of the poor communications that were common in Orange County, both between city governments and between city governments and the county government. Further evidence of a local orientation is seen in the resistance to regional governance in the years leading up to the bankruptcy. The Orange County cities and county government could not reach agreement on a council of governments for Orange County. The cities and county government officials were also reluctant to be involved in Southern California regional agencies, such as the Southern California Association of Governments and the Air Quality Management District.

The city data indicate that most of the municipal governments in Orange County were experiencing population changes that would lead to fiscal pressures. Twenty-two of the thirty-one cities experienced double-digit growth rates in the 1980s. Cities such as Irvine, Mission Viejo, and Tustin were rapidly gaining new residents who were moving to their new homes and planned communities. Older, large cities such as Santa Ana, Anaheim, and Garden Grove had large influxes of foreign immigrants. The percentage of the city population that was white and non-Hispanic had become 23 percent in Santa Ana, 57 percent in Anaheim, and 55 percent in Garden Grove. Many of the cities in the northern portion of the county had experienced an increase in both the Hispanic and Asian populations because of foreign immigration. Thus, many cities were facing external conditions that would place fiscal pressures on the delivery of municipal services. Voters in these cities wanted to maintain services but would be unwilling to have their taxes increased. Orange County's cities and special districts were thus as much in search of new revenues, without an increase in taxes, as was the county government. This is one reason most of the local governments invested funds with Bob Citron.

LOCAL FOCUS AND REGIONAL APATHY

Orange County residents tend to focus their attention on their city or area while ignoring the overall region. This reflects the local political views that are common in suburban regions. Many residents believe that city government does a good job of representing their local interests. They would prefer to see their cities have more power and the county government less power over their daily lives. The public's apathy toward the county government had an enormous role in the financial crisis.

Responses to the questions asked in a survey about local government indicate that most Orange County residents preferred the current system of fragmentation and local political authority. Fifty-six percent of residents said "the current system of county government and city government sharing responsibilities for solving problems" was effective, while 39 percent described it as ineffective. However, if given a choice, most would prefer to give their city governments more power. Fifty-eight percent said they would prefer to give their city governments more responsibility in the community, while only 28 percent said they would like to see the county government with more responsibility than it already had. There are no differences between Republicans and Democrats in this heavy leaning toward a more local orientation.

Moreover, 63 percent said they would oppose "the merger of county government and city governments into one large countywide government." Only 29 percent would support a regional government. At least six in ten Republicans and Democrats are opposed to having one countywide government (see Appendix B, Table B-4).

About six months before the bankruptcy made headlines, a random sample of 600 Orange County voters were asked, "When it comes to Orange County's leaders, what names come to mind?" This was an open-ended question that allowed up to three responses. Fifty-six percent of Orange County voters drew a blank and could think of no one. Twenty-two percent could think of only one leader, 11 percent named two, and only 11 percent mentioned three people whom they considered Orange County leaders.

Relatively few residents named the members of the Board of Supervisors or other county government officials when asked to name their county's leaders. Eleven percent named Supervisor Tom Riley, 11 percent mentioned Supervisor Gaddi Vasquez, 8 percent named Supervisor Harriet Wieder, and 10 percent mentioned Sheriff/Coroner Brad Gates (see Appendix C, Table C-2). Less than 3 percent named Supervisor Roger Stanton, Supervisor William Steiner, District Attorney Mike Capizzi, Clerk/Recorder Lee Branch, or Treasurer/Tax Collector Bob Citron. This means that when the bankruptcy took place, there were no public figures seen as county leaders.

The survey also asked questions to elicit the name identification and popularity of each of the five members of the Board of Supervisors. In the same survey, voters were asked if they had "a favorable or an unfavorable opinion" of each of the five supervisors in Orange County politics, or if they "didn't know enough about them to have an opinion." The majority of Orange County voters said that they didn't know enough about each county supervisor to have an opinion. The "don't knows" ranged from 58 percent to 78 percent. About one-quarter had favorable opinions of Tom Riley, Gaddi Vasquez, and Harriet Wieder. The unfavorable views ranged from 11 to 18 percent for these three county officials. One in six had a positive impression of Roger Stanton and William Steiner, while 6 and 9 percent, respectively, had unfavorable opinions. The supervisors were not even well known in their districts. The county's top officials, then, were largely unknown to residents when disaster struck in 1994 (see Appendix C, Table C-3).

One can contrast the invisibility of county government leaders in Orange County with the high profile of mayors in big cities such as

San Francisco and Los Angeles. When asked about Mayor Frank Jordan, 45 percent of San Francisco voters had a favorable opinion, 50 percent had an unfavorable opinion, and only 9 percent of voters had no opinion (*San Francisco Chronicle*, 1995). As for Mayor Willie Brown, 63 percent had a favorable opinion, 19 percent an unfavorable opinion, and 18 percent no opinion (*San Francisco Chronicle*, 1996). When Richard Riordan was a candidate for mayor of the city of Los Angeles, 32 percent had a favorable opinion, 43 percent had an unfavorable opinion, and 25 percent had no opinion (KCAL, 1993). The relative invisibility of county government leaders is striking. It reflects the fact that city governments have more day-to-day contacts and meaning for the average resident than county government. The five supervisors, even within their own local districts, are not viewed as having the same kind of significance to voters as their mayor.

It is possible that Orange County's voters could not recall the names of particular supervisors, but could still have an overall positive impression of the actions of the five-member county board. In the same 1994 survey, voters were asked to evaluate the Orange County Board of Supervisors on a number of dimensions. About one in four gave the board excellent or good ratings "in terms of providing overall leadership." Half gave them fair ratings for this issue, and 15 percent said they did a poor job in leading the county. Once again, there were no differences between Democrats and Republicans. The positive ratings for overall leadership were six points lower than in a similar 1992 survey. One in four also gave the Orange County Board of Supervisors either excellent or good ratings "in terms of representing the views of local residents." Forty-two percent said they did a fair job, and 27 percent said they were poor on this dimension. This means that as many voters ranked them in positive as in negative terms for representing the views of residents. There were no differences between Democrats and Republicans in these judgments toward the all-Republican Board of Supervisors. A 1992 survey had also found that 30 percent of Orange County voters thought the supervisors did well in representing the views of local residents. In general, then, the ratings that the Orange County Board of Supervisors received from voters were mostly mediocre along key dimensions of job performance (see Appendix C, Table C-4).

It is important to note that the county supervisors' ratings were well below those achieved by the city government. While the questions were not identical, about four in ten gave their city governments excellent or good ratings for solving problems in their community. In contrast, only one in four said that the county supervisors were doing a similarly good job in either providing overall leadership or representing the views of local residents. This again reflects the local orientation of Orange County residents and their tendency to favor the actions of their city officials over their county officials.

Other job ratings of the county supervisors were also low. Twenty-nine percent said the Orange County Board of Supervisors did an excellent or good job in "maintaining integrity and high ethical standards." A similar number gave them poor ratings on this dimension. The county supervisors received their best rating of all for "fostering the county as a place to do business." Forty percent said they did an excellent or good job with this task. The number with positive feelings, however, had slipped dramatically by 29 points since a 1988 survey (Times Orange County Poll, 1994a).

The May 1994 survey also asked about several countywide elected officials who were on the June primary ballot. The sheriff/coroner and the district attorney were in uncontested races, so voters were asked to rank their job performance. Sheriff /Coroner Brad Gates had the highest popularity and name identification of any county official, including the members of the Board of Supervisors. Fifty-one percent said he was doing an excellent or good job, one-third said his performance was fair, and only 10 percent rated him as poor. Also significant is the fact that only 8 percent had no opinion about the sheriff's job performance. Both Democrats and Republicans gave the sheriff/coroner high ratings. The fact that voters had a favorable view of Sheriff Brad Gates was to play an important role during the early stages of the bankruptcy. This was the county official who took one of the lead roles in managing the fiscal emergency.

The district attorney was much less well known than the sheriff. Only 34 percent gave District Attorney Mike Capizzi either an excellent or good rating. Twenty-three percent said he did a fair job, and only 7 percent rated him as poor. A third did not know enough about Capizzi to rate his job performance. There were no significant differences across party lines. In the election for the county's clerk/recorder, which involved incumbents for this merged office, about half of the voters had no opinion about how they would cast their votes. Thus, most other elected county officials generated as little public interest as the supervisors (see Appendix C, Table C-5).

As for the treasurer/tax collector election, this was a relatively high-profile campaign, but many voters apparently tuned it out. John

Moorlach had accused Bob Citron of making dangerous financial investments in search of high yields for the local government funds. For months the stories about this campaign had appeared in both major newspapers. Two weeks before the election Citron led by a two-to-one margin, but 36 percent of the voters had no opinion. Republicans and Democrats gave the current treasurer, a known Democrat in Republican Orange County, a healthy lead.

A local orientation among residents is fairly common in the context of the political fragmentation that takes place in suburban regions. What was unique to Orange County in the 1990s was a decline in residents' satisfaction with the public services they were receiving from local government. The majority of residents were still rating their parks and recreation, police protection, and streets and roads in excellent or good terms. Seventy-one percent gave positive ratings to their parks and recreation, 59 percent to police protection, and 58 percent to streets and roads. But the positive evaluations were down more than ten points from a decade earlier for each of these local public services. Even more dramatic was a seventeen-point decline in the evaluations of local public schools. Twenty-eight percent gave their local public schools excellent or good ratings in the 1991 survey, compared with 45 percent a decade earlier (see Appendix B, Table B-5). The increasing urbanization in the county—in particular, the larger population sizes, higher densities, and changes in ethnic and racial diversity of Orange County's cities—was closely tied to the lower public service ratings (Baldassare and Wilson, 1995). These results offer evidence that local governments were straining to keep pace with the service demands of their residents. In this context, local elected officials sought extra revenues by investing their government funds in the county pool.

SUMMARY

Orange County today is very different from its portrayal as a white, middle-class suburban region. It is the fifth most populous county in the United States, having reached a size of 2.5 million residents after many decades of rapid population growth. Recently the county has been a major site of immigration from Asia and Mexico, and this is leading to significant racial and ethnic change. Rapid growth and increasing diversity have placed demands on local governments to provide both more and different public services. The county had an economic boom in the 1980s, followed by a severe recession. In the early 1990s the job market shrank, business declined, incomes stagnated, and housing values dropped. The mostly middle-class residents were in no mood to raise taxes. As a result, local governments struggled to raise the revenues they needed to provide services.

The political profile in Orange County is often described as very conservative and Republican. In actuality, though, most residents from both major parties express more moderate views that are conservative on fiscal issues and liberal on social issues. At the heart of the voters' opposition to tax increases is a distrust of government officials and the perception that there is a lot of waste in government spending. Residents want their elected leaders to reduce taxes, but they do not want cuts in middle-class services. They believe that services can be maintained or increased by increasing the efficiency of local government bureaucracies. Local elected officials needed to find ways to meet these demanding requirements by their voters.

At the time of the fiscal crisis, the structure of local government in Orange County was one of layers upon layers of political fragmentation. The members of the Board of Supervisors were focused on their local districts. The countywide elected officials, such as the treasurer/tax collector, had little oversight and considerable autonomy. There were thirty-one cities, more than two dozen local school districts, and over one hundred local special districts without any real ties to county government or each other.

County residents were locally focused and apathetic toward county government. Most were unaware of the supervisors and could not name a county leader. Few had focused on the county treasurer's race, despite the serious allegations raised against Bob Citron. In the early 1990s there was a decline in the perceived quality of local services. City and county officials, who were interested in pleasing their constituents and extending their political careers, would be in search of new revenues for improving local public services. They could not raise taxes or cut services. In this context, many local officials were attracted to the interest income promised by the county treasurer.

Orange County had a combination of demographic, economic, political, and governmental features that help to explain why the fiscal crisis occurred in this suburban region in 1994. Many of these features are not unique. Orange County simply had more extreme versions of the characteristics found elsewhere in California and throughout the nation's populous suburban regions. It also had a treasurer named Bob Citron, whose actions were the catalyst for this event. We conclude from this that the Orange County financial crisis could be repeated in other locales at other times.

CHAPTER 3

The California Context

From Proposition 13 to Fiscal Crisis

Orange County does not exist in a vacuum. It is highly influenced by the trends that are occurring throughout California. Orange County's population and employment growth generally follow the statewide cycles. Its county government is also highly dependent upon the state government. Sacramento is a major source of funding, and it determines in large part the range of county services that are provided. Thus, fiscal changes at the state level have profound local impacts. This chapter reviews the California context before the Orange County bankruptcy.

The story begins when Proposition 13 was passed by the state's voters in 1978. It continues over the next decade as the state government imposed new rules for counties in terms of their revenues, expenditures, investments, and programs. It ends in 1994 with the state in a severe recession and budget crisis. All of these state trends created conditions without which the Orange County financial crisis would not have occurred.

PROPOSITION 13 AND ITS LEGACY

It would be impossible to fully understand the Orange County bankruptcy without looking at Proposition 13 and its legacy on local fiscal policy. The county government may not have turned to their county treasurer for new revenues from interest income without the loss of property tax funds. Local officials could have raised local taxes to pay for the debt incurred by the bankruptcy except for the fact that voter approval was required. The bankruptcy recovery plan may not have taken such a long, stressful, and complicated route if there were fewer restrictions on how the county governments could use the money they received from the state government.

Proposition 13 marks the beginning of a new era in California fiscal governance. This 1978 initiative had profound significance for the fiscal relations between the state and its local governments. The amount and sources of funding for county governments were changed by the imposition of severe limits on what was once their major source of tax revenues. The fiscal relations between the state government and the county government were also permanently altered, placing the county governments in a much more dependent position. Proposition 13 forced the state agencies, county governments, cities, local special districts, and local school districts to reach new agreements on how to provide local public services to California residents.

Proposition 13 was a citizens' initiative. It passed by a wide margin in the California primary of June 1978. There were several parts to this state law. The property tax rate was limited to 1 percent of the sales price. Property assessments were limited to a 2 percent annual increase until the property was sold again. Current property assessments were rolled back to 1975–1976 levels. Proposition 13 placed the burden of dividing the local property taxes that were collected each year on the state legislature. The new law also made it more difficult to raise taxes. A two-thirds vote from the state legislature was required to pass any new state taxes. Two-thirds voter approval at the ballot box was needed for the passage of new local special taxes (Legislative Analyst, 1993a, 1995a).

The implications of Proposition 13 were profound. Property taxes were reduced and future revenue growth from this source would be severely limited. There was an initial loss of $7 billion as a result of the 57 percent reduction in property tax revenues throughout the state. County governments were particularly reliant on property taxes as a revenue source. On average, before Proposition 13 the county governments received about a third of their funding from property taxes, half from state and federal sources, and about a sixth from the sales tax, fees, and other sources (Raymond, 1988, pp. 1, 5).

County governments would either have to find other revenue sources to compensate for the loss of property tax income or cut their local services. However, many of the services they provided were mandated by the state or federal government. The state legislature, which was re-

TABLE 3-1   STATE AND LOCAL GOVERNMENT
TAX AND SPENDING RESTRICTIONS
FROM 1978 TO 1994

1978	Proposition 13: Limited property tax rate to 1 percent; legislature responsible for dividing property tax among local entities; two-thirds voter approval required for new local special taxes
	SB 154: One-year "bailout" program to offset local property tax revenue losses under Proposition 13
1979	Proposition 4: Imposed spending limits on state and local governments and schools; required states to reimburse local entities for mandated costs
	AB 8: Permanent "bailout" program; "buyouts" of county health and welfare costs; property taxes shifted from schools to cities, counties, and special districts
1982	AB 799: Transferred responsibility for providing health care for the medically indigent from state to counties
1988	Proposition 98: Established minimum state funding level for K-12 schools and community colleges
1992	Proposition 162: Repealed "snack tax" and prohibits future sales tax on food items; AB 2181 in 1991 had raised sales tax from 4.75 percent to 6 percent and allowed tax on snack foods
1993	Proposition 172: Imposed half-cent sales tax; dedicates revenue to local public safety

SOURCE: Legislative Analyst (1995a, 1996a).

quired by Proposition 13 to divide the property tax revenues among the local entities, passed a one-year "bailout" in 1978. The SB 154 bill set up the formal procedure for the state government to allocate local property tax funds to county governments. It also provided financial relief for the county governments by taking over all or a portion of the costs of several health and welfare programs. In exchange, the county governments were required to maintain certain services, such as police and fire protection, at specific levels. The state economy was in good shape in the late 1970s and the state budget had a surplus. The state was able to reallocate surplus funds in order to help pay for county services (Raymond, 1988, pp. 6–10).

Proposition 4, the so-called Gann spending limit, was passed by the state's voters in a special election in November 1979. This statewide initiative generally limited spending by state and local governments to the "proceeds of taxes." Spending growth would be adjusted each year for population growth and inflation. This new state law placed a ceiling on state and local government and school spending each year. The Gann spending limit also included a provision requiring the state government to reimburse the local governments for mandated services (see Table 3-1).

That same year the state legislature also passed a permanent bailout program for the loss of property taxes from Proposition 13. The AB 8 bill shifted the property taxes from the local school districts to the counties, cities, and special districts. It also made permanent the transfer of certain expenses for health and welfare programs from the counties to the state government. This legislation also had a "deflator" provision. This required that local governments would receive less funding whenever the state revenues fell short of expectations (Raymond, 1988, pp. 10, 11). The possibility of the counties losing funds that were provided in the bailout was not an immediate concern while the economy was growing and there were surplus funds in the state budget. The issue of the counties losing their financial support was, however, to resurface when the state government faced a serious budget crisis in the early 1990s.

Proposition 13 and the bailout legislation that followed had a significant impact on county revenues. County government revenues fell by 13 percent in the first few years after Proposition 13 passed. Property tax revenues declined throughout the state by 44 percent. For county government budgets, this meant that property taxes declined as a revenue source from 34 percent to 22 percent. The county government's relationship with the state also changed. The share of the county budget that was derived from state funding increased from 22 percent to 33 percent (Raymond, 1988, p. 10).

The ways in which the state legislature decided to allocate funds for the permanent bailout has had an effect on the counties that is still felt today.[1] Table 3-2 summarizes the fiscal relief provided by AB 8 for the five most populous counties in the state. Los Angeles received by far the most fiscal relief from the state. However, it is much larger than any other county. Orange County received the lowest amount of fiscal relief funds in this group. There were smaller counties that received more money from the state, such as Alameda, Santa Clara, and San Diego. But the fiscal relief from Proposition 13 was not on a per capita basis. The state legislators took into account the property tax rates before Proposition 13. Orange County had the lowest property tax rate among the five largest counties. It was considerably lower than the rates in Los Angeles, Alameda, and Santa Clara counties. In fact, Orange County had the lowest property tax rate in the state. The state legisla-

1. Some Orange County leaders make the argument that the distribution of property taxes was unfair and that the decision was politically motivated by the Democratic leaders in the state legislature against the Republicans from Orange County.

TABLE 3-2   BEFORE AND AFTER PROPOSITION 13
Property Tax Rates and State Fiscal Relief for the Five Most
Populous California Counties

	County Tax Rate (1977–1978)	AB 8 Fiscal Relief (1979–1980)	Population (1980)
Los Angeles	$4.24	$682,565,000	7,500,300
Alameda	3.07	85,241,000	1,109,500
Santa Clara	2.22	65,422,000	1,300,200
San Diego	1.83	64,930,000	1,873,300
Orange	1.33	58,717,000	1,944,800

SOURCE: State Controller (1978); Green (1979); California Department of Finance (1996a).

ture also took into account the costs of running county programs that were funded by these higher tax rates. That is the reason given for why Orange County did not fare as well as other counties in terms of the state's fiscal relief.[2]

Orange County officials have always been bitter about the state's allocation plan. Some county leaders blamed partisan politics for this funding decision. They argue that the Republicans who represented Orange County were punished by the Democrats who controlled the state legislature. Other local leaders have gone so far as to say that the unfavorable allocation of property taxes by the state legislature was a cause of the financial crisis that resulted in bankruptcy. It led the county officials to look elsewhere for revenues and allow their treasurer to take risks to increase the interest income.

Although the state government was generally in the position of taking over the financial responsibility for county programs, there were some important exceptions. The AB 799 legislation in 1982 transferred the responsibility for providing health care for the mentally ill from the state to the county government. The risk for counties was that this category of local government spending had the potential to grow in the future. In fact, the medically indigent population did increase rapidly when large numbers of foreign immigrants moved into the state, adding to the county's fiscal problems.

Another fiscal trend after Proposition 13 was the voters' use of "earmarking" of state funds and new taxes. This was a further reflection of the voters' lack of trust in their elected officials. Proposition 98, passed in

2. I am grateful to Fred Silva for providing this information and insight about the state fiscal relief to counties after Proposition 13.

1988, required a minimum state funding guarantee for local public schools and community colleges. A certain proportion of any new state tax revenues would also have to be dedicated to the state's K-12 school districts and the community college system. As for limiting general tax revenues, in 1992 Proposition 162 repealed a "snack tax," which was part of an overall sales tax increase passed by the state legislature the year before to help move the state toward a balanced budget. This citizens' initiative also took away the state's ability to place a sales tax on food items in the future. The following year the state passed Proposition 172, which earmarked a half-cent sales tax for local public safety. The voters had also passed a state gasoline sales tax increase in 1990, through Proposition 111, with the funds dedicated specifically to transportation improvements.

Voting requirements for increased taxes, which date back to Proposition 13, provided demanding hurdles for state and local governments trying to raise new revenues. For instance, a two-thirds vote is needed for the state legislature to increase its general taxes or special taxes. Local taxes require support from a majority of the voters or a majority of the local governing board, which is the Board of Supervisors in county governments. Special taxes require a yes vote from two-thirds of the local voters. Approval of state bonds requires a majority of voters for general obligation bonds and a majority of the state legislature for other bond offerings. Local bonds require a two-thirds approval of the voters for general obligation bonds, such as local school or park bonds. A majority vote from the local governing board is needed for other bonds. In practical terms, strict voting requirements to increase local taxes or bonds limit the county's fiscal options. A two-thirds majority would place many tax increases or bond offerings out of reach. The voting requirements for increased taxes had implications for how Orange County would be able to raise funds to manage its financial crisis. This raised new doubts on Wall Street about the abilities of local governments in California to pay off their debts.

Proposition 13 was not the end of the tax revolt. In retrospect, it was just the beginning. The era of fiscal conservatism is still unfolding. Throughout the 1980s and early 1990s there have been incremental changes in tax and spending policies that were made through state legislation and citizens' initiatives. These have added new complications to the ways in which state and local governments can go about raising taxes and spending money. The end result is that the finances of county government are on shakier grounds since 1978. As Alvin Sokolow, a political scientist at the University of California–Davis, noted at the tenth anniversary of the passage of Proposition 13, "County budgets . . . are greatly affected by the budget games at the state. Local governments are too linked to the state. This further lessens their autonomy" (Hahn, 1988, p. 7). In 1996 the voters struck again and passed Proposition 218, adding more restrictions to the passage of new local taxes. This is discussed later in the book.

DEMANDS ON COUNTY GOVERNMENTS

What can county governments do? In order to understand the implications of the Orange County bankruptcy, we review the current roles, funding, and expenditures for county governments in California.

County government is not well understood. Edwin Epstein described it as a "shadowy operation whose existence is nearly forgotten, save for the quatra-annual election of a largely unknown county supervisor and the twice-yearly reminder when property tax payments must be sent to a remote figure—the County Treasurer and Tax Collector" (Raymond, 1988, p. vii). This is certainly an ironic statement, given the impact that the Orange County treasurer had in 1994. Monterey County Supervisor Barbara Shipnuck adds, "Most people orient themselves toward their city councils, yet in many ways, county supervisors have a more immediate effect on their lives" (Hahn, 1988, p. 37).

Counties are officially political subdivisions of the state government. Their operations combine both state and local functions (see Harvey, 1993, p. 244). In California the local functions are divided between the county governments, city governments, special districts, and local school districts. The state government mandates many of the tasks of county governments. Over time, the county's leaders have determined fewer.

The functions of county government cover a wide variety of services. They are required to provide welfare and public assistance programs, such as Aid to Families with Dependent Children, mostly through federal and state funds. County governments are in charge of local public safety programs, including the offices of the county sheriff, district attorney, probation, courts, county jails, flood control, and fire protection. There are a variety of environmental programs in the county's domain, including pollution control, zoning and land use regulations, and environmental management. There are several important public health tasks at the county level, such as sanitation; hospital care for the medically indigent; and mental health, drug abuse, and alcohol abuse programs. There are recreation programs, such as the maintenance and operations of county parks, beaches, and other recreational facilities. The counties have a variety of public works projects, including freeway construction and road maintenance.

The counties are also charged with general government tasks, such as record keeping, maintaining vital statistics, tax collecting, voter registration, and management of local elections. They also have an education function, including the operation of a county library system and a county education department, which runs special programs for local school districts and is in charge of maintaining statewide standards. Finally, there are the miscellaneous tasks that are the responsibility of county governments, such as animal control, agricultural regulations, building inspections, and ambulance services.

Another major function of county governments is the provision of local services in the unincorporated areas. Within the city limits, most municipal governments in the state are in charge of providing police protection, parks, libraries, street maintenance, land use zoning, health clinics, and waste disposal for their residents (Harvey, 1993, p. 246). However, some areas of the county have residents living outside the city limits of all of the municipalities. There are large numbers of residents living in vast unincorporated areas, especially in the urbanizing counties of the state. The counties have to provide what is generally expected of a city government in these areas, including such functions as police, parks, libraries, street repair, and land use.

It is important to note that the county government and city governments are not the only local governments that provide needed services within a county's borders. Local school districts have their own governing bodies and funding sources, and they are in charge of implementing local public education according to the standards set by the state government. There are also special districts that provide services such as transportation, water, utilities, and air pollution regulation. The geographic areas of these special districts vary from tiny locales to very large regions.

At the time of the bankruptcy, the major sources of revenues for the county governments in California were state agencies. They provided 42 percent of county revenues (see Table 3-3). Next are the federal funds, which account for 22 percent of a county's money. This means that about two out of three tax dollars are received from federal and state sources. Fifteen percent of county funds were from property taxes in 1994. This is down sharply from the roughly one in three tax dollars

TABLE 3-3   REVENUE SOURCES AND
EXPENDITURES OF COUNTY GOVERNMENTS
IN CALIFORNIA, 1994

	All California Counties	Orange County
Types of Revenue Sources		
State agencies	42.1%	39.0%
Federal and other intergovernmental	22.2	15.4
Property taxes	15.4	13.3
Services, charges	12.2	15.3
Interest, rental revenue	2.8	12.0
Licenses, permits, fines	2.7	3.9
Sales and other taxes	2.6	1.1
Total amount (millions)	$25,592	$1,798
Categories of Expenditures		
Public assistance	40.7%	32.6%
Public protection	26.8	38.1
General government	8.8	10.0
Health and sanitation	17.2	14.2
Public ways and facilities	3.5	2.0
Education, recreation, other	3.0	3.1
Total amount (millions)	$25,785	$1,587

SOURCE: State Controller (1994).

from property taxes in the 1970s before Proposition 13 passed. About
12 percent of a county government's funds are from payments for services and other kinds of charges. Much smaller amounts are generated
from interest income, property revenue, licenses, permits and fines, and
the sales tax and other taxes. All together, county governments
throughout the state received about $25.6 billion in funds in 1994.

The fifty-eight county governments in California now spend most of
their money on a few large programs. About 41 percent goes to public
assistance programs and 27 percent goes to public protection. These
two categories amount to about two-thirds of all county expenses.
Seventeen percent is for health and sanitation spending, while 9 percent
goes toward general government functions. County programs obvi-
ously play a critical role in the lives of poor residents, although many
services touch the middle class. The expenditures of county governments in California totaled about $25.8 billion in 1994. These are

telling numbers, indicating that the county revenues fell short of what was needed to pay for all of the county services that were mandated by the state and federal governments.

In 1994 the Orange County statistics for revenue sources and expenditures were quite exceptional. Fifty-four percent of the revenues in Orange County came from state and federal sources, compared with 64 percent for the state average. Thirteen percent of the funds were from property taxes, a figure that is also lower than the percentage of revenues for other counties. To make up the difference, Orange County received 12 percent of its revenues from interest and rental revenue, compared with less than 3 percent for the statewide average. This was largely a result of the interest income that was generated by Treasurer Bob Citron's investment activities. These statistics show that Orange County had become highly dependent on the county pool to make up for less in outside revenues.

The ways in which Orange County chose to spend its money also varied from other county governments in the state. Public protection was the major budget category, accounting for 38 percent of the county budget, compared with a statewide average of 27 percent. Orange County was less likely to spend its money on public assistance; specifically, 33 percent of the budget went for local welfare programs compared with 41 percent for county governments throughout the state. Orange County spent about $1.6 billion and received about $1.8 billion in revenue in 1994. There was a budget surplus in Orange County while the rest of the counties in the state faced a deficit. This helps to explain why Orange County had such a strong credit rating only a few months before the treasurer's investment pool collapsed and the county went into bankruptcy.

To have a complete picture of how county governments operate, one also has to take into account the fact that the general fund's sources include both intergovernmental revenues and general-purpose revenues. The intergovernmental revenues are provided for specific programs and must be spent only for those purposes. About 60 percent of the county's general fund dollars have to be spent on specific programs, such as health and welfare programs for the state and federal governments. However, this does not mean that the county government is free to spend the other 40 percent of their revenues as they choose. Some of the funds have to be used to pay for state-mandated programs that are not fully funded by the state government. Other funds are allocated to programs that are essential, such as jails and police protection.

The county governments do not have a lot of flexibility as to how to spend their money. Barbara Shipnuck noted, "The legislature adopted legislation indicating that they would send money back to the counties from the state surplus. But instead of the counties being able to use these funds with a great deal of discretion, the money had a lot of strings attached. Now, counties find themselves in control of budgets that are ninety percent driven by state requirements" (Hahn, 1988, p. 38). This would present a problem for Orange County as it sought to balance its budget during the fiscal crisis.

DEREGULATION OF THE COUNTY TREASURER'S INVESTMENTS

All county governments have to do something with their cash on hand. The treasurer is responsible for investing these funds so that they will earn interest income. In California, local school districts are required to deposit their funds in the county pool. Some cities and special districts voluntarily invest in county pools. The county pool was looked upon as a nontax revenue source for local governments after Proposition 13.

The state government has the authority to regulate the ways in which the county government can invest its cash on hand. For many decades the state's laws have tightly regulated the kinds of investments that county treasurers could make. For instance, the county treasurers were required to make deposits in commercial banks, savings and loans, credit unions, and industrial loan companies in addition to a narrow range of other, safe options. These regulations concerning the county treasurer were changed as a result of the state laws enacted after Proposition 13 passed.

In 1979 the state legislature made a fateful decision about local investment deregulation that would bring on the Orange County financial crisis in 1994. A year after Proposition 13 became law, the legislature passed AB 346. This allowed local agencies to purchase or sell securities under repurchase agreements or reverse repurchase agreements. Two years later SB 1152 expanded the types of investments that a local agency could make to include guaranteed portions of Small Business Administration loans. In 1983 AB 695 and AB 323 allowed a local government to increase the amount of its fund that could be invested in commercial paper from 15 percent to 30 percent and increased the amounts that could be invested in banker's acceptances from 30 percent to 40 percent. A year later SB 2095 authorized local

TABLE 3-4   STATE LEGISLATION ON LOCAL
TREASURER'S INVESTMENTS

1979	AB 346: Authorized county treasurers to invest in repurchase agreements and reverse repurchase agreements; county treasurers need approval from the Board of Supervisors
1981	SB 1151: Expanded the types of investments that a local agency can make to include guaranteed portions of Small Business Administration loans
1983	AB 695: Increased the amount of a local agency's money that may be invested in commercial paper from 15 percent to 30 percent
1983	AB 323: Increased the amount of a local agency's surplus funds that can be invested in banker's acceptances from 30 percent to 40 percent
1984	SB 2095: Authorized local agencies to invest in certain mortgage securities
1986	SB 2595: Expanded the types of securities and obligations in which a local agency can invest its surplus funds or funds in custody to include medium-term corporate notes
1987	SB 962: Increased the amount of the local agency's surplus funds that may be used to purchase medium-term corporate notes from 15 percent to 30 percent
1988	SB 1883: Revised the collateral requirements for local agency surplus cash deposits by deleting the prohibition against the use of mortgage loans with negative amortization
1992	AB 3576: Authorized county treasurers to invest up to 20 percent of their portfolios in several forms of highly rated collateralized mortgage instruments

SOURCE: State Senate (1995).

agencies to invest in certain mortgage securities. In 1986 state bill SB 2595 expanded the types of securities that a local government could invest in to include medium-term corporate notes. The next year SB 962 further added to the list of acceptable securities and increased the proportion of funds that could be invested in medium-term corporate notes. In 1988 SB 1883 allowed local governments to use mortgage loans with negative amortization features as collateral. In 1992 AB 3576 was enacted, and this state bill authorized county treasurers to invest up to 20 percent of their portfolios in collateralized mortgage instruments. This legislation is summarized in Table 3-4.

These are only nine of the state bills that deregulated the county treasurer's investments. A state senate report (1995) prepared for the investigation of the Orange County bankruptcy lists nineteen bills that the state legislature has passed since 1979 that have changed the rules governing and thus affect the security of county investment funds. The same report concluded that AB 346, allowing the use of reverse repurchase agreements, and AB 3576, permitting investments in collateralized mortgages, were the most significant for understanding the collapse of the Orange County Investment Pool.

These changes at the state level opened the door to the risky strategies followed by Bob Citron. County treasurers were permitted to leverage their investment funds, that is, borrow money based on the principal on deposit by local governments. They could then use the borrowed money to buy longer-term notes and derivatives that would raise the interest income. The overall impact of following such an investment strategy was that there was a higher risk that the value of the principal could decline. Only local agencies that can afford to lose some of their principal, or that have the time to wait for their funds during a financial market downturn, should invest heavily in high-risk funds. In reality, very few local agencies would publicly admit to taking such risks with taxpayer money.

Why did the state government move to deregulate the activities of the county treasurer? It should be noted that this was a significant change that occurred slowly and incrementally over a thirteen-year period, rather than an intentional policy decision made at one point in time. There were probably several reasons for this trend in the 1980s and early 1990s. Some of the factors involved state and local government in California, and others were related to developments in the private sector.

For example, county government officials had asked the state government to give them more fiscal autonomy and independence. The deregulation of the treasurer's investments was seen as another step toward giving local elected officials the ability to make decisions about local affairs. Another factor is that state and local governments were looking for some new local revenue sources after Proposition 13 passed. The ability to earn a higher yield on surplus funds meant that county governments could tap a new source of extra income without asking the local voters or the state legislature.

Another factor was the general trend of deregulation of financial practices throughout the United States. In the 1980s a host of new investment opportunities became available to average citizens, businesses, and local governments. The standard investments such as money market accounts, certificates of deposit, Treasury bills, and savings accounts gave way to trading in stocks, bonds, futures, and derivatives. Local treasurers were thus following a societal trend when they turned to riskier securities to increase their interest income. The white-collar fraud that surfaced when the savings and loan industry was deregulated, including embezzlement and cover-ups (Calavita and Pontell, 1992), has parallels with the Orange County bankruptcy.

Finally, there was the effective lobbying of the financial industry in the state legislature. Many investment companies and financial brokers stood to make money by being able to sell their financial instruments to county treasurers. The investment firms were active in supporting the state bills that deregulated the local treasurer's operations. Some observers have also pointed out that investment firms helped to fund the campaigns of county officials and state legislators who were the supporters of state bills to expand the types of allowable investments for local government funds.[3]

It is remarkable, in retrospect, that the state government would also loosen the restrictions on the county treasurer's investment reporting at the same time it was passing state bills to allow for more risky investing. But they did. For fifty years SB 133 had required the county treasurer to issue quarterly reports to local agencies that had cash in county investment funds. In 1983 SB 389 changed this regulation so that the local treasurer had to issue quarterly reports only when the local agency paid for them.

The state passed AB 1073 in 1984 and reinstituted investment reporting. This was after the City of San Jose had lost millions in risky investments under conditions that were similar to what would happen in Orange County a decade later. This state law had a "sunset clause" effective January 1, 1991, which meant that the law governing the local treasurers would revert back to the 1983 law unless the state legislature extended the new state mandate. Legislation for the 1990–1991 state budget suspended the requirement for investment reports. On January 1, 1991, the law returned to its 1983 form, and local treasurers were no longer required to provide investment reports to local agencies. In fact, SB 443 loosened the requirements for quarterly interest reports even if local agencies asked for them (see Table 3-5).

Why would the state government drastically reduce the investment reporting requirements? Once again, the state was giving local governments more autonomy and greater control over their actions. The state

---

3. Bob Citron has been credited with authoring some of the state legislation that relaxed the investment rules for county treasurers.

TABLE 3-5   STATE LEGISLATION ON LOCAL
TREASURER'S INVESTMENT REPORTING

1933	SB 133: Required local treasurers to issue quarterly investment reports to local agencies that had money on deposit
1983	SB 389: Required the local treasurer to issue quarterly reports only when the local agency asked for them
1984	AB 1073: Passed after the City of San Jose lost substantial money on investments; mandated an annual statement of the treasurer's investment policy, a monthly report on the types of investments for the local agencies, and a detailed monthly report if repurchase agreements or reverse repurchase agreements were involved; included a "sunset clause" reverting to the 1983 law on January 1, 1991
1990	1990–1991 state budget suspended the 1984 state-mandated investment reports
1991	On January 1 the 1984 law reverted to its 1983 form (SB 389) because of the "sunset clause"; local treasurer's investment reports suspended from 1991 to 1994
1993	SB 443: Made the requirement for quarterly interest reports permissive, even if the local agency asked for them

SOURCE: State Senate (1995).

was also offering local governments a way to save money by not having to produce reports. The initial change in state law occurred during the early fiscal stress of Proposition 13. The reporting requirement was dropped again when counties were facing fiscal difficulties in 1991.

A major question raised by the state deregulations is the extent to which the new investment risks were understood by the county, city, special district, and school district officials who were placing funds in county investment pools. The fact that state lawmakers passed the bills allowing such investments could have been seen by some as an endorsement of their use and a signal that their principal was safe. Other local officials may have known the risks and looked the other way. The idea of making more money from interest income on cash deposits was just too appealing to resist. In any case, it is important to note that the Orange County bankruptcy would not have occurred if the state government had not changed the rules governing the counties' investments.

FROM BOOM TO BUST

California has been gaining new residents at a rapid pace for many decades. This was an enormous challenge to state and local governments operating under tax and spending limits. The population was about 20

million in 1970, 24 million in 1980, and 30 million in 1990. The state
population increased to 32 million by 1994. California is by far the
most populous state in the nation (California Department of Finance,
1996a). The state's rapid growth from 1980 to the early 1990s was
largely a result of historic levels of immigration from Asia and Latin
America. Immigration occurred during some of the best and worst of
economic times. These demographic and economic changes placed severe strains on the state's ability to provide health, education, and welfare services. They would have important consequences on the fiscal
health of all California counties.

The rate of immigration has been phenomenal. From 1980 to 1994
the state gained about 2.8 million residents through legal immigration
(California Department of Finance, 1997). Over 200,000 foreign immigrants were arriving each year in the early 1990s (Johnson, 1996, p. 34).
One-fourth of the population growth of the state since 1980 can be directly attributed to legal immigration; births account for most of the rest.

The statistics on legal immigration do not take into account the large
numbers of undocumented immigrants who were also arriving in
California at the same time. Estimates of the number of illegal immigrants entering California between 1980 and 1993 range from 1.4 million to 2.0 million. Between 1980 and 1985 the net undocumented
immigration was under 100,000 a year; this grew to well over 200,000
a year by the late 1980s and then fell to below the level of 100,000 per
year in the early 1990s (Johnson, 1996, pp. 68–71). [4]

The changes in racial and ethnic composition since 1980 reveal a
dramatic shift over just a decade and a half. In 1980 67 percent of California residents were non-Hispanic whites, 19 percent were Hispanic,
7 percent were black, and 7 percent were Asian (California Department
of Finance, 1996b, 1996c). In 1994 54 percent were non-Hispanic
whites, 28 percent were Hispanic, 10 percent were Asian, and 7 percent
were black. The percent of the California population that was non-
Hispanic and white had dropped by thirteen points from 1980 to 1994,
while the proportion that were Asian or Hispanic increased by twelve
points.

These demographic trends would have an impact on state tax revenues. Older, more middle-class, and higher-tax-paying segments of the
population were now a smaller percentage of the total population.

4. Johnson (1996) documents a range of illegal immigration flows using a variety of
statistical sources in what is certainly the most comprehensive study to date.

Younger, lower-income, and more welfare-dependent groups of new immigrants represented a larger share of the population. By 1994 24 percent of California's population was foreign born. There were a total of 7.7 million foreign-born residents in California. One out of every three foreign-born residents in the United States was living in California in 1994 (California Department of Finance, 1997).

These population trends had major cost implications for county governments. Foreign immigrants tend to be younger, and their presence is felt acutely in the local public schools and public health institutions. Foreign immigrants, especially the undocumented immigrants, tend to have low incomes, which creates high demands for social, health, and welfare services. Most of the immigrant population that moved to California in the 1980s and early 1990s could be found in six counties: Los Angeles, Orange, Santa Clara, San Diego, San Francisco, and Alameda (California Department of Finance, 1997). It is thus interesting to note that both Orange County and Los Angeles County saw their governments face severe fiscal problems by late 1994.

The state and local governments could generate the tax revenues needed to expand public services as long as the economy was growing at a rapid pace. In the 1980s California's employment numbers were phenomenal. There were over 3 million jobs created in California between 1983 and 1990, a growth rate of 29 percent. The rate of employment growth was thus outpacing the rate of population growth (Employment Development Department, 1996). The state's economy took a severe turn for the worse in the early 1990s. There were a number of factors in the California downturn, including the national recession, the loss of aerospace and defense industry jobs after the Cold War ended, the downsizing occurring in large corporations, and a sharp decline in real estate values. More than 400,000 jobs were lost in California between 1990 and 1993. Over a quarter million jobs were lost in the traditionally higher-paying manufacturing industries. The recession was so severe and widespread that only a few industries experienced increases in their labor force. Unemployment increased from 5.8 percent in 1990 to 9.4 percent in 1993 (Employment Development Department, 1996). Still, the immigrants moved to the state, and demands for services were increasing.

Trends in income distribution in California were occurring that would also seem to place pressures on both state revenues and state expenditures. There was growth in median household income in the state and the nation in the early 1980s, though it was faster in the nation

(Reed, Haber, and Mameesh, 1996). However, median household income began to stagnate in California around 1987. During the recession in the 1990s the median household income fell at a sharper rate in California than in the rest of the nation. There was a widening gap between the household incomes of the wealthy and the poor. One of the major causes of the growing income inequality was the recession. The income trends no doubt also reflect the rapid growth of the immigrant population. The worsening financial situation for the poor would add to the state's revenue problems. This would increase health and welfare spending while reducing tax revenues.

There were also more pressures on state government expenditures after the Los Angeles riots in 1992 (Baldassare, 1994). The costliest outburst of urban violence in this century occurred after the police officers accused of beating Rodney King were found not guilty by a mostly white jury. Following several days of unrest in the South Central area of Los Angeles in the spring of 1992, residents throughout the state began to identify crime as the biggest problem. The public turned to their local and state officials for efforts to make them feel safer. They called for more police protection in their neighborhoods. Voters wanted stiffer penalties for crimes and no parole for repeat offenders. State and local government officials responded by expanding police protection and increasing the punishment for crimes. Elected officials committed large sums of money to more police, local jails, and state prisons. They did so at a time when they were having problems paying for programs already in place.

State government was faced with the worst of all possible combinations by the early 1990s. There continued to be a growth of expenditures because of an increase in population that was fueled by historic levels of foreign immigration. There were shrinking revenues because of higher unemployment. There were demands for public services created by the severe recession, worsening poverty, and an epidemic of crime fears. The state's leaders were left with difficult choices that all had political risks. The rapid pace of economic growth that had allowed the state government to operate under the fiscal constraints of Proposition 13 was gone. The funding of bailouts for local governments through excess revenues or state surpluses was no longer an option.

Moreover, local governments were also in a fiscal bind. Many of the counties experiencing the highest rates of foreign immigration were the same places seeing massive layoffs in large companies, the aerospace and defense industries, and the real estate industry. Los Angeles and Orange counties were particularly hard hit by the economic downturn in the 1980s, and they were also the major destinations for Asian and Mexican immigrants. Local governments had a major fiscal problem on their hands. This time, they could not expect the state government to be of much help.

THE STATE'S FISCAL CRISIS

The governor and state legislature were faced with a difficult situation by 1991. The combination of a severe recession and rapid immigration was taking its toll. The state's revenues were growing at a slower rate than its spending. There was no end in sight to the slowdown in tax revenues. Nor was there any sign of moderation of the increases in major state expenditures. Officials would have to do something about the ballooning state deficit. Their decisions had major impacts on county governments.

State leaders could raise taxes, cut state spending, shift costs to local government, or redirect the state revenues that were being sent to local governments as part of the bailout for Proposition 13. Because of the restrictions placed on their actions by state initiatives, raising taxes was not an easy task in the state legislature. It was also a road that was full of political dangers in a state dominated by antitax voters. There were also limits on how much spending could be cut because of federal mandates to provide certain services, such as programs for foreign immigrants and welfare recipients. The governor and state legislature reached an agreement to use several approaches at their disposal to try to close the state's budget gap. Their actions were to have significant consequences for county governments.

In 1991 there were three state bills that raised tax revenues in the state. The state sales tax rate was raised from 4.75 percent to 6.0 percent through AB 2181. Legislation also eliminated the sales tax exemptions for certain foods—for example, the so-called snack items—as well as periodicals such as newspapers. This had the effect of raising approximately $3.85 billion. Also, SB 169 increased the income tax rates for high-income taxpayers and reduced certain tax exemptions and tax credits. This created an additional $880 million in new tax revenues. Finally, AB 758 changed the fee structure for vehicle licenses. This raised another $770 million (Legislative Analyst, 1993a). Together these state bills increased tax revenues by $5.5 billion a year.

The state also sought to lower its expenses by shifting more of the responsibility for health and social service programs to the counties. What the state was doing, in part, was reversing some actions it had taken a decade earlier to help the counties overcome the problems they faced after Proposition 13. It was also transferring future expenses for the growing needs for health and social services, created by an exploding population of low-income foreign immigrants, from the state to the local governments.

This "program realignment" was accomplished through bills AB 758, AB 948, and AB 1288 in 1991. The state placed the county governments in charge of all mental health service delivery, which included community-based mental health programs, state hospital services for mental patients, and institutions for mental diseases. The counties would also take control of public health programs, including county health services and local health services. The state also gave the counties the responsibility for indigent health, including the Medically Indigent Services Program and the County Medical Services Program. The cost of the Local Block Grants Program was also transferred to the county. Finally, the state also changed the state and county cost-sharing ratios for a number of jointly funded health and social programs. For instance, in the past the county may have paid 75 percent of the expenses, and it would reduce this amount to 50 percent in the future. These health and social services included California Children's Services, AFDC-Foster Care, Child Welfare Services, In-Home Supportive Services, the County Services Block Grant, the Adoption Assistance Program, and the Greater Avenues for Independence Program (Legislative Analyst, 1995a, p. 4).

The county governments were to receive about $2 billion in new revenues generated from the increases in the sales tax and in vehicle license fees to pay for their increased county expenditures. Table 3-6 indicates that the increased expenses caused by shifting programs to the counties and changing the cost-sharing ratios were higher than the new tax funds that were received from the state sales tax and vehicle license fees. In addition, the legislative analyst (1995a, p. 3) reports that the new county revenues have fallen short of the additional expenses for each year since the legislation was enacted. The result of the program realignment, then, is greater fiscal strain for county governments.

The budget deficit continued, and the state government was forced to take further actions to increase its revenue base in 1992 and 1993. Two bills were passed that had serious implications for the financial health of county government. The effect of this state legislation was to

TABLE 3-6   PROGRAMS TRANSFERRED FROM
THE STATE TO COUNTIES IN 1991
All Figures in Millions of Dollars

Costs Shifted to Counties	
Mental health	750
Public health	506
Indigent health	435
Local block grants	52
Total costs	1,743

County Cost-Sharing Ratio Changes	
California children's services	30
Social services	441
Total costs	471

Additional County Revenues (January 1992 estimate)	
State sales tax	1,350
Vehicle license fee	712
Total additional county expenditures	2,214
Total additional county revenues	2,062
Revenue shortfall for counties	152

SOURCE: Legislative Analyst (1995a).

TABLE 3-7   PROPERTY TAX REVENUE REDUCTIONS FOR
LOCAL GOVERNMENTS IN 1992 AND 1993

1992	SB 617: $1.3 billion in property tax revenue shifted from local governments to schools, reducing the amount of the state general fund spent on public education
1993	SB 1135: $2.6 billion in property taxes shifted from local governments to schools; counties lose approximately $2 billion, cities about $300 million, special districts and redevelopment agencies about $300 million

SOURCES: *San Francisco Chronicle* (1992); *Cal-Tax News* (1993).

take back some of the bailout funds that had been allocated to the county government after Proposition 13. This fundamentally changed the contract and relationship between the state and its local governments.

Table 3-7 summarizes the two state bills that reduced the property tax revenues for local governments. In 1992 SB 617 shifted $1.3 billion in property tax revenues from local governments to local school districts. The local governments that lost tax funds included cities, counties, and special districts. This allowed the state government to reduce the amount it spent on public education. In 1993 SB 1135 transferred $2.6 billion in property taxes from local governments to local school districts. The counties lost approximately $2 billion in property taxes. The cities and special districts each saw their level of funding drop by about $300 million. The transfer of $3.9 billion from the local governments to local school districts occurred in two stages, both in the 1992–1993 fiscal year and the 1993–1994 fiscal year. The state legislation that authorized the property tax transfer was also permanent (Legislative Analyst, 1995a, p. 3); there was no sunset clause. County governments could anticipate receiving a lower amount of property tax revenue until the state legislature decided to change the law again.

The state budget was still deeply in the red in 1994, despite all of these actions. This placed severe constraints on state government spending. The legislative analyst (1994, p. 2) had estimated in May of that year that the state would have a $4.6 billion budget deficit in the 1994–1995 budget. This included a $2.2 billion carryover from the 1993–1994 budget and a $2.4 billion shortfall in the 1994–1995 budget. The tax revenues improved from that dismal forecast as the economy improved. Still, the governor and state legislature had to agree to a state budget that included a two-year plan for ending the deficit spending. The state would begin the fiscal year in July 1994 by carrying forward a $1.6 billion deficit. The next fiscal year would start with a $668 million deficit. If all went well, by July 1996 there would be a small surplus (see Table 3-8).

This dismal budget scenario was based on a number of optimistic and fairly controversial assumptions. It was expected that the federal government would provide California with $3.6 billion to pay for foreign immigration assistance programs over these two years, when no such promises were made. There was also an assumption that the state would continue to see a modest economic recovery for two consecutive years, even though the economy continued to be in the doldrums. The state expected only a modest growth in expenses to pay for the state's programs, despite the fact that others were predicting continued growth in the populations of foreign immigrants and young children. In the event that these expectations were off base, the state budget also included a "trigger" mechanism that would put into effect automatic spending cuts for most categories of state spending. The only programs

TABLE 3-8   THE STATE BUDGET, 1994 AND 1995

	Estimated General Fund Condition (millions of dollars)	
	1994–1995	*1995–1996*
Prior year balance	−1,619	−688
Revenues and transfers	41,892	45,442
Total resources available	40,273	44,776
Expenditures	40,941	44,399
Fund balance	−688	375
Reserve	−1,020	23

SOURCE: Legislative Analyst (1994).

that would be spared were those protected by the state constitution, such as K-12 public education or programs required by federal law (Legislative Analyst, 1994).

Demographic trends in California were having an impact on the budget process. Up until the late 1980s, the working-age population was growing at a faster rate than the school-age population. This meant that "tax payers" were increasing in number more than "tax receivers." This trend began to reverse in the early 1990s for several reasons. The lower birth rates in the 1960s and 1970s resulted in a slowdown of the working-age population. A sharp decline in this key demographic and economic group was expected between the 1980s and the 1990s. In the meantime, the school-age population was increasing rapidly, from about 15 percent in the 1980s to 40 percent in the 1990s (California Department of Finance, 1991). The increase in the number of children was a reflection of the higher birth rates for recent foreign immigrants. It was widely known by state leaders during the 1990s budget crisis that "receiver populations" such as school-age children, the elderly, and those who depend on state aid would be growing rapidly. The big fear was that there might not be enough state funds available to pay for the future service needs.

Thus, even in the midst of a state budget deficit, there was talk of an even worse "looming budget crisis" in California (see Carroll, McCarthy, and Wade, 1994). Ninety percent of the state's $41 billion budget in 1994 was allocated to spending on health and welfare, prisons and corrections, public education from kindergarten to high school, and public colleges and universities. The problem that many envisioned was a rapid increase in the first three categories of state spending. The health and welfare population would grow because of the increase in the elderly population, foreign immigrants, and the poor. The prison population would explode because the state's voters had passed a "three strikes" measure, which required repeat criminal offenders to have long prison sentences. The number of students enrolled in the state's public school system was anticipated to grow by 30 percent in the 1990s as a result of demographic trends. Nearly half of the state's budget would be allocated to public education by 2002, since that spending is mandated by the state constitution based on Proposition 98, and there would be little left to pay for health, welfare, and higher education. The state government in 1994 thus viewed severe fiscal austerity as a permanent condition.

The issue of illegal immigration became a heated topic in California as the state budget crisis worsened during the 1990s. The governor's office blamed the federal government for not doing more to reduce illegal immigration into California. Moreover, the governor's office complained that the state and local governments were not being reimbursed for the federally mandated services that were being provided to illegal immigrants. In fiscal year 1994–1995, the cost for federally mandated programs such as education, incarceration, and health care was estimated at $2.4 billion. Further, $1 billion was spent on state general services for illegal immigrants, such as police protection, road and park usage, and environmental protection. Then there were estimates that the children of illegal immigrants cost the state another $900 million for education, health, welfare, and state services. The governor's office assumed that the tax revenues generated by illegal immigrants living in California amounted to only $700 million because of their low wages. Thus, the total cost of illegal immigrants was estimated to be $2.7 billion (Romero and Chang, 1994).

The governor sought to counteract the effects of illegal immigration on the state budget in two ways. First, there was an attempt to lobby the federal government to pay for more services to illegal immigrants. In November 1994 a state initiative was passed by the voters seeking to deny illegal immigrants many public services. However, both of these efforts had little bearing on the state budget crisis in the early 1990s.

In sum, the state's budget crisis had large implications for county governments. Their costs increased when the state transferred some health and social services. Their revenues shrank when the state took back some of the property tax funds from the Proposition 13 bailout.

The state had eliminated the chances of raising local taxes, however slim they may have been, when it increased state taxes in 1991. The state government was having long-range problems with budget deficits in mid-1994. It signaled to the local governments that they could expect no fiscal relief from the state government for several years. They would have to find new revenues or cut spending.

ORANGE COUNTY'S SOLUTION

Orange County, like other county governments, saw its program expenses increasing while its state revenues were dwindling in the 1990s. It was faced with a loss of property tax revenues, as the state kept some of its funds. It had higher expenses because of the program transfers from the state to the county governments. The county had a large and growing immigrant population, and the immigrants' service needs were placing more pressures on the county budget. Given the circumstances, county leaders could either raise new revenues or reduce their expenditures. The state and federal mandates prevented them from reducing programs for the poor. The middle-class voters would revolt if the services they used were cut. They needed more revenues.

For county leaders, the possibility of raising taxes to increase revenues seemed remote. First, there were the practicalities imposed by Proposition 13. It was unlikely that voters would raise their taxes so that local governments could restore funds. The state government had just raised the sales tax, state income tax, and motor vehicle fees. It was now even less likely that voters would support another tax hike.

In Orange County the solution seemed simple enough. The county government embarked on a growing reliance on interest income from the county pool as the state government reduced its property tax funding. As shown in Table 3-9, based on the sources of general county funds, the property tax revenues were stable between 1989 and 1992. There was a $10 million loss of funds in the first stage of the property tax transfer. By the 1993–1994 fiscal year, the county government was receiving $100 million less in property taxes from the state than it had in the 1991–1992 fiscal year.

The county government compensated for these losses through interest income generated by the Orange County Investment Pool. The interest income had steadily increased from $37 million to $82 million between 1989 and 1993. Then the interest income rose by over $100 million to

TABLE 3-9   ORANGE COUNTY'S SOURCES OF
GENERAL COUNTY FUND REVENUES
Millions of Dollars

	1989–90	1990–91	1991–92	1992–93	1993–94
Property taxes	236	236	239	229	138
Interest income	37	48	60	82	206

SOURCE: State Controller (1990, 1991, 1992c, 1993, 1994).

$206 million in the year the state drastically reduced its level of property tax funding. The county government leaders had become dependent on the investments of the county treasurer to bail them out of the difficult fiscal situation in which they had been placed by the state government.

SUMMARY

The California context is a major factor in understanding the events that unfolded as Orange County slid into fiscal crisis in 1994. Some of the state's conditions were causal factors in the fiscal decisions that led up to the bankruptcy. Poor fiscal conditions would make it difficult for the state government to come to the aid of Orange County in its time of need. State conditions would also set the parameters for the solutions that were possible for resolving the Orange County bankruptcy.

The tax and spending restrictions that began with Proposition 13 in 1978 are critical elements in the Orange County story. First of all, county governments lost their major source of local revenues, property taxes, and their right to raise local taxes without asking the voters. As a result, the county governments became highly dependent on the state government to provide the funding that they needed for a wide array of local services.

Although they receive little recognition for their efforts, county governments in California have a large number of important roles. They are the ones who deliver many of the health and welfare programs to the poor that are mandated by the state and federal governments. They offer a variety of local services to all residents. The county budgets were tight after they received a Proposition 13 bailout from state government. County revenues were largely restricted to certain uses by state and federal agencies.

After Proposition 13, the state government offered the county governments a rather unorthodox way to raise their revenues. The state deregulated the investments of the county treasurers in a series of state bills from the late 1970s to the early 1990s. The new state rules made it possible for county treasurers to buy longer-term instruments and to leverage the funds they were receiving from local agencies. This new freedom was given to local governments because it offered county treasurers an opportunity to make more money with their cash on hand. This would help to compensate for the loss of property tax funds after the passage of Proposition 13. Bob Citron was one of the county treasurers who took advantage of this opportunity.

California has experienced rapid population growth since Proposition 13 passed. Much of the recent growth is a result of foreign immigration. The result has been increasing demands for health, education, and welfare programs. The state's economy went from boom to bust in a decade and a half. The state budget deficit was ballooning, and tax increases and spending cuts could not close the deficit gap. The state legislature responded in the 1990s by breaking the contract it had made in the bailout of county governments after Proposition 13. The state government took back some of the funds it had previously given to county governments.

Orange County responded to the state's funding cutbacks by embarking on a strategy of using the state's loose restrictions on treasurer investments. The treasurer followed a risky strategy to increase the country's interest income to compensate for the declining state aid. The county leaders hoped that, by taking this route, they could avoid spending and service cuts or proposals for tax increases, all of which would have stirred anger among their fiscally conservative voters. The schools, cities, and other local governments put their money into this financial venture. For a while the new post–Proposition 13 fiscal strategy seemed to work. The outcome was a financial disaster of historic proportions for local governments in Orange County by the end of 1994.

CHAPTER 4

Events Leading up to the Bankruptcy

The Orange County financial crisis came suddenly, but not without warning. Throughout 1994 there were people saying that the county treasurer was taking too many risks with the Orange County Investment Pool. Why did no one look into his actions until it was too late? It may have been because Citron's financial transactions were so complicated that only the experts were able to follow his strategy, because he had a successful track record that kept his critics in check, or because he was highly secretive. For county officials, it was easier not to question and to accept the high interest earnings. The magnitude of the financial problem was thus underestimated by almost everyone. Even those who had a suspicion of difficulties were surprised at the size of the losses.

This chapter examines the important events leading up to the financial calamity in December 1994. This was not the usual bankruptcy scenario of a troubled central city with declining revenues and rising expenditures. The local governments in Orange County were considered highly creditworthy up until the very end. Their downfall was the result of an overwhelming desire to live beyond their means by increasing their local revenues. They could not say no to the interest income that was gained through risky investments.

THE ORANGE COUNTY INVESTMENT POOL

By the beginning of 1994, the Orange County Investment Pool was an accident waiting to happen. The size of this government fund had

TABLE 4-1   AMOUNT OF TOTAL
INVESTMENT IN THE ORANGE COUNTY
INVESTMENT POOL

Date	Amount Invested (billions)
January 31, 1991	$ 5.1
January 31, 1992	6.9
January 31, 1993	10.5
January 31, 1994	20.9

SOURCE: California State Auditor (1995).

grown enormously, mostly because the fund had become highly leveraged. Moreover, the financial instruments that were being purchased
with borrowed money were highly volatile. In sum, big risks were being
taken with funds from many local governments (see Jorion, 1995).

Table 4-1 summarizes the growth of the Orange County Investment
Pool during the 1990s. The fund more than quadrupled, from about $5
billion in 1991 to almost $21 billion in 1994. Moreover, the fund
nearly doubled in size between 1993 and 1994, when it grew from
$10.5 billion to $20.9 billion. The Orange County Investment Pool was
a "commingled" fund, with money on deposit from the county and
other local public agencies. The use of a commingled fund allowed local
governments to pool their money and purchase securities that would be
unavailable to smaller investors. This was a way to earn higher yields
for local governments (California State Auditor, 1995, p. 2).

How did the Orange County Investment Pool grow to be so large in
such a short period of time? First, local public agencies flocked to the
fund that promised the best investment returns in the state. In all, there
were 194 investors when the fund crashed in late 1994. Next, many of
the local public agencies placed more and more money in the fund as a
way of increasing their interest earnings. In fact, some even borrowed
money with the expectation that they could increase their revenues with
the "spread" between the money they owed and the money they would
earn from higher yields. Although the rush to place money on deposit
in the county pool may seem like foolishness, there was also some des-
peration in these actions. The growth of fund deposits was coincidental
with the state government's rollback of property tax revenues from
counties, cities, and special districts to resolve the state fiscal deficit. The
Orange County Investment Pool provided an opportunity to gain new
revenues to replace the lost state dollars.

The major reason that the pool grew to be so large, however, was the borrowed money. Table 4-2 indicates that $7.6 billion of the total fund was placed on deposit by the 194 local agencies. The other $13 billion consisted of funds that were borrowed from Wall Street using the original investments as collateral. The Orange County Investment Pool thus became a fund that was highly leveraged. For every three dollars used to purchase securities, about two dollars was borrowed money.

There is major consensus that this leveraging was the main reason for the Orange County financial disaster. U.S. Treasury Undersecretary Frank Newman said, "Orange County got into financial trouble because it was highly leveraged." Arthur Levitt, chairman of the Securities and Exchange Commission, said, "The fault lies in a failed investment strategy involving the use of borrowed money for speculation." A *Wall Street Journal* editorial agreed, stating, "Bob Citron got into trouble simply by borrowing short to go long" (Merrill Lynch, 1995, p. 4-1).

The county treasurer borrowed these huge sums of money through financial transactions with Wall Street firms called "reverse repurchase agreements." The use of reverse repurchase agreements, which were once outlawed, was allowed by state legislation after Proposition 13 passed. The agreement works as follows. A security that the county government owns is held by an investment broker as collateral for a short-term loan. The county government then uses the borrowed money to buy another security. The county agrees to pay back the short-term loan, and, if it does not, the security held by the investment broker as collateral can either be kept or sold. The high yield that was achieved by the Orange County Investment Pool is mostly attributed to the use of these reverse repurchase agreements (California State Auditor, 1995, p. 11).

The county treasurer was very taken with his past success. He once boasted to the Board of Supervisors, "We have perfected the reverse repo procedure to a new level" (Office of the Treasurer–Tax Collector, 1991) and showed that his investment yields were consistently higher than those of the state treasury. Citron's "perfected" strategy was based on multiple borrowing on the same security to increase the leveraging of the county fund.

The California state auditor (1995, pp. 11–13) provides a simplified version of the very complex financial scheme followed by Bob Citron. First, the county treasurer buys a short-term bond in the amount of $1 million that pays at 6 percent and uses this as collateral to borrow about that same amount of money from a brokerage firm at 5 percent, to be paid in 180 days. Then, using the borrowed money, the county treasurer purchases a longer-term bond that pays 7 percent and then uses the longer-term bond as collateral for another 180-day loan at 5 percent. Finally, using this borrowed money, the county treasurer buys a longer-term bond at 7.5 percent and uses this bond as collateral for another 180-day loan.

The strategy used by Citron, as summed up in the quote from the *Wall Street Journal* editorial, was "borrowing short to go long." Such a strategy requires a stable interest rate environment. Moreover, sizable profits are possible if interest rates decline, since the cost of borrowing would decrease and the value of the long-term investments would increase. This accounts for the great success of the Orange County Investment Pool in the 1980s and early 1990s. But if interest rates begin to increase, then there could be sizable losses as the cost of short-term borrowing grows and the value of the long-term bonds that are purchased begins to steeply decline. In fact, this is what caused the financial collapse of the Orange County Investment Pool in 1994.

Another important element of the Orange County Investment Pool's risk was the purchase of derivatives and other complex financial instruments. Table 4-2 indicates that at least four out of ten dollars were invested in structured or floating-interest-rate securities. The Orange county treasurer was particularly taken with the "inverse floaters." In his annual financial statement to the Board of Supervisors in the fall of 1993, Citron explained, "Inverse floaters are indexed to produce a higher yield when interest rates remain steady or decline. An example of an inverse floater is a U.S. government security that pays interest at a rate of 10 percent minus the 6-month LIBOR. The security would earn a current yield of 6.69 percent. If interest rates declined ½ percent . . . our investment yield would increase from 6.69 percent to 7.19 percent" (Merrill Lynch, 1995, p. 11-7). The treasurer did not provide examples to show the negative consequences. The value of inverse floaters sharply declines whenever interest rates increase.

One other problem with the Orange County Investment Pool involved the liquidity of the funds. The current county treasurer, John Moorlach, calculated that the average duration of the securities in the portfolio was 2.3 years (Moorlach, 1996, p. 2). This is because Bob Citron had bought long-term securities with high yields. However, most of the large sums of money that were owed through the reverse repurchase agreements had to be paid back in 180 days, or six months. In

TABLE 4-2   ORANGE COUNTY INVESTMENT POOL,
NOVEMBER 1994

	Amount (billions)	Percent
Leveraging		
Original investment of 194 agencies	$ 7.6	37
Investments borrowed against	13.0	63
Total investments	$20.6	
Risks		
Inverse floaters	$ 6.6	32
Other structured notes	1.7	8
Fixed-rate notes	9.7	47
Unknown	2.6	13
Total investments	$20.6	

SOURCE: California State Auditor (1995).

addition, some of the 194 public agencies who had invested in the funds may have had a much shorter time frame in mind for withdrawing their funds than 2.3 years. The county treasurer was not prepared for a run on the money by the Wall Street lenders or the pool participants.

In 1994 the Orange County Investment Pool had turned into a risky business. The California state auditor, in a report after the bankruptcy, calculated the risk level in the Orange County Investment Pool. The auditor used a "duration score," which is a measure of how vulnerable a fund's principal is to interest rate increases. A passbook savings account receives a duration score of 0, since its principal is not affected by higher interest rates. The risk level in the Orange County Investment Pool increased significantly between 1991 and 1994, from a score of 2.7 to 7.4, as the fund ballooned in size and the county treasurer took on an aggressive investment strategy. By comparison, the typical money-market funds for local governments, which seek to achieve investment yields with short-term, high-yield securities, have a score of 1.8. The bond funds designed for high-risk investors have a score of 4.5, which is much lower than the 7.4 rating of the county's funds before the bankruptcy. Funds for high-risk investors typically purchase lower-quality or "junk" bonds and longer-term securities that pay high yields but can sharply decline in value. They are only for private investors who can afford to lose some of their principal. The duration score of 7.4 for the Orange County

Investment Pool in 1994 points out how ill suited the fund had become for local governments.

Bob Citron was not following the basics of sound investment policies. Safety of the principal and liquidity of the funds should be of primary importance, and yield should be of less significance (California State Auditor, 1995, pp. 9–10). It would seem all the more important to follow this strategy since the investors were 194 local agencies.

The treasurer acted with considerable autonomy in making these investment decisions. There was little oversight from other county officials. In 1993 the county auditor-controller wrote to the Board of Supervisors and said, "Because of the County's current high rate of return I believe it is extremely important that you thoroughly understand the related risk and find it acceptable" (Merrill Lynch, 1995, p. 14-1). In the same letter the auditor-controller said that he had only general conversations with the treasurer and was not in a position to make a judgment. John Moorlach (1996, p. 1) summarized the oversight by county officials in saying, "Interactions between the Supervisors and the Treasurer's Office were minimal. In the last few years, Mr. Citron provided an annual written report to the Board and monthly accountability statements were not provided." The Board of Supervisors, county administrative officer, and auditor-controller later pleaded ignorance when asked why they allowed the kinds of investments that the county treasurer was making to obtain high yields.

There are some questions about the county pool that may never be answered. For example, why did Citron make these risky investment decisions? Some say that he relied heavily upon the advice of Michael Stamenson, the broker at Merrill Lynch who sold many of the securities to the county treasurer. Citron is also said to have listened to the advice of other economic experts at that brokerage house. But there is contrary evidence suggesting that Merrill Lynch made timely warnings to the treasurer and suggested that he seriously rethink his investment strategy. Some say that Citron pretty much acted on his own intuition and research. He reported to the Board of Supervisors a year before the bankruptcy that he was convinced that "higher interest rates are not at all sustainable" (Merrill Lynch, 1995, p. 8). Moreover, as John Moorlach (1996, p. 5), the new county treasurer, wrote, "And, if the current Grand Jury transcripts are to be believed, Mr. Citron also utilized a mail order astrology service and a psychic."

LOCAL GOVERNMENT INVESTORS

One feature of the Orange County bankruptcy that greatly complicated both the response to the emergency and the search for solutions is the fact that there were so many local government investors in the Orange County Investment Pool. It wasn't just the county government that had lost money and had funds tied up in a frozen government pool. Investors included the county, school districts, most cities, and many special districts. The chances that the bankruptcy would paralyze the county were greatly increased by the fact that so many deliverers of public services were pool participants.

It is perhaps one of the great ironies of the financial crisis that, despite the political fragmentation and local orientation, most local governments in Orange County were members of the Orange County Investment Pool. Such involvement would not have been possible if the county had called upon all of the local public entities to join with them in a regional governing body. The local governments were drawn into the investment pool, some despite their misgivings toward county government, by the high yields that were being paid. In a sense, it was the fiscal conservatism of the local voters and the fiscal austerity imposed by state government that drew them to this appealing source of new revenues. Also, local governments did not need to exhibit any cooperative behavior with the county or other local agencies in order to be in the investment pool, at least until they had to work in the tangled world of the county bankruptcy.

Who were the local government investors in the Orange County Investment Pool? State law authorizes that the county's funds be deposited with the county treasurer. In California the law also requires that the school districts in the county give their money to the county treasurer. Cities and special districts can voluntarily deposit their excess funds with the county treasurer, as long as their elected officials approve of this arrangement and the county treasurer is willing to accept their funds (California State Auditor, 1995, p. 1). The Orange County Investment Pool in December 1994 included money from the county government and its agencies, all of the local school districts, and most cities and local special districts. There were also a handful of local government investors from elsewhere in California.

Table 4-3 lists the largest pool investors at the time of the bankruptcy. The County of Orange was the largest investor, with about $2.8 billion in the pool. The Orange County Transportation Authority, the

TABLE 4-3   LARGEST INVESTORS IN THE
ORANGE COUNTY INVESTMENT POOL, 1994

	Amount (millions)	Percent of Pool
County of Orange	$2,760.3	37.2
Orange County Transportation Authority	1,092.9	14.7
Orange County Sanitation District	441.0	6.0
Orange County Employees Retirement System	133.4	1.8
Orange County cities		
Irvine	198.1	2.7
Anaheim	169.6	2.3
Santa Ana	150.7	2.0
Orange County school districts		
Irvine Unified	105.8	1.7
North Orange County Community College	98.9	1.6
Newport-Mesa Unified	82.4	1.3
Capistrano Unified	75.0	1.2
Orange County water districts		
Irvine Ranch	300.9	4.1
Orange County	118.4	1.6
Total amount from largest investors	$5,727.4	78.2

SOURCE: *New York Times* (1994a).

regional transportation agency, had the second largest amount of money, with about $1 billion in deposits. The third largest investor was the Orange County Sanitation District, with $441 million. The Orange County Employees Retirement System had $133 million in the investment pool. Several of the bigger cities had voluntarily placed large amounts of money in the investment pool. Notably, Irvine, Anaheim, and Santa Ana each had more than $150 million in the county fund. Several of the school districts, which were required to use the county pool, also had large investments. These included Irvine Unified, North Orange County Community College, Newport-Mesa Unified, and Capistrano Unified, which each had $75 million or more in the fund. Also, several of the special districts had made large deposits. The Irvine Ranch Water District had $300 million, and the Orange County Water District had $118 million invested in the Orange County Investment Pool. Together these thirteen local public entities had $5.7 billion invested and accounted for over three-fourths of all the county funds that were on deposit.

It is interesting to note that Irvine tops the list of large investors in multiple categories. It was the city with the most money invested in the pool. Irvine also had the school district with the most funds and the water district with the largest investment. However, it is not the largest city in Orange County. Irvine was a city experiencing rapid population growth and thus a demand for more public services. It was also a city in which its predominantly middle-class residents had high expectations for the kinds of public schools and services they received in their planned communities. Irvine was also a mostly Republican city where voters had rejected local tax hikes in the past. Irvine was a perfect example of a fiscally conservative, middle-class city that was living beyond its current means by increasing its revenues through the investment fund.

However, Irvine was not the only city that had its funds in the county pool. As shown in Table 4-4, twenty-nine of thirty-one cities had at least some money on deposit. (The amounts given are slightly different from those in Table 4-3 because of the time of reporting and the source.) Only Garden Grove and San Juan Capistrano had no money in the fund.[1] Laguna Hills, Tustin, and Westminster had less than $1 million in the county pool; eleven cities had from $1 million to under $10 million invested; and twelve cities had from $10 million to under $100 million on deposit. Three cities had $100 million or more in the county pool.

Some of the smaller cities had investments that were nearly the size of their annual budgets, including Buena Park, Dana Point, Fountain Valley, Laguna Niguel, La Palma, Placentia, and San Clemente (*Orange County Register,* 1995a). Undoubtedly, the knowledge that the county pool was paying higher returns was what drew many of the cities into the fund. For instance, Citron's 1992–1993 annual financial statement noted that the county pool was paying 8.52 percent compared with 4.71 percent for the state treasury (Office of the Treasurer–Tax Collector, 1993). There probably would have been political risks if local officials did not choose to have their city's funds in the high-yielding pool.

All of the twenty-eight local school districts had their surplus funds invested in the county pool as required by law. Table 4-5 indicates that thirteen school districts had between $1 million and under $10 million on deposit, fourteen had between $10 million and under $100 million in the county fund, and one district had over $100 million in the

---

1. Gary Hausdorfer, who was the mayor of San Juan Capistrano until the end of 1994, was later an active participant as a negotiator and facilitator in the discussions between the county and the city governments.

TABLE 4-4   ORANGE COUNTY CITIES: AMOUNT
OF FUNDS IN THE ORANGE COUNTY
INVESTMENT POOL, 1994
All Figures in Millions of Dollars

Anaheim	169.0
Brea	9.0
Buena Park	28.0
Costa Mesa	3.1
Cypress	5.8
Dana Point	15.8
Fountain Valley	30.8
Fullerton	18.3
Garden Grove	0
Huntington Beach	43.6
Irvine	208.0
La Habra	8.2
La Palma	5.5
Laguna Beach	7.6
Laguna Hills	0.9
Laguna Niguel	18.1
Lake Forest	9.6
Los Alamitos	2.1
Mission Viejo	18.7
Newport Beach	16.2
Orange	28.2
Placentia	20.7
San Clemente	33.3
San Juan Capistrano	0
Santa Ana	151.0
Seal Beach	2.1
Stanton	3.0
Tustin	0.2
Villa Park	1.3
Westminster	0.1
Yorba Linda	13.5

SOURCE: *Orange County Register* (1995a).

Orange County Investment Pool. Because of the state law, some of the school districts in cities that shied away from the county pool, such as Tustin, had considerable sums of money on deposit. (The amounts differ slightly from those in Table 4-3 because of the time of reporting and the source.) Three school districts had amounts invested in the pool that were almost equal to their annual budgets for the same year. These were the districts of Irvine Unified, Newport-Mesa, and Placentia–Yorba Linda. All of these schools are located in affluent areas. They are in cities that are predominantly Republican and fiscally

TABLE 4-5   ORANGE COUNTY SCHOOL
DISTRICTS: AMOUNT OF FUNDS IN THE
ORANGE COUNTY INVESTMENT POOL
All Figures in Millions of Dollars

Anaheim City	8.2
Anaheim Union	19.4
Brea-Olinda	7.5
Buena Park	4.4
Capistrano	74.0
Centralia	7.6
Cypress	6.8
Fountain Valley	5.5
Fullerton	5.0
Fullerton Union	24.0
Garden Grove	54.3
Huntington Beach	8.9
Irvine	106.0
La Habra	13.2
Laguna Beach	6.8
Los Alamitos	12.0
Magnolia	5.7
Newport-Mesa	81.0
Ocean View	8.8
Orange	19.3
Placentia–Yorba Linda	84.0
Saddleback	66.0
Santa Ana	49.0
Savanna	3.5
Tustin	12.0
Villa Park	1.3
Westminster	13.5
Yorba Linda	13.5

SOURCE: *Orange County Register* (1995a).

conservative. This is more evidence that the county pool was used to gain high yields and extend revenues to meet the high expectations of middle-class residents.

Some local government investors were so anxious to use the county fund to generate more revenues that they went out and borrowed money to place in the fund. These investors were involved in their own leveraging. Their idea was to make money on the spread between the interest on the money they borrowed and the interest they would earn from the county pool. This subgroup of local government investors included the county, cities, school districts, and special districts. In all, about $1.2 billion of the money deposited in the fund was borrowed money (see Table 4-6). The county itself borrowed $600 million to

TABLE 4-6 TAXABLE DEBT ISSUED FOR
INVESTMENT IN THE ORANGE COUNTY
INVESTMENT POOL

County of Orange	$ 600,000,000
Cities	207,155,000
Schools	193,715,000
Special districts	161,360,000
Total	$1,162,230,000

SOURCE: California State Auditor (1995).

place in the fund for the purpose of raising more tax revenues. This proposal was submitted by the county treasurer and approved by the Board of Supervisors after the June 1994 election. The official statement of the $600 million note offering was submitted on July 8, 1994 (Merrill Lynch, 1995, pp. 17-1, 10), and included some discussion about how the county fund had yielded between 7.80 and 8.85 percent in the past four fiscal years. What was not included in the financial statement was any mention of the fact that more money was being borrowed to invest in a fund that was already highly leveraged and whose principal had declined sharply in the higher-interest-rate environment. The omissions about the high risks involved in this bond offering were to raise legal and ethical issues after the bankruptcy.

The county government was not the only local government investor seeking to squeeze more earnings out of the investment pool through leveraging. Cities borrowed over $200 million to deposit in the funds. This included $95 million from Anaheim and $62 million from Irvine. School districts borrowed almost $200 million to place in the county pool. This included about $50 million each from the affluent districts of Irvine Unified, Placentia–Yorba Linda, and Newport-Mesa. Special districts also borrowed $162 million in the hopes of making some profits in the county pool. The Orange County Flood District took on an additional $100 million in taxable debt specifically for the purpose of investing in the county's pool (California State Auditor, 1995, p. 3).

The Orange County Investment Pool was serving a variety of needs. This is to be expected, given the financial capabilities of the county government, small and large cities and school districts, and many kinds of special districts in the county. Some were using the Orange County Investment Pool as a checking account. They would need quick and frequent access to their funds for payrolls and operating expenses. Others were longer-term investors and would not need their funds until they began projects. Each of the local government investors had different financial needs that would have to be considered once the county declared bankruptcy and the county pool was frozen.

The extent to which local government investors were themselves following the principles of prudent investment is also open to question. Some claimed ignorance as to the high-risk nature of the pool. Others pointed to the assurances of safety made by the county treasurer. Some said that the state had sanctioned the treasurer's actions by authorizing the use of high-risk investments. Many of the local government investors praised the work of Citron and his risky efforts to raise the amount of interest income. The general manager of the Orange County Sanitation District wrote in late 1993, "I want to express our appreciation for your outstanding investment earnings. . . . We are also grateful for the reverse repo transactions you make on our behalf" (Merrill Lynch, 1995, p. 12-23). The county administrative officer wrote at about the same time, "Mr. Citron has made extra efforts to create significant new revenues to replace property tax revenues shifted to the State. . . . In my opinion, Mr. Citron deserves the acknowledgment of your Honorable Board for these efforts" (Merrill Lynch, 1995, p. 6-1).

It is fair to say that the pool participants were not given a lot of information with which to fully judge the risks of the county pool. Moorlach (1996, p. 4) quoted local government officials as saying that "Mr. Citron didn't like outsiders coming in and looking in his portfolio" and "The county staff isn't forthcoming with answers . . . their attitude seems to be we don't have time, just send your money and trust us." They placed their trust in the county treasurer to keep their money safe and to give an honest accounting of their earnings. The treasurer's office was later found to be skimming interest from pool deposits and crediting these funds to the county. The discovery of these illegal actions would shatter whatever trust the local officials had left in their county government.

THE FEDERAL RESERVE BOARD

Nothing had a more immediate impact on the Orange County Investment Pool than the federal government. The financial securities that were purchased, and the leveraging strategy that was followed, resulted in the pool's value being highly sensitive to interest rate changes. The Federal Reserve Board has a major impact on interest rates.

In retrospect, the past successes of Citron came at a time when the Federal Reserve Board was seeking declining or stable interest rates. Simply put, the principal value of interest-bearing bonds rises when interest rates fall. In the early 1980s interest rates were very high. For the most part, they fell to lower levels during the decade. In the early 1990s the United States faced a severe recession with no end in sight. The Federal Reserve Board moved interest rates well below the levels that had been seen over the previous decades. Those who had purchased long-term bonds were in the position of seeing their investments rise in value as interest rates fell significantly. Those with the most interest-sensitive investments, and investors who had borrowed money to purchase even more of the interest-sensitive investments, were rewarded with great profits.

Citron learned his trade in the financial scenario of falling interest rates. After the state legislature deregulated the activities of county treasurers, he bought bonds that increased in value as the interest rates were trending downward in the 1980s. He bought even riskier or more interest-sensitive bonds that gained even more in value, such as longer-term notes, as the interest rates moved down in the 1990s. He also borrowed money so that he could purchase even more of the interest-sensitive investments. This is why his fund paid high interest rates to local government investors. Citron had been making a long series of large, one-way bets on falling interest rates.

The downfall came when Citron was unable to foresee and adapt to a rapidly changing financial environment. In 1994 interest rates were no longer headed downward. On February 4, 1994, the Federal Reserve Board made the first of six increases in the Federal Funds Rate. This was only a quarter-point increase, from 3 percent to 3.25 percent, but it spooked the bond market since many had bet on declining interest rates. They had purchased long-term bonds, and borrowed money to buy long-term bonds, assuming they could be sold at a profit. Interest rates of all kinds began to move upward as investors started selling their long-term bonds. Citron was an investor who had placed large bets on lower interest rates. He did not follow the others and sell his holdings. He was still a buyer and was betting on lower interest rates by year's end.

Interest rates continued their ascent when the Federal Reserve Board raised the Federal Funds Rate by another quarter point on March 22. The new target funds rate was at 3.5 percent. In less than a month, on April 18, the Fed raised the Federal Funds Rate by another quarter

TABLE 4-7   CHANGES IN THE INTENDED
FEDERAL FUNDS RATE, 1994

Date	Change	New Target Funds Rate
February 4	+.25 point	3.25%
March 22	+.25 point	3.50%
April 18	+.25 point	3.75%
May 17	+.50 point	4.25%
August 16	+.50 point	4.75%
November 15	+.75 point	5.50%

SOURCE: Federal Reserve Bank (1996).

point, to 3.75 percent. There had been three upward moves in less than two months. Bond investors became more nervous. These interest rate hikes signaled to many investors that the Federal Reserve Board was very concerned that the economy was growing too fast and that there may be higher inflation on the horizon. Since the Federal Reserve Board had described itself as serious about fighting inflation, and because it was moving aggressively to increase interest rates, there was a feeling in the bond market that further interest rate increases during the year were likely. This further lowered the principal value of long-term bonds as more nervous investors sold their holdings.

Those who sold because they anticipated higher interest rates in the near term proved to be right. The Federal Reserve Board's next step was even more drastic. Within a month of the previous increase, on May 17, the Fed increased the Federal Funds Rate by a half point, to 4.25 percent. Interest rates had risen by one and one-quarter points in 1994. This was three weeks before the Orange County treasurer's election and the challenger, John Moorlach, was telling anyone who would listen that the Orange County Investment Pool had suffered big losses and was in grave danger. From what is now known, Moorlach's statements at the time had a lot of validity.

After winning the election, Bob Citron continued to make more big bets. He convinced the Board of Supervisors to allow him to borrow money to place in the fund. He had hopes that interest rates would move down in late 1994 and that he could recoup his earlier losses. What happened was that interest rates increased by another one and one-quarter points. On August 16 the Federal Reserve Board increased interest rates by a half point, to 4.75 percent. Then, on November 15, they increased the Federal Funds Rate by another three-quarters of a point, to 5.50 percent (see Table 4-7).

The interest rate increase of two and one-half points in the course of nine months in 1994 had a devastating effect on the principal value of the Orange County Investment Pool. The drastic change in the financial environment, caused by the Federal Reserve Board actions, is what ultimately brought on the panic among the Wall Street lenders that led to the county government declaring bankruptcy. What made the experts even more nervous about Orange County was that Citron had continued to borrow their money to purchase more bonds on the assumption that interest rates would turn lower by the end of the year. No one knows for sure what his motivation was for these risky actions. He may have been rattled by the criticisms in the county treasurer's race. He could have felt pressure to make up for the mounting losses for the nearly 200 local government investors in his pool. He may have felt the need to take desperate actions to provide the interest income he had promised to the county government. He may have been advised, or thought he had seen the evidence himself, that the economy was cooling off and that interest rates would move lower by the end of the year. If he had knowledge about lower interest rates late in 1994, it was contrary to most of the conventional wisdom on Wall Street. After many rate increases, the financial world was assuming that the Federal Reserve Board's next actions would again be upward.

Citron had learned the tools of his trade in a unique financial environment of declining interest rates. He was unable to adjust to the drastically changing conditions. He was not a financial wizard. He did not even have a college degree in business or finance. Nor did he have years of experience as a bond trader with a Wall Street firm. He was an investor who had never weathered a financial storm anything like the rapid interest rate increase that he faced in 1994. He was a county treasurer who had learned that the one way to make big money for the local governments was to bet on lower interest rates. The Federal Reserve Board's actions exposed his naive views.

THE ORANGE COUNTY TREASURER'S RACE

Over the years there had been many rewards for Citron as he followed a risky strategy of providing high-interest income for local governments. The voters had reelected him to several terms. The Board of Supervisors praised his ability to provide additional revenues for the county during trying fiscal times. Local governments flocked to his pool. Local elected officials credited Citron for providing them with the

funds they needed to improve their cities, schools, services, and infrastructure. The local newspapers wrote glowing stories about his long
track record of providing high interest earnings to local governments.
The county treasurers around the state treated him with the esteem and
respect that is typically given to a "financial guru" on Wall Street.

The campaign for county treasurer in 1994 was the first time serious
doubts were raised about the investment practices of Citron. The challenger, John Moorlach, forcefully brought his message to the voters,
local newspapers, and the Board of Supervisors. The county treasurer,
he said, was taking great risks with the taxpayer's money. The fund had
suffered large paper losses. Many dismissed him as a political oppor-
tunist and partisan politician. Some even charged that, by speaking out,
Moorlach was doing damage to the county's credit ratings. But the allegations of risky ventures created some doubts among the local government investors. Some of the Wall Street firms that had lent money to
the Orange County Investment Pool also took notice.

The county treasurer's election was to take place in June 1994. In a
January 14 press release in which he announced his plans to seek reelection, Citron was described as the sixty-eight-year-old "dean of
county elected officials" who "has served six distinguished terms as
Orange County's only elected Treasurer–Tax Collector." The press release called Citron a "nationally-recognized money manager" whose
policies "generated billions of dollars in tax relief for local taxpayers"
and "California's top public investor." Orange County Supervisor Tom
Riley, the chair of the board at the time, praised Citron for "guiding our
ship through such turbulent fiscal times." Citron himself was quoted as
saying, "The investment strategies and programs that have carried
Orange County's annual interest rate on tax dollars to the highest levels in the state and the nation must be continued" (Merrill Lynch, 1995,
pp. 12–25, 26). The race was defined by Citron around the theme of
maintaining high yields for the Orange County Investment Pool.

Compared with past campaigns, Bob Citron had real competition in
the 1994 election. He was opposed by John Moorlach, a thirty-eight-
year-old certified public accountant who was a partner in a private firm
and lived in Costa Mesa. Local races do not have partisan labels on the
ballot, but this one was really a contest between Republicans and
Democrats. Moorlach was a local Republican Party official who had the
support of some, but not all, of the leading Republicans in the county.[2]

---

2. John Moorlach was the treasurer of the Orange County Republican Party.

Republicans in high places, such as some members of the Board of Supervisors, were supporting the reelection of the Democrat Citron.

The treasurer's race heated up in April and May. Moorlach accused Citron of making investments that placed the county's investment fund at considerable risk. Citron answered that this was not true, pointing to his long record of providing local governments with high yields on their investments. On April 13 the City of Tustin withdrew $4 million from the county fund for the stated reason that they were uncomfortable with the risks involved in reverse repurchase agreements. Citron countered that this move was "for purely partisan political purposes" and was motivated by the fact that the city councilman who called for the change was an ally of Moorlach. One of the local newspapers downplayed this event as "a move shrouded in politics" (*Los Angeles Times* Orange County Edition, 1994a). But the campaign issue of the dangers lurking in the Orange County Investment Pool had been defined.

As the county treasurer's election became perceived as a partisan battle, Moorlach's criticisms of Citron's policies tended to be viewed with less credibility. The race did have such elements. The Republicans wanted to unseat the only Democrat who currently held office. The campaign committee for Moorlach included a long list of Republican congressmen and state legislators. Citron had made the political mistake of funneling his campaign contributions to Democratic candidates, and this partisan action had upset the head of the Orange County Republican Party (*Los Angeles Times* Orange County Edition, 1994b). The Republicans were determined to win the treasurer's race.

Some elected officials were complaining that Moorlach's statements about the Orange County Investment Pool were hurting the county's finances. His criticisms of Citron's investment tactics had now surfaced in the local news media, the *Wall Street Journal,* and several financial trade publications. State Senator Marian Bergeson said she withdrew her endorsement for fellow Republican Moorlach for this reason. In early May Orange County Sanitation District officials complained that the adverse publicity about the county fund had increased their costs of financing new debt. The Irvine Water District also complained about higher costs due to increased doubts about the county fund. County officials said that they had to delay a bond refinancing until jittery investors were calm, and one official said, "I've never had to have so many conversations with them [i.e., Wall Street firms]." An Irvine Ranch Water District official summed up the impact of Moorlach's allegations as follows: "The danger was in possibly creating a run on the pool" (*Los Angeles Times* Orange County Edition, 1994c). The local government officials generally lined up in support of Citron, and some openly criticized the Republican Moorlach for raising issues that could place their pool funds in jeopardy.

In mid-May Moorlach stepped up his attacks on Citron and raised even more questions about the safety of the Orange County Investment Pool. After reviewing documents provided by the county treasurer's office, Moorlach announced he had concluded that the fund was in real danger of a major loss because of rising interest rates. He cited the fact that there had already been calls for $300 million in collateral on the reverse repurchase agreements because the principal value of the long-term securities the county owned had sharply declined. He said that future collateral calls could be even larger. The county treasurer's office countered by saying that, although it was true that there had been collateral calls in recent months, the county investment fund had paid them and had sufficient liquid assets to weather the current interest rate environment (*Los Angeles Times* Orange County Edition, 1994d).

On May 31 Moorlach sent an eight-page letter to Supervisor Tom Riley, the chair of the board, and outlined his concerns about how interest rate rises were adversely affecting the county pool. Moorlach had calculated that the fund had lost $1.2 billion since interest rates began to rise in February 1994. He called the county treasurer's investment strategy "a major bull-market bet in the middle of a bear market." Moorlach claimed that the approach taken by Citron would work only if there were declining interest rates over several years, which was impossible to predict. Supervisor Riley dismissed the criticisms as without merit on the basis of advice he received from financial experts. Matthew Raabe, the treasurer's assistant, described them as "a last-minute chance to get publicity" (*Los Angeles Times* Orange County Edition, 1994e).

The county treasurer won reelection on June 7, 1994, by a comfortable margin. Bob Citron received 61 percent of the vote while John Moorlach got only 39 percent. Citron won by 75,000 votes in what was a low-turnout primary election (see Table 4-8). The incumbent had a big lead in preelection surveys, capturing the support of both Republicans and Democrats, but many voters had been undecided. The accusations that were raised by the challenger ultimately seemed to have no effect on the election outcome.

TABLE 4-8   ORANGE COUNTY VOTERS'
PREFERENCES FOR TREASURER, JUNE 1994

	Vote	Percent
Bob Citron	209,630	61
John Moorlach	133,754	39

34% voter turnout in June 1994

SOURCE: Orange County Registrar of Voters (1994).

The treasurer's election in 1994 was, in part, a referendum on the investment policies that Bob Citron had followed for nearly two decades. The local elected officials rallied to his support when his practices were attacked. The voters seemed to brush aside the criticisms by Moorlach. The Democrat who described himself as "providing tax relief for local taxpayers" had beaten the Republican. In the end, the status quo of taking risks with the county pool to increase local revenues had been preserved.

Even though he won the election, Citron said that the campaign had taken a great toll on him. He was a sensitive, shy, and reclusive individual. He was not used to having his policies attacked in public. Citron took the campaign issues that surfaced very personally. He viewed his opponent as attacking his character. Those who knew Citron said he had become emotional and defensive. He had decided that he would never run for office again (*Los Angeles Times* Orange County Edition, 1994c). Citron may have felt that he had something to prove after winning this election. The experience seemed to have made him more determined to follow his risky investment strategies.

FINANCIAL MELTDOWN

The financial meltdown of the county pool began on February 4, 1994 (see Appendix A, Table A-1). This is when the Federal Reserve Board set the course to raise interest rates. The county treasurer's race, from March through early June, brought to light the extent to which the county pool was being adversely affected by the Federal Reserve Board's actions. For the first time, the Wall Street lenders and the local government investors were expressing nervousness about the status of the county pool.

Still, a week after his reelection, on June 14, Bob Citron received the approval of the Board of Supervisors for a $600 million bond for the

express purpose of investing this money in the pool to earn more interest income. The Board of Supervisors also approved a $100 million
bond for the Orange County Flood District to be used for the same
speculative investment purposes. A month later the City of Irvine voted
its approval of a $62 million bond to raise funds that would be placed
in the Orange County Investment Pool to earn extra interest income. In
August Orange County's debt received an Aa1 rating from Moody's.
Orange County was given the highest rating of any county in the state
(*Orange County Register,* 1995a).

Citron was apparently well aware that the county fund was deterio-
rating. In the early fall he began diverting interest into special funds and
moving around some of the money-losing securities to protect the
county government from even bigger losses. This was done at the expense of the other pool participants (*Orange County Register,* 1995b).
These were the illegal activities that resulted in his criminal conviction.

The county treasurer's office did not admit that the investment pool
was in trouble until October 1994. Bob Citron stated in an interview on
October 13 that the county fund was losing money because he had made
a wrong-way bet on interest rates. Still, he assured the local government
investors that their funds were safe and that they were in no danger of
losing money on their principal. But less than two weeks later Assistant
County Treasurer Matthew Raabe paid a visit to County Administrative
Officer Ernie Schneider without the consent of Citron. Raabe informed
Schneider that the county pool was in deep trouble. This meeting took
place after Raabe, speaking for the county treasurer, had assured the
local government investors that there was cash on hand to pay any outstanding debts and process normal requests for pool withdrawals.

The financial condition of the pool went from bad to worse in
November as interest rates rose. In the early days of the month, the
assistant treasurer informed the county administrative officer and the
auditor-controller that the Orange County Investment Pool was near
collapse because of the prospects of collateral calls for the reverse repurchase agreements. Local business leaders were paying visits and making
telephone calls to county elected officials, urging them to look into the
rumors they were hearing on Wall Street. The county government hired
an outside consultant to evaluate the financial condition of the pool in
early November. This was no quick and easy task, given the complex nature of Citron's transactions and the size of the pool. The consultant's
report of November 16 indicated that the county pool had thus far suffered a paper loss of about $1.5 billion because of rising interest rates.

It was when the huge paper loss was discovered in mid-November that the county treasurer began to relinquish autonomy over the day-to-day decisions involving the investment pool. The county government had put together a "crisis team" of top county officials that included the county administrative officer, the auditor-controller, the assistant treasurer, and financial and legal experts. They had tried to keep the severity of the problem a secret and downplay the crisis, but they were not successful. There were more rumors on Wall Street. The investment firms that had lent the county treasurer large sums of money, and that held billions of dollars in securities as collateral, wanted their money back. Local government investors had suspicions that something was wrong. The Irvine Ranch Water District was requesting to withdraw millions of dollars. There were signs of panic over the financial state of the county pool.

County officials spent the final days of November trying to seek the financial cooperation of the pool participants and Wall Street investors. They tried to convince both of these parties that the financial problem was still only a paper loss. On November 29 the assistant treasurer asked the ten largest pool participants not to withdraw their funds from the county pool. They did not. On November 30 county officials talked to the Wall Street lenders. Their goal was to get the investment firms to extend their loans and not liquidate the collateral. The reaction on Wall Street was cool. CS First Boston asked for a refund on a $110 million bond within one week (*Orange County Register,* 1995b).

There continued to be rumors that the Orange County Investment Pool was in serious trouble. In an attempt to calm the Wall Street investors, the county government made a public announcement after the stock market closed on Friday, December 2, that the county pool did indeed have a $1.5 billion paper loss. This would buy the county government a few days, until the markets opened again on Monday morning, to try to avert a run on the county pool by the Wall Street firms and the pool participants.

The crisis team went to work trying to get financial assistance from the Wall Street firms. But on Saturday, December 3, the crisis team learned that their effort to avert a financial disaster had failed.[3] The Wall Street firms they had sought help from were said to have decided to sell off the collateral they held from the county pool when the market opened on Monday (*Orange County Register,* 1995a). At this point

---

3. This was discussed at the now infamous dinner at Prego Restaurant in Irvine. According to one of the participants, "We were all very depressed. . . . We quickly ordered dinner, hardly anyone had an appetite" (*Orange County Register,* 1995a, p. 6).

TABLE 4-9 THE BROWN ACT AND
SUPERVISORS' MEETINGS

1953: The Ralph M. Brown Act governs the rights of the public to attend and participate in meetings conducted by local legislative bodies, such as boards of supervisors, city councils, and school boards.
- A meeting includes any congregation of a majority of the members of the legislative body on any matter related to their local jurisdiction.
- For regular meetings, public notice must be given seventy-two hours in advance.
- For special meetings, twenty-four-hour public notice must be given.
- Emergency meetings, with public one-hour notice, are allowed only in case of work stoppage or crippling disaster.
- Closed meetings are allowed only in special circumstances, such as to discuss employees, litigation, or labor negotiations.
- Criminal penalties can be applied to members of local legislative bodies for attending meetings in violation of the Brown Act.

SOURCE: State Senate (1989); California Attorney General's Office (1994).

the county leaders who made up the crisis team agreed that their only hope was to focus their efforts on a liquidation of the risky investments in the county pool.

The next day, Sunday, December 4, the Board of Supervisors were called to the county government building and separately briefed in their offices by members of the crisis team. The supervisors could not meet as a group to discuss this important matter because of a California law called the Brown Act (see Table 4-9). The Brown Act forbids a majority of the Board of Supervisors to meet without public notice. Regular meetings must be announced seventy-two hours in advance, and special meetings require a twenty-four-hour public notice. The financial disaster taking place was not accounted for in the allowances for "emergency meetings" or "closed meetings." This law is designed to give the public an opportunity to attend and provide input to local legislative meetings. Most of the county officials who were involved in these crisis meetings expressed frustration with the Brown Act and their inability to hold group meetings at this time.

There were two decisions made at the briefings of the members of the Board of Supervisors. First, County Administrative Officer Ernie Schneider would ask for the resignation of Bob Citron. That same day he made a visit to Citron's house, explained to him the deepening crisis, and then asked for and received his resignation. The motivation behind this move was to assure the investors that the situation was being managed. But it may have had the opposite impact, since the county pool had been a one-man show. Second, the crisis team would try to sell off the investments in the county pool. That effort failed later in the day when there were no buyers for the county pool.

On December 5, in another failed attempt to prevent a panic run on the funds, the County of Orange asked the Securities and Exchange Commission to freeze the Orange County Investment Pool. The federal agency refused to act, however, saying this was a local financial matter and was not in their jurisdiction. The county was facing a deeper crisis as more loan payments were due and the Wall Street firms were refusing to lend them any more money. On December 6 the investment firm of CS First Boston seized over $2 billion in collateral that it held through reverse repurchase agreements with the Orange County Investment Pool. To the County of Orange, which could no longer borrow money to meet its obligations, this was a signal that the other Wall Street investment firms that had lent them money would follow suit and liquidate the county securities that they were holding as collateral. This action by CS First Boston is credited with precipitating the Orange County government bankruptcy.

At about 5:00 P.M. on December 6, the Orange County Board of Supervisors filed for bankruptcy protection under Chapter 9 of the bankruptcy code. Orange County became the largest U.S. municipality to file for bankruptcy. County officials had done so after seeking legal advice from a corporate bankruptcy attorney. Chapter 9 is designed for political subdivisions of the state, such as counties. It had been rarely used and its consequences were hard to anticipate. The Board of Supervisors filed separate petitions for the County of Orange and for the Orange County Investment Pool.

The stated purpose of the bankruptcy filing was, in the words of Supervisor Tom Riley, the chair of the board, to allow the county to face its financial problems "in an orderly manner." Their intention was to prevent a run on the investment pool by freezing the funds in the pool, thus preventing the local government investors from withdrawing their money and the Wall Street firms from taking any more of the securities that they held as collateral. The bankruptcy also meant that the county could wait to pay its bills, such as contracts with outside vendors and other operating expenses. There was no question that the local government investors and vendors would not receive their money any time soon. But there were allowances in the bankruptcy that seemed to exclude the reverse repurchase agreements between the Wall Street

TABLE 4-10   INVESTMENT FIRMS WITHDRAWING
COLLATERAL FROM THE ORANGE COUNTY
INVESTMENT POOL
All Figures in Billions of Dollars

Before Bankruptcy (December 6, 1994)	
CS First Boston	2.6
After Bankruptcy (December and January)	
Merrill Lynch	2.0
Morgan Stanley	1.6
Prudential	1.0
Nomura	0.9
Smith Barney	0.8
Paine Webber	0.6
Paribas	0.6
Sanwa	0.5
Fuji Securities	0.5
Bank of America	0.3

SOURCE: *Los Angeles Times* Orange County Edition (1995b).

firms and the county treasurer (*New York Times*, 1994a). In fact, many
Wall Street firms withdrew their collateral in December and January
(see Table 4-10). Nomura Securities, Prudential, Smith Barney, and
Morgan Stanley all sold collateral in the days right after the bankruptcy
(*New York Times*, 1994b). The actions of these investment firms were
the basis of suits from the county government. The outcome of this litigation is still uncertain, but it is clear that the bankruptcy filings did
not have the intended impact of stopping the Wall Street firms from
withdrawing the collateral.

At the time of the bankruptcy filing, there was a considerable
amount of second-guessing about the wisdom of this drastic move.
Some argued that there was a more orderly way to resolve the problem,
such as placing an oversight committee in charge of the funds (*New
York Times*, 1994a). Others argued that a bankruptcy filing would
damage the county government's credit rating for years. A study conducted by Miller, Merton, and Lexicon, Inc. (1996) that was commissioned by Merrill Lynch sought to answer the question of whether or
not the financial condition of the fund made it necessary to declare
bankruptcy and liquidate the fund. The authors concluded that there
were sufficient funds in the county pool, and that there was no need to
declare bankruptcy.

The news about the bankruptcy filing and the freezing of the deposits in the Orange County Investment Pool came as a big surprise. The response was one of shock and uncertainty in Orange County. County government officials, county employees, city governments, school districts, and local special districts did not know where they stood financially. Local residents who heard the news that their county government had gone bankrupt struggled to comprehend the meaning of this seemingly absurd statement. Orange County had become an object of curiosity and scorn by the national media.

PUBLIC REACTIONS

Public reactions to the financial crisis were monitored though a series of public opinion polls for the *Los Angeles Times* Orange County edition. I conducted the first survey a few days after the county declared bankruptcy. These surveys offered a way to gauge residents' awareness and perceptions of the local crisis, assess their views on the performance of county elected officials, and provide a way to ask local residents about the impacts of the financial meltdown. They also offered a mechanism for testing the public's acceptance of various solutions that were being proposed, such as raising taxes.

A random telephone survey of 600 Orange County adult residents was conducted from December 9 to 11, 1996. The first response of the public to the Orange County bankruptcy was one of anger more than fear. Four in ten adult residents described themselves as "very angry" about the actions of local officials that led to the Orange County financial crisis. Three in four said they were feeling "very angry" or "somewhat angry." As for the remaining residents, two in ten described themselves as "not too angry" or "not at all angry," while 4 percent were not sure.

In contrast, less than three in ten said they were worried about the events of the past week. This was the response when they were asked about their feelings toward the loss of $1.5 billion in the county investment pool, the resignation of Treasurer Bob Citron, and the bankruptcy filing to halt the withdrawal of investors' funds. About two in three said they were feeling "very worried" or "somewhat worried." About one in three residents said they were "not too worried" or "not at all worried" about the county's fiscal problems (see Appendix C, Table C-6).

The anger at local officials for leading Orange County into bankruptcy extended into the ratings of the Board of Supervisors. Only one in ten said they had a "great deal" of confidence in the ability of the Board of Supervisors to solve the county's financial crisis. Four in ten had "some" confidence in their local legislative body. Nearly half said they had "very little" confidence or "none" that the Board of Supervisors could solve the crisis. The responses of the Democrats and Republicans were about the same.

Most residents were also unimpressed with the board's handling of the county's financial crisis in the last week. Only 4 percent said they had done an excellent job, while 16 percent gave them credit for doing a good job under pressure. Thirty-five percent gave them a job rating of only fair, 34 percent said they had done a poor job of managing the county financial crisis thus far, and 11 percent were not sure. Democrats and Republicans gave similar evaluations (Times Orange County Poll, 1994c).

Surprisingly few residents placed all of the responsibility for the bankruptcy with the county treasurer. Most spread the blame around to several sources. When asked who they thought was most to blame for the financial crisis, 21 percent named Bob Citron. Nearly as many, 16 percent, named the Board of Supervisors. Seven percent named either the Wall Street companies that sold the investments to the county, County Administrative Officer Ernie Schneider, or the schools and other local government investors. However, 42 percent of the county residents said that all of these individuals and institutions were to blame for the financial crisis. Most could not identify one of them as more responsible than the other (Times Orange County Poll, 1994c).

The lack of serious panic about the bankruptcy was evident in the perceived impacts of the crisis. Three in ten expected that county services will have to be reduced "a lot" because of the investment fund losses. Yet only 17 percent thought that their city services would be significantly reduced, and 22 percent thought that funding for their local school programs would be reduced a lot. More residents were expecting some cuts in county and city services and the local schools, though not drastic in nature. Two in ten residents were anticipating little or no impact on county services, and about a third expected little or no effect on city services or school programs.

Relatively few residents thought that the bankruptcy would have a great impact on their own finances. One in six said they were "very worried" that they or a family member would be hurt financially as a result of the county's investment fund crisis. A quarter described themselves as "somewhat worried." However, more than half were either "not too worried" or "not at all worried" about there being any personal financial impacts of the Orange County bankruptcy. In general, lower-income residents worried the most about the personal impacts of the crisis (Times Orange County Poll, 1994c).

One reason for the lack of immediate concern about the bankruptcy is that only 17 percent of the respondents said that they or a member of their family depended on the county, a city, a school district, or another local agency for a salary, a contract, or some other form of payment (see Appendix C, Table C-7).

Most residents believed that recent events would have an effect on the county's economy and national image, but many seemed to view the financial crisis as a short-term problem that was not of a highly serious nature. Seven in ten said the bankruptcy would have a negative effect on job opportunities and the economy in Orange County, but only 32 percent said it would have a "very negative effect." Similarly, three in four said the financial crisis will have a negative effect on the county's image and prestige, but only 38 percent said it would have a "very negative" effect. When asked what the county would be like five years in the future, only 24 percent thought it would be a worse place to live than it was before the bankruptcy. Forty-two percent expected the county to be in about the same shape as it was before the bankruptcy, 29 percent thought it would be a better place, and 5 percent were not sure.

As another indication of the lack of serious public concern about the financial crisis, only 7 percent said the bankruptcy had made them think "very seriously" of moving out of Orange County (Times Orange County Poll, 1994c).

The public's reaction at the outset was one of anger toward their county officials for causing the crisis rather than concern about the personal impacts of the bankruptcy. They clearly displayed no willingness to make personal sacrifices to help resolve the crisis. Local residents were overwhelmingly opposed to raising their taxes to help restore the Orange County Investment Pool funds that were lost. Eight in ten said they opposed this action; only one-sixth were in favor. There were similar responses among Democrats and Republicans. The public gave only a lukewarm endorsement even to a state government bailout. Fifty-two percent said they favored asking the state for money to help Orange County out of its financial problems, while 41 percent were opposed and 8 percent were unsure. Again, the responses of Republicans and Democrats were about the same. These poll results gave county officials their first signal that the local voters were not very interested in helping their county government out of the $1.5 billion investment fund losses and the bankruptcy filing. They would have to look elsewhere for solutions to this fiscal problem (see Appendix C, Table C-8).

SUMMARY

This chapter has examined the series of events that led up to the Orange County government bankruptcy on December 6, 1994. The Orange County Investment Pool had grown into a $20.9 billion fund in just a few years. Citron had the fund highly leveraged and was using the borrowed money to purchase risky investments. He followed this strategy in order to increase the interest income for the county and other local governments. There were 194 pool participants, including the county government, twenty-nine of the thirty-one cities, all of the local school districts, the regional transportation agency, and most of the local special districts. Citron's investments worked when interest rates were falling, but it collapsed when the Federal Reserve Board raised interest rates in 1994.

The first whiff of trouble came out during the county treasurer's race. The challenger, John Moorlach, described the investment practices as unsafe. The Wall Street firms and pool participants took notice of the problems. The financial crisis worsened in the fall, after Citron continued to borrow money to bet on lower interest rates. The county declared bankruptcy to stop a run on the county pool by the Wall Street lenders and pool members. The Wall Street firms still seized the collateral they were holding on the county's loans. The pool participants found that their deposits had been frozen.

The financial crisis exposed the political fragmentation of local government in Orange County. The Board of Supervisors, the county administrative officer, and the auditor-controller had no control over the actions of the elected county treasurer. In 1987 the county auditor-controller said, "Currently, the County's investment strategy is designed and carried out by one person, the County Treasurer. . . . As noted in the Grand Jury report dated June 26, 1985, there appears to be little or no review of investment activity by the County Board of Supervisors, Chief Administrative Officer, or Auditor-Controller"

(Merrill Lynch, 1995, p. 13-2). The formation of an investment committee including several county officials was recommended. These and other warnings were all ignored. By the time county officials were told there was a problem, it was far too late.

Further, the county government, cities, school districts, and special districts in the county pool did not have open lines of communication with the county's leaders. Nor did these local governments have a history of cooperation with each other. Local governments would now have to find a way to cooperate in a fiscal crisis.

The public's initial reaction to the bankruptcy was anger rather than fear. They focused their blame for the event on several sources, including the Board of Supervisors, rather than just the county treasurer. They were not very worried. Voters were in no mood to pay more taxes to bail their county out of the bankruptcy. County officials, who now had to cope with a fiscal emergency in county government, also faced the prospects of working with local government representatives and residents who were angry at them.

CHAPTER 5

Response to the Fiscal Emergency

Orange County's elected officials woke up with a big headache on the day after their government declared bankruptcy. The Orange County Investment Pool was a sinking ship. The fund could lose more money if there was another interest rate hike. In the meantime, the government could not declare bankruptcy, close its doors, and expect its customers to go elsewhere. The county government was in charge of providing many public services to its residents, some of whom lived in life-threatening circumstances. Also, the frozen pool was not one that involved wealthy private investors who could wait to get their money back. The pool participants were scores of local agencies that provided needed services such as schools, garbage collection, water, roads, sewers, libraries, buses, health clinics, and police protection. The county and the other local government investors also had employee payrolls, bills to pay, and more loans coming due in the weeks ahead.

This chapter looks at the response to the fiscal emergency in Orange County. It shows how the county government reshaped itself to overcome its fragmentation and how scores of local governments managed to work together despite their local orientation. The public's reaction to the ongoing crisis is also of interest, since the fate of a tax increase for bankruptcy recovery would be in their hands. What also emerges is a new role for the state government. There would be no state loans or financial help, as was the case in New York. California was in no position to offer a bailout to Orange County.

DARK DAYS

There was no outpouring of sympathy for Orange County during the dark days in early December. The national media came down very hard on the "poor little rich county" that had gambled with taxpayer money and gone bankrupt. Late-night comedians made jokes about this strange turn of events. Bob Citron had changed Orange County into "Lemon County" to the outside world. The bond investors were infuriated by the news that this municipality was refusing to meet its obligations. Local governments were supposed to honor their debts with "full faith and credit," including raising taxes if need be. The idea that a local government had chosen to walk away from its promises was also maddening to private investors who held bonds. Political writers who viewed Orange County as the home of a selfish style of affluence and conservatism now gloated that this so-called suburban paradise was getting what it deserved. No one seemed too worried about the harm to local residents, since most had the notion that this was a wealthy county where people would cope.

The Orange County bankruptcy made headlines in the major newspapers from coast to coast. The local crisis also sent ripples through the nation's financial markets. Large municipalities were not supposed to go bankrupt. There were fears on Wall Street that deeper problems might be brewing in the municipal bond market.

The financial condition of Orange County government actually worsened after the bankruptcy was declared on December 6. Because of the county government's unwillingness to meet its obligations, its credit rating fell from being one of the top-rated local governments in California to "junk" bond status. To make matters worse, Orange County government defaulted on a $110 million pension bond that came due on December 8. Several Wall Street firms that had lent money to the county pool through reverse repurchase agreements began to sell off the securities they held as collateral.

At that time, a particularly damaging internal report was released. It indicated that the county auditor-controller had issued a warning to the Board of Supervisors a year ago that the county treasurer needed more oversight. There were also questions as to whether there was sufficient cash in the pool to allow for emergency withdrawals because of the leveraging. The county government, cities, local school districts, and special districts needed at least some of the funds that were tied up in the pool in order to pay their bills and to continue to provide services to their residents. There was little or no confidence that the county officials now in place could stabilize the Orange County Investment Pool (see Appendix A, Table A-2).

The state government had become very concerned about the Orange County bankruptcy. The governor, state legislature, state controller, state treasurer, and state auditor were all closely watching as the events unfolded. Counties are, after all, political subdivisions of the state government. These two branches of government are thus highly interdependent when it comes to revenues, expenditures, and services. The state's interest was also driven by the fact that the municipal bond market was now rethinking the creditworthiness of all state and local government agencies in California. Many years earlier Proposition 13 had limited local government funding and the ability to raise local taxes when the need arose. But it was the Orange County bankruptcy that exposed, for the first time, the severity of these state restrictions.

Some state leaders feared that the Orange County bankruptcy would have a "domino effect" on access to borrowing. State Treasurer Matt Fong noted during the crisis, "The state and local governments in California borrow billions of dollars in the bond market each year . . . . This borrowing activity will become more expensive to the extent that the Orange County crisis causes investors to question the ability of public agencies in California to honor their debt obligations" (California Debt Advisory Commission, 1995, p. 11). California leaders were concerned that they might have to add sinking credit ratings to the list of financial woes facing the state government.

There was talk that other California counties were about to fall because they too had followed risky investment practices. A survey after the bankruptcy by Moody's Investors Service found that fourteen of the fifty-eight counties in California were using leveraging and derivatives. There were six counties whose pools were inherent with significant risks, including Monterey, Placer, Solano, Sonoma, San Bernardino, and San Diego (New York Times, 1994c). The San Diego County fund, which included over $3 billion, had dropped by more than 10 percent in value during the month that Orange County declared bankruptcy. In addition, eight small counties in California had claimed extreme fiscal stress in the fall of 1994 and asked the state government for a $15 million bailout. Their problems were the result of changes in revenues and expenditures (*New York Times,* 1995a). Moreover, Los Angeles County faced a deficit of over $1 billion, mostly because health care costs for indigents were exploding while revenues were declining. The state government badly wanted the Orange County fiscal crisis to be contained.

At this point there was no sign that the state government would intervene. Instead, there was finger pointing between the state and Orange County about how they should have found a way to work together to avoid the bankruptcy filing. In a hearing, State Senator Killea asked a member of the Board of Supervisors about a newspaper report that said, "County leaders—whatever that means—county leaders accused state administrators of not coming to the county's aid, despite repeated pleas for loans and even a bailout. State leaders say they were rebuffed in their attempts to help out" (Senate Special Committee on Local Government Investments, 1995a, p. 74). The supervisor denied any knowledge of such conversations with state officials. Whatever the facts, the state and county leaders were off to a shaky start in trying to resolve the Orange County crisis.

THE SELLING OF THE
ORANGE COUNTY INVESTMENT POOL

The most immediate problem facing Orange County government after the bankruptcy was what to do with the Orange County Investment Pool. The only county official who had any real knowledge about the pool was the former county treasurer, Bob Citron. He had gone into seclusion. No one in the treasurer's office had the experience with complex investment securities or the familiarity with Wall Street investors to step into this crisis. Nor were the members of the Board of Supervisors, the county administrative officer, the county auditor-controller, or any other county officials in a position to take the leadership role with the county pool. Someone outside the county government would have to take charge of these troubled investments.

Fortunately for Orange County, the governor had taken a keen interest in the financial crisis. He had been briefed by business leaders and county officials from the outset. There were strong ties between Pete Wilson and Orange County Republicans. Many helped with his reelection campaign in 1994. Wilson won by landslides in Orange County during both of his gubernatorial elections, and the Orange County vote put him over the top in a close win in 1990. The governor had also appointed Bill Steiner to the Board of Supervisors. In early 1995 Wilson was planning to run for president. He was going to need a lot of support from Orange County Republicans. He did not need a bankruptcy in Orange County to spoil his political ambitions.

The governor provided very timely assistance to Orange County. He convinced a former member of his administration to oversee the Orange County Investment Pool. On December 8 the Board of Supervisors moved to appoint Tom Hayes, the former state treasurer and state auditor-general, for a ninety-day period. He was currently the president of a private municipal securities firm. Hayes was a trusted and respected financial advisor. His conditions in taking the job were that he would report directly to the Board of Supervisors, be given the full responsibility of restructuring the Orange County Investment Pool, and have oversight of the county treasurer's office. The governor had accomplished a new kind of "state intervention." The county government had retained the former state treasurer as the overseer of the failed investment fund.

Hayes reported to a state senate hearing about his tasks and his early days as the "turnaround manager" of the Orange County Investment Pool. He said, "When I arrived there, I found a portfolio that was highly leveraged, that was mismatched between the cash needs of the county and the length of the maturity of the investments, that have over 60 percent concentration of derivative products" (Senate Special Committee on Local Government Investments, 1994, p. 6). He found the county pool in bad shape. Its risky holdings left open the prospect that it could lose more money. Hayes saw his assignment as one of restructuring the large and risky county portfolio into a short-term money-market fund that was designed for local government investors.

The Board of Supervisors also hired the Salomon Brothers investment firm to help Hayes. The firm would determine the financial loss to the county portfolio if the holdings were liquidated on December 12. After several days at work, the firm estimated the loss to be about $2 billion. However, the losses would increase by another $300 million if there was another one-point increase in interest rates. The Federal Reserve Board had a meeting scheduled in late January.

Tom Hayes recommended to the Board of Supervisors that something be done soon to stabilize the Orange County Investment Pool. He wanted to increase the cash holdings so that local government investors could withdraw the funds they needed, eliminate some of the riskier interest-sensitive securities that were held in the pool, and shorten the average maturity from approximately four years to about 180 days. He also asked the supervisors to have Salomon Brothers manage the county fund so that they could begin the sale of the risky and long-term securities that were held. The supervisors approved his request, as did the bankruptcy court. Hayes stressed that his goal was to restructure the county fund "in an orderly manner, not conduct a fire sale" (Senate Special Committee on Local Government Investments, 1994, p. 7). But this would have the look of a quick sale, given the valid worries about rising interest rates.

The liquidation of the pool assets would not be an easy task. The fund was huge and complicated. The Orange County Investment Pool included 206 securities and 198 reverse repurchase agreements at the time of the bankruptcy. This included $646 million in cash. Based on current market value, there were $11 billion in fixed income securities, $222 million in collateralized mortgage obligations, $556 million in floating-rate notes, $4.8 billion in inverse floating-rate notes, $1.5 billion in index-amortizing notes, and $135 million in dual-index notes. The remainder of the fund consisted of about $13 billion in reverse repurchase agreements (Miller, Merton, and Lexicon, Inc., 1996, Table 1).

There were some who saw the pool liquidation strategy as one of "buying high and selling low." In mid-December Hayes stressed that the financial markets were receptive to the Orange County offerings and that the liquidation was proceeding with sales in the price range that he had expected. He also said that he would take longer than ninety days to complete the pool restructuring, or withdraw the securities from being offered for sale if the financial markets deteriorated. At the same time, Hayes stressed the danger of mounting losses if the county pool was not restructured in time for a possible interest rate hike when the Federal Reserve Board met again in late January.

Salomon Brothers sold the securities in the Orange County Investment Pool between December 15, 1994, and January 20, 1995. They were able to rid the portfolio of its derivatives and long-term bonds. They raised cash and shortened the maturity of the portfolio so that the local government investors would be able to withdraw most of their money. After the sale of securities, however, what was once a paper loss became quantifiable. The good news was that the amount of the loss was below the $2 billion estimates in December. The bad news was that the county pool now had a real loss of $1.64 billion. The county government, cities, school districts, and special districts had their first assessment of how much money they had lost in the county pool.

The decision to sell off the assets was one that is second-guessed by financial experts. Interest rates peaked in February 1995, when the Federal Reserve Board raised rates a half point. For the rest of the year, rates declined. Miller, Merton, and Lexicon, Inc. (1996) analyzed the liquidation of the portfolio between December 15, 1994, and January 20, 1995, and the investment of the proceeds in short-term money-market securities. They compared how the original investments would have performed over time with how they performed as money-market securities. If the county pool had not been liquidated, they claimed, the losses that the pool had suffered would have been greatly reduced by June 1995 and eliminated a year later, in January 1996. Comparing the original portfolio to the money-market portfolio after the liquidation, they estimate that the "opportunity cost" of the change in investment strategy was more than $1.4 billion by June 1995 and $1.76 billion by January 1996. Still, it is important to note that few experts were predicting that interest rates would stabilize in early 1995. Hayes did the "damage control" and stopped the fund losses. That was his assignment.

The recruitment of Tom Hayes by the county supervisors to have full authority to manage the investment pool, and his acceptance at the urging of the governor, was an important turning point in the Orange County crisis. The county pool had been turned into a safe, short-term money-market fund with adequate cash for local government withdrawals. Hayes was a highly credible figure for the county, local, and state government and the financial markets. One state senator credited him with lifting morale in the county government and "doing a bang-up job for the people of Orange County," and another added, "Your presence there has been very reassuring" (Senate Special Committee on Local Government Investments, 1994, pp. 20, 24).

NEW FISCAL CONDITIONS

The liquidation of the Orange County Investment Pool was the end of an era. No more would the county government live beyond its means through interest income. The shortfall in interest income would force the county to revise its current budget. It would also have to revise its budget plans for the following year. Someone had to make unpopular decisions about budget cuts during the fiscal emergency.

TABLE 5-1   SOURCES OF COUNTY REVENUES
FOR THE GENERAL FUND, FISCAL YEAR 1995

Interest earnings	34.8%
Property taxes	25.7
Motor vehicle fees	21.1
Fund balance available	11.9
Sales taxes	3.7
Other	2.8

SOURCE: County of Orange (1995a); *Los Angeles Times* Orange County
Edition (1995c).

In Orange County the total budget for county government for fiscal
year 1995 included $3.73 billion in revenues. The largest single cate-
gory involved revenues for the general fund, which were about 44 percent of the total budget (Arthur Andersen, 1995). The general fund
includes public services such as police protection and law enforcement,
health services, and social and community services, as well as government operations. Some of these programs are state or federally mandated, and others are not. About $1.18 billion, which is 72 percent of
the revenues for the general fund, were intergovernmental and other
special-purpose revenue sources. These include federal and state funds
that are restricted in use for specific county services.

The remaining $463 million, or 29 percent of the general fund, are
county revenues that are unrestricted. The county revenues for the general fund are used to pay for a variety of state-mandated services as well
as other county programs. The county revenues for the general fund
were strongly affected by the collapse of the county pool.

Table 5-1 indicates the expected sources of revenue for the general
fund in fiscal year 1995. The largest category of funding was supposed
to be interest income from the Orange County Investment Pool. The
treasurer's investments were expected to generate $161 million, which
was more than a third of the general fund budget. The revenues from
property taxes were declining, as a result of state government reductions in these funds to the counties, and would only be $119 million,
or about a quarter of the budget. Motor vehicle fees made up $98 mil-
lion of the general fund revenues, or about one-fifth of the general fund.
Less than one-fifth of the general fund revenues came from other
sources, including $17 million in sales taxes, $13 million in miscellaneous revenues, and an available fund balance of about $55 million. It
is safe to say that no other county government in the state would have
depended so heavily on interest earnings.

Of course, there was no possibility that the county pool would generate the $161 million in funds that were budgeted to pay for programs and government operations now that the pool had collapsed. Nor would it be possible to find other sources of general fund revenues to replace the expected interest earnings within a short period of time. The state government was not going to increase the property tax revenues or the motor vehicle fees, given the budget shortfalls it faced. The other fund sources were quite small. The bankruptcy and the restructuring of the Orange County Investment Pool came at about the midpoint of the 1995 fiscal year. This meant that there were insufficient unrestricted funds to pay for the county programs for the current year.

By early January it was apparent that there would be a shortfall of $170 million in general fund revenues. Instead of $463 million in funds, there was now expected to be only $293 million for the year in progress. Most of the $170 million shortfall was due to the loss of $161 million in interest revenues from the county pool (Arthur Andersen, 1995). There would also be a smaller amount of property tax revenues from the state. Other revenues were revised downward because of the recession. The $170 million loss meant that the general fund expenses for fiscal year 1995 would have to be reduced by 37 percent. There would need to be immediate and large budget cuts. The deficit also pointed to the need for severe cuts in the general fund budget for the 1996 fiscal year. A permanent restructuring of county government would be needed unless the voters agreed to raising taxes.

In mid-January it was possible for the pool members to calculate their dollar losses from the liquidation of the Orange County Investment Pool. About $7.5 billion had been deposited in the county pool by the county government and local government investors. The loss after the liquidation was about $1.7 billion, or almost 23 percent of the county pool's value. The county government was by far the largest single investor in the pool, with about $2.4 billion. This amounted to a third of the pool deposits. Almost every element of the county government had money invested in the county pool. The agencies whose revenues are generally restricted for specific purposes, including fire protection, harbors and beaches, roads, and airports, had $1.4 billion invested. About $900 million of county government funds came from special revenues, capital projects, enterprise, internal service, and other sources. There was also about $100 million in idle cash from the general fund that had been invested in the county pool (Arthur

TABLE 5-2 ORANGE COUNTY INVESTMENT
POOL LOSSES FOR 194 AGENCIES
All Figures in Billions of Dollars

	Investment Balance	Cash Available	Losses
County	2.4	1.9	0.5
Schools	1.0	0.8	0.2
Cities, transportation, and special districts	4.1	3.1	1.0
Total	7.5	5.8	1.7

SOURCE: County of Orange (1995a).

Andersen, 1995). The county government had lost about $500 million in the county pool. For now, these pool funds were frozen.

However, the total noncounty investment in the county pool was even larger; it amounted to $5.1 billion, or about two-thirds of the pool. The loss for all of these local government investors was $1.2 billion. The local school districts had about $1 billion that was required by the state to be placed in the county government's fund. The schools' share of the losses amounted to about $200 million. The cities and special districts had $4.1 billion that they voluntarily deposited in the county fund. This included $1 billion for the cities, $1.5 billion for transportation, $500 million for the water districts, $450 million for sanitation, and the balance for other agencies. The cities, transportation, and special districts had about a $1 billion loss (see Table 5-2). Again, all of these local governments were unable to access their deposits in the county pool.

The calculation of the losses in the county pool raised a number of crucial questions. Some wondered what the implications of the dollar amounts lost would be for the delivery of local services and local government operations. There was also the issue of whether the county government, cities, school districts, and special districts would be able to receive the frozen funds in time to pay for ongoing services and operations. Another concern among these shaken pool participants was when they would be able to withdraw their remaining funds from the county pool that had failed them.

Local government investors had lost real money in a pool despite promises of safety of principal and high yields. This became a complex political issue as well as a financial one. The local governments wanted to be made whole again. The local elected officials did not want to take less and be blamed for losing the taxpayer's money. However, they were

TABLE 5-3   COUNTY OF ORANGE
SHORT-TERM DEBT, 1995

	Maturity Date	Principal and Interest (millions)
Delinquent property tax (Teeter) notes	June 30, 1995	$ 179
Taxable notes	July 10, 1995	613
County cash flow notes, series A	July 19, 1995	177
County cash flow notes, series B	August 10, 1995	32
Total		$1,001

SOURCE: County of Orange (1995a).

asking for $1.2 billion from a county government that was bankrupt.
Many leaders began to fear that lawsuits would proliferate as pool investors turned their anger on the county government. A pool agreement
would have to be reached between the local government investors and
the county government, or there would be more financial chaos and a
greater likelihood of service disruption.

The county government had other big financial problems looming
on the horizon. In about six months there would be $1 billion of debt
coming due (see Table 5-3). This included almost $200 million in Teeter
notes, which are funded by delinquent property taxes; $600 million in
taxable notes; and about $200 million in short-term borrowing that is
designed to help the county with its cash flow cycles. The county government would have to come up with a way to pay back the principal
and interest to these bondholders between June 30 and August 10,
1995. But the county government did not have the money. They would
find it very difficult to borrow that much in such a short time after declaration of bankruptcy. The county leaders thus faced the possibility of
a massive default on county government bonds. Such an event would
have severe implications for any future borrowing. Somehow, this default had to be avoided.

The state offered little help in response to Orange County's distress.
The governor's spokesman said, "The bottom line . . . is the state has
shown leadership and provided a hand to the county when it needed
it . . . but the state is not in a position to bail out the county" (*Los
Angeles Times* Orange County Edition, 1995e). Their most generous effort was to shorten the delivery time for state funds. State Controller
Kathleen Connell said, "I will continue to do whatever I can to assist

with the immediate crisis. . . . I have, for example, already accelerated payments to the Orange County School Districts, to the community colleges in Orange County, and to the county itself to ease the liquidity crisis" (California Debt Advisory Commission, 1995, p. 12). Supervisor Gaddi Vasquez added in a state senate hearing, "The Orange County Transportation Authority did, in fact, receive some state assistance, not in any form of bailout monies but monies that were already on route to Orange County . . . to assist us, to provide for transportation projects to keep them moving" (Senate Special Committee on Local Government Investments, 1995a, pp. 74–75).

MAINTAINING LOCAL GOVERNMENT SERVICES

The local governments' finances were a tangled legal mess after the bankruptcy. It was hard to know which county agencies were short on funds and how much they would need to keep all of the county programs and services functioning. Moreover, the local governments that had invested in the county pool now had their funds frozen. Some of them had cash flow problems and needed their money right away to avoid disruptions in services, while others expected to need access within a short amount of time. It was clearly no longer business as usual for local governments in Orange County.

The political fragmentation in county government, and lack of coordination between the county government and the local governments that made up the county pool, would be formidable barriers to making decisions. The county's employees were in a panic mode. Rumors were rampant in the county's Hall of Administration. Many wondered if they had lost their jobs or would be receiving their next paycheck. The Board of Supervisors could not meet as a group to discuss the problems, because of the Brown Act, except in public sessions that were punctuated by angry speakers who wanted them to be recalled. Moreover, there was little trust in the county officials because of the huge investment losses that had been suffered. This would affect the deliberations with local officials about how to handle the distribution of funds in the now-frozen county pool.

The county government would have to find a way to shrug off its fiscal problems and keep operating. At a time when the local governments were very upset with the county leaders, they still needed to sit down together and make decisions about how to dispense the funds in the county pool and avoid shutdowns in schools and services.

The county government took an important step to maintain county programs and cut the budget in the wake of the fiscal emergency (see Appendix A, Table A-2). The Board of Supervisors appointed an Operations Management Council after consultation and urging from the top management in the county government.

The county team included Sheriff Brad Gates, District Attorney Mike Capizzi, and Health Care Agency Director Tom Uram. The Operations Management Council provides a relevant example of how this county government overcame its politically fragmented structure in a time of crisis. The Board of Supervisors pooled the powers of two countywide elected officials and an appointed director of a large agency. The sheriff had a lot of experience with making decisions during emergencies. He was used to working in fires, floods, and other disasters. Gates was also the best-known and most popular figure in county government, according to the public opinion polls. The district attorney commanded a considerable amount of respect since he was in the midst of criminal investigations of the county officials who were involved in the bankruptcy. The Health Care Agency director would represent the county's programs that were designed to benefit the poor and dependent populations. The Operations Management Council represented a departure for Orange County. There was a deliberate centralization of authority and delegation of power over the county's agencies. The establishment of this group turned out to be a critical move in addressing the financial crisis.

The Operations Management Council interviewed each of the county department heads and agencies to determine their immediate cash needs. The elected and appointed heads were told they would be treated as equals. By all accounts, this appointed group received the cooperation they needed from all agencies. The information from the three-person team went directly to the Board of Supervisors. They then asked the county administrative officer to take appropriate actions. The council is credited with preventing major breakdowns in county service delivery.

The Operations Management Council also made the first attempts at cutting the budget to compensate for the loss of interest income. This group filed a report within a month from when they began interviewing department and agency heads. They recommended about $42 million in budget cuts for fiscal year 1995. Their plan resulted in the elimination of 700 county jobs through layoffs, leaving vacant positions unfilled, transfers and retirements, and the loss of contract and temporary employees.

Most of the budget cuts were in public protection, general government services, and community and social services. These were the county agencies that depended on interest revenues from the general county fund (*Los Angeles Times* Orange County Edition, 1995f). State and federal mandates prevented such cuts in health and welfare spending.

Making these decisions about employee reductions was a vital task that was provided by a new structure in county government. There had to be some immediate staffing cuts because of the revenue shortfall. The other county leaders at the time would not have gained the kind of support and cooperation that the Operations Management Council did in order to gather the information that was needed. The council's efforts resolved some budget issues for the current fiscal year and, equally important, provided a framework for the decisions that needed to be made on the next county budget.

The local government investors had an equally challenging task after the bankruptcy. They could not access the county pool. They were not a cohesive group that had worked together in the best of times, and these were very tense moments. In fact, the combination of Orange County cities, schools, special districts, and non–Orange County agencies provided a great deal of political fragmentation. On December 14 the U.S. bankruptcy court in Los Angeles provided this shocked group with the organizational structure they needed for accessing funds and maintaining local services.

The U.S. bankruptcy court appointed the Orange County Pool Participants Committee. This group included a representative from the Orange County Sanitation District, the City of Irvine, the Orange County Water District, the Transportation Corridor Agencies, the Orange County Transportation Authority, the Orange County Department of Education, the City of Mountain View, and legal counsel. The purpose of the pool committee was to represent the various types of government investors inside as well as outside (i.e., Mountain View) Orange County. The committee members represented agencies with some of the largest deposits for their respective types of local government. The chair of the committee was from the Orange County Transportation Authority, which had over $1 billion in the pool.[1] The mix of agencies represented,

---

1. The Orange County Transportation Authority had a board that included both city elected officials and members of the Board of Supervisors. This placed Stan Oftelie, the chief executive officer of this organization, in a unique position as chair of the Pool Participants Committee.

and their large deposits, would give the committee clout with the county government and the other local government investors.

Within two weeks of the bankruptcy, the court authorized the emergency release of about $152 million so that certain local governments could distribute payrolls. The county released these funds. Most of this money went to the local school districts. The state auditor, explaining how the decision process worked, said, "My understanding is that it will be done in concert with the bankruptcy court, and clearly it would include Tom Hayes who is here, his advisors from Salomon, and the attorney for the Board of Supervisors, Mr. Bennett, and they would go forward and say, these are the numbers the people are telling us the needs are. The Auditor has validated them as being reasonable" (Senate Special Committee on Local Government Investments, 1994, p. 39). These were the formal steps taken to allow for orderly withdrawals from the county pool.

There were also many individuals who made these tense and difficult discussions work. After all, the local government needs could not be easily identified, and there was considerable distrust of the county government. The attorney for the County of Orange, Bruce Bennett, and the attorney for the Pool Participants Committee, Patrick Shea, shared the goals of seeking consensus and avoiding litigation. Tom Hayes took the lead role for the county government. He was viewed by all sides as an impartial outsider sent by the governor. The county government involved Dan Young and Gary Hausdorfer in the negotiations. They had a lot of credibility as former mayors and board members of the regional transportation agency. The Board of Supervisors, the treasurer's office, and the county administrative officer stayed in the background.

On December 22 the bankruptcy court judge approved an agreement between the county government and the Pool Participants Committee to release up to $1 billion of the funds on a hardship basis, if the withdrawal is approved by the Pool Participants Committee. This clearly simplified the withdrawal process and speeded the delivery of funds. Three weeks after the bankruptcy took place, when the county pool funds were frozen, the Pool Participants Committee granted its first hardship approvals of about $60 million. By the end of December this committee was meeting regularly to review, discuss, and approve the hardship distributions. There were hardship and emergency distributions amounting to $428 million by the time the bankruptcy was a month old. On January 19 the pool committee approved $555 million in disbursements from the county pool (Orange County Investment Pool, 1995a, 1995b).

The committee structure created by the bankruptcy court was what allowed the cash to flow from the funds to the local government investors to the needed local services. It also created cohesion among a diverse group of pool participants. Moreover, it joined the county government and the local governments in a cooperative venture. It prevented lawsuits. These positive experiences laid the groundwork for the more complex issues that would take place in the negotiation of an overall pool settlement.

There were also efforts by the private sector and nonprofit organizations to make sure that essential local services were maintained after the bankruptcy. On January 12 the United Way of Orange County announced a $450,000 emergency loan program. This was to provide interest-free loans to nonprofit organizations who had cash flow problems because of delays in receiving funds from county government. Seven corporations in Orange County provided $50,000 each, while the United Way offered $100,000 for this program (United Way of Orange County, 1996).

POLITICAL FALLOUT FROM THE FISCAL EMERGENCY

The shock of the county government's declaring bankruptcy was wearing off by the end of January. Nothing terrible had happened. There were no school closings or disruptions in services. Still, the public was receiving some disturbing news. They learned that the real loss in the county pool was $1.64 billion. The county government was talking about budget cuts, layoffs, and possible bond defaults. City leaders criticized county officials for not supervising the county treasurer's risky practices.

To test the public mood at this juncture, I conducted a random telephone survey of 600 Orange County adult residents between January 20 and 23 for the *Los Angeles Times* Orange County edition. The bankruptcy was a month and a half old. In response to an open-ended question at the start of the survey, six in ten residents named the financial crisis and bankruptcy as the top problem facing Orange County. Never before had one topic so dominated the list of concerns in a public opinion survey. The top public policy topics over the past ten years, such as the economy, crime, and traffic, were hardly mentioned. The financial crisis was the top county issue for all demographic groups.

Most of the residents thought that the fiscal problems now in evidence would be around for some time. Only 10 percent predicted that the financial crisis would end within a year, while one in three thought it would be resolved in less than two years. Six in ten thought it would take two years or more for the financial crisis to end, and a quarter of the residents thought it would take five or more years before it was all settled (Times Orange County Poll, 1995b).

The political heat on the county leaders was growing. Fifty-one percent of residents now said that they were "very angry" with the actions of county officials. This was an increase of twelve points since the December survey. Nine in ten expressed at least some anger toward the county officials over the financial crisis. Two in ten mentioned the Board of Supervisors and one in six named the treasurer when asked who was most to blame for the financial crisis. Very few residents pointed specifically to the investment brokers, local government investors, or the county administrative officer. About half were still saying that multiple sources were primarily responsible for the financial crisis. However, fewer were pointing to Bob Citron and more were blaming the Board of Supervisors compared with the December survey. Recent news about the lack of oversight of the county treasurer seemed to be resulting in the placement of more blame with the Board of Supervisors (see Appendix C, Table C-9).

There was considerable support for removing the county officials who were present when the financial crisis began. Nearly half favored the recall of supervisors Gaddi Vasquez, Roger Stanton, and Bill Steiner. These were the three remaining members of the Board of Supervisors who were serving in 1994. The other two members, Tom Riley and Harriet Wieder, had retired at the end of the year. There was little difference in the responses concerning these three board members, indicating that many in the public believed that it was the Board of Supervisors in general who had failed rather than a particular person. Fifty-three percent also favored the removal from office of the county administrative officer, Ernie Schneider, which was similar to the sentiment against the supervisors. At that time 49 percent also wanted to appoint John Moorlach as county treasurer. Moorlach was the challenger in the June 1994 election who had criticized the investment practices of the county treasurer. The Democrats and Republicans had similar reactions toward their county government leaders.

County residents were not very impressed with the governor's performance. Three in ten said that Pete Wilson was doing an excellent or good job in responding to the county financial crisis, while four in ten gave him fair ratings and a quarter said he was doing a poor job. Two in ten Democrats and about only a third of Republicans gave him positive marks during the crisis. This was in a county that had overwhelmingly voted for Pete Wilson only two months earlier, when the governor ran for a second term.

Orange County residents were also given a list of alternatives for resolving the $170 million shortfall in county revenues for the general fund for the current year. Few Democrats or Republicans favored tax increases alone to resolve the budget deficit. A third favored spending cuts only, and 15 percent wanted to raise user fees. Only 4 percent said they supported a tax increase and no other efforts. Four in ten favored a combination of cuts, user fees, and taxes (see Appendix C, Table C-10).

In a follow-up question, 60 percent said they favored increasing county fees as a way of maintaining the current level of funding for county services. The county fees that had been included were library fees, real estate fees, and impoundment fees for cars. Six in ten favored a reduction of 10 percent or more in the county government's workforce and budget. Many said they would be willing to see some cuts in the budget for parks and recreation, waste management, roads and transportation, or public health.

The privatization of county services and selling of the county's assets also had some appeal as solutions to the financial crisis. Six in ten believed that contracting out government services to private companies would be a good way to save the county money because private companies can provide services more cheaply and efficiently. Fifty percent of Orange County residents were in favor of selling John Wayne Airport, which was perhaps the county government's most valuable asset.

There was strong opposition to raising taxes in order to pay back the private investors who had bought Orange County bonds that were coming due. Eighty percent were opposed to raising taxes for this purpose. However, at this time, there was more support for raising taxes earmarked for specific services. About half said they supported a tax increase to maintain the current level of funding for local public schools (53 percent) and for law enforcement and fire protection (48 percent). The results provided little hope for those who supported a tax increase as the solution. The response indicated a bare majority support for a tax hike only for services essential to residents.

There were no signs of grave concerns about the bankruptcy by the public at large. About a quarter were "very worried" about the financial crisis, similar to the December survey. One in six were "very worried" that they or a family member would be hurt financially as a result of the bankruptcy. One in five said they had heard or read something about cuts in local services or school programs that would directly affect them. About a third expected major cuts in county services, while fewer than a fourth anticipated that their city services or local school programs would be reduced a lot. Other responses indicated that the public had become more negative toward the local economy and owning an Orange County home. But to place these views in perspective, only one in ten were very seriously thinking about leaving the county or sending their children to private schools (Times Orange County Poll, 1995b).

The support for Proposition 13 was unwavering. Fewer than one in five agreed with the argument that the financial crisis was caused in part by Proposition 13, which made it so hard to raise taxes that schools and local governments were forced to make risky investments to get enough money to pay for their operations. Republicans and Democrats both were largely unwilling to hold Proposition 13 responsible. Two in three residents said that the financial crisis came about in part because the county government was overstaffed and had wasted taxpayer money for years (see Appendix C, Table C-11). Trust in Proposition 13 held steady as confidence in government declined. The public signaled its approval for budget cuts and changes in the county leadership.

THE CHIEF EXECUTIVE OFFICER: BUDGET CUTS AND HOUSE CLEANING

The Orange County Board of Supervisors needed to shake up the county government leadership and reestablish some public trust. By late January the risky investments in the pool had been liquidated. The pool members who needed funds were making withdrawals. Local services were being delivered and public schools remained open. The imminent sense of danger surrounding the fiscal emergency had passed. Yet there were tough issues just ahead, such as the budget shortfall, an overall settlement for the pool members, the possibility of a loan default, and the politically incorrect move of calling for new taxes to get out of the bankruptcy.

In late January the Board of Supervisors took the first step by removing Ernie Schneider from the position of county administrative officer. For the time being, he was a county employee in limbo waiting for reassignment. They appointed Tom Uram of the Health Care Agency as interim county administrative officer. Their next goal was to find someone quickly, preferably from outside the county government, to take on the new role of chief executive officer. The responsibilities would include managing the budget cuts, cleaning house of the tainted county officials, and developing a long-term plan for restructuring county government. Over the next few weeks the Board of Supervisors looked at several candidates, including a turnaround expert given the name "Ming the Merciless" for his ruthless budget cuts.[2]

The county supervisors appointed a local, William Popejoy, to this new post on February 10 (see Appendix A, Table A-3). His financial experience in the private sector included the leadership of a failing savings and loan institution in Orange County a decade earlier. The effort was ultimately unsuccessful. He was a wealthy county resident and an affable business leader who brought credibility, honest answers, and a fresh perspective. He had no prior experience working in government. Popejoy had also agreed to take on this challenging new job with no salary. His pay rate would be highly popular with residents in this fiscally conservative county (*Wall Street Journal*, 1995).

The new chief executive officer moved quickly to clean house. Two weeks into his new job, Popejoy fired the former county administrative officer, Ernie Schneider. He arranged for the termination of Assistant Treasurer Matthew Raabe, who worked for Citron. He asked for and received the resignation of the county counsel, Terry Andrus. Popejoy also asked for the removal of the auditor-controller, Steve Lewis, but Lewis refused to give up his elected office. Lewis's term would not expire until 1998.

Popejoy's efforts were aimed at removing the major county officials involved in the bankruptcy. The exceptions were supervisors Vasquez, Stanton, and Steiner, who were among the board members who hired him. A few weeks later, in another effort to boost public approval, the board appointed John Moorlach as the county treasurer. Popejoy learned important lessons about the structure of county government through this exercise of power. He did not have the authority to fire a county elected official whom he did not trust. His every move would require the approval of a majority of the Board of Supervisors. This was unfamiliar territory for a corporate executive.

2. A leading finalist for the chief executive officer position was Sanford Sigiloff, who was known in the private sector as a corporate turnaround expert. However, he had asked the Board of Supervisors for high compensation to take the county government position (*Orange County Register*, 1995a).

TABLE 5-4   DECLINE IN COUNTY REVENUES
FOR THE GENERAL FUND
All Figures in Millions of Dollars

	Fiscal Year 1995: Original	Fiscal Year 1996: Proposed	Change
Interest earnings	161	10	(151)
Property taxes	119	121	2
Motor vehicle fees	98	101	3
Fund balance available	55	15	(40)
Sales taxes	17	18	1
Other	13	10	(3)
Revenue estimate	463	275	(188)
New revenue estimate	293		
New budget deficit	170		

SOURCE: County of Orange (1995a); *Los Angeles Times* Orange County Edition (1995c).

In March 1995 Popejoy turned his attention to the county's financial matters. One of the priorities was to develop a budget for fiscal year 1996, which would begin in just a few months. Ernie Schneider, the former county administrative officer, had warned the Board of Supervisors in August 1994, "We should be concerned that interest income and one-time revenues are financing a significant portion of the budget. The FY 1995 interest income projection represents 35 percent of the available financing and is our single largest source of discretionary revenue" (Merrill Lynch, 1996, p. 13-5). These warnings had, of course, fallen on deaf ears. The fiscal year 1995 budget proved to be significantly off target because of the lost interest income. Table 5-4 summarizes the original sources of general fund revenues from county sources in fiscal year 1995. It also compares these figures with the preliminary budget estimates for fiscal year 1996. There was a budget shortfall of $170 million because of the lower interest earnings in 1995. The county revenues would shrink by 41 percent for the next year. This was largely the result of losing about $150 million in interest income. Other revenue sources of income would grow very little.

The chief executive officer proposed a new round of large budget cuts. The expenditures for public protection, general government, and community and social services would each be reduced by about 25 percent. Health services would take a 35 percent cut, and insurance and reserves would be reduced by 98 percent. All of the other expenditures in the general fund budget would be cut by 45 percent (see Table 5-5).

TABLE 5-5 THE COUNTY GENERAL FUND FOR
FISCAL YEARS 1995 AND 1996: BUDGET
REDUCTIONS AND JOB LOSSES

County Budget Reductions (millions)

	Fiscal Year 1995	Fiscal Year 1996	Percentage Change
Community and social services	$ 74	$ 54	−27
Health services	40	26	−35
General government	81	61	−25
Public protection	160	121	−24
Insurance and reserves	88	2	−98
Other	20	11	−45
Total expenditures	$463	$275	−41

County Government Job Losses

	Layoffs	Vacancy Deletions	Total
Community and social services	731	259	990
Health services	36	103	139
General government	151	96	247
Public protection	68	61	129
Environmental resources	54	43	97
Insurance and reserves	0	4	4
Total	1,040	566	1,606

SOURCE: County of Orange (1995a); *Los Angeles Times* Orange County Edition (1995d).

Altogether, there would need to be 1,040 layoffs and 566 vacancy deletions on top of the budget cuts that were made earlier for the current fiscal year. Table 5-5 indicates that the job losses would not be equally distributed across county government. Seventy percent of the layoffs and vacancy deletions, or 1,129 of the 1,606 job losses, were in community and social services and health services. Some complained that the budget cuts were aimed at the poor and the immigrants. These groups were heavily dependent on county programs, but they did not have a voice in these local fiscal decisions.

The Board of Supervisors approved the budget cuts and staff reductions on March 7. The chief executive officer in describing these effects said, "We started with 18,000, we're coming down to 13,000. Services will be cut back dramatically. Basic needs in some areas will not be met. The facts are, we cannot print money, we have to live with this budget of $275 million" (Committee of the Whole, 1995, pp. 11–12). The county government had learned what it was like to balance a budget without interest income.

The county budget cuts thus far were limited to balancing the county budget in fiscal years 1995 and 1996. As Popejoy noted, "It doesn't provide one penny . . . to help meet our bond repayments this summer. . . . We have no excess cash flow to meet those bond payments" (Senate Special Committee on Local Government Investments, 1995b, p. 37). Then, there was also the matter of the money that was owed to the cities, school districts, and special districts that had funds in the Orange County Investment Pool.

Popejoy explored all of the revenue sources that would allow the county to pay its debts. He turned to his experiences in the private sector for creative ideas. He first looked into the possibility of selling assets. The county's most valuable assets were the airport and landfills. But it could take years to find buyers, and even longer to gain approvals for such complex transfers from public hands to private firms. The county did not own enough real estate to sell and raise large amounts of cash. Popejoy sought an out-of-court settlement with the Wall Street firms that the county had sued, but could not reach a settlement. He explored leaseback arrangements and cost savings through the privatization of county services, but these efforts would not generate enough funds.

Popejoy was aware that the county was running out of time to make the bond payments in the summer. He concluded that a sales tax increase was the only way that the county government could generate the revenues needed to borrow money and pay its debts in a short amount of time. Reluctantly, he proposed to the Board of Supervisors in mid-March that they place a tax increase measure on the June ballot.

ORANGE COUNTY INVESTMENT POOL SETTLEMENT

There were many reasons why the county government and local governments needed to reach an overall settlement on the Orange County Investment Pool. Many local public agencies needed full access to their large cash deposits. There was the possibility of "ripple effects" resulting in bankruptcies and defaults among the cities, school districts, and special districts that could not withdraw their funds. A settlement was also necessary in order to avoid lawsuits between the pool investors and the county government. The prospects of litigation meant that the bankruptcy could become more much more costly and take many years to resolve.

The county government and the local investors seemed to want a settlement on the investment pool from the start. So did the attorneys representing both sides. However, there was a major stumbling block to an agreement. The local government investors wanted 100 percent of their funds returned. They publicly argued that they had been promised that the money was safe. They privately worried that it would be the end of their political careers if they were held responsible for not getting back all of the money.

The private sector in Orange County was instrumental in helping the county government and local governments reach an agreement. The Orange County Business Council had been keeping a close eye on events. They had reached the conclusion that the financial crisis could hurt the county's economy and business owners. For some companies, such as the large landowners and developers in the county, the implications of the bankruptcy were even more alarming. They faced the prospects of declining land values, slow real estate sales, and problems with their lenders. They could ill afford to leave their fates in the hands of local government leaders. This was a time for action.

The Orange County Business Council decided to focus its efforts on the investment pool settlement. The council appointed a three-person task force on January 20 to assist in negotiations between the county government and the investment pool committee. The members included Gary Hunt of the Irvine Company, George Argyros of Arnel Development, and Tom Sutton of Pacific Mutual. Gary Hunt was a high-ranking executive for the largest landowner in the county. He had taken the lead role in engaging the business community in the financial crisis from the beginning. He was highly knowledgeable about city, county, and state government. He also had strong ties to Governor Wilson. George Argyros was a real estate developer. He had just led a successful countywide initiative campaign to convert the El Toro Marine Air Base into a commercial airport. He was highly active in civic affairs and politics. Tom Sutton was chairman and chief executive officer of one of the largest private employers in Orange County. He also had recent experiences with bankruptcies and financial settlements through his efforts on behalf of his company and the insurance industry. His company was active in public affairs and charitable giving. These three business leaders offered a perspective from outside of local government, yet they were familiar with Orange County. They knew a great deal about finance and business negotiations. They differed in their politics but all were pragmatists. Their

TABLE 5-6   COMPREHENSIVE
SETTLEMENT AGREEMENT

	School	Nonschool
Per Dollar		
Cash	0.77	0.77
Recovery notes	0.13	0.03
Senior claims	—	0.09
Repayment claims	0.10	0.11
Total	1.00	1.00
In Millions of Dollars		
Cash	783	3,161
Recovery notes	132	123
Senior claims	—	370
Repayment claims	102	452
Total	1,017	4,106

SOURCE: County of Orange (1995a).

recommendations would command a high level of respect within county government and local governments.[3]

The business leaders convened daily meetings with the representatives of the county government and local governments, their attorneys, and several other business executives with expertise in local government. Ironically, the attorneys representing the two sides in the Orange County Investment Pool negotiations were from San Diego and Los Angeles counties. The business leaders represented for the local governments a trusted source of "reality checks" about the bankruptcy. For instance, they were able to convey the idea that investors do not receive 100 percent of their funds after a financial collapse. They offered a perspective on what is a "good deal" in such circumstances. They stressed to everyone on both sides the importance of reaching a pool settlement so that the people and businesses in Orange County could move forward.

Remarkably, the negotiating team for the Orange County Business Council reached an agreement in less than three weeks. They publicly announced the plan on February 7 and received the unanimous endorsement of the Board of Supervisors the same day. The agreement is outlined in Table 5-6. For all pool participants, the county government

3. All three business leaders were residents of Newport Beach, which was one of only two Orange County cities that passed the sales tax measure.

would agree to return 77 cents on the dollar in cash for their deposits in the Orange County Investment Pool. The local school districts would receive another 13 cents on the dollar with recovery notes from the county that they could redeem for cash; the remaining 10 cents of each dollar would be in the form of repayment claims to be paid at a time when the county government received more funds through a lawsuit or a revenue increase. For the cities and special districts, there would be 3 cents on the dollar in recovery notes. Another 9 cents on the dollar would be in the form of senior claims, meaning that they would take precedence over other county debts. The remaining 11 cents of each dollar would be repayment claims. The pool participants that accepted this plan would, in return, agree not to sue the county government.

The plan's appeal for the local government investors was that it provided most of their money immediately. It also gave them political cover by stating that they could ultimately receive all of their money. The schools were treated better than the cities and special districts, since they alone were provided with 90 cents of each dollar in cash and redeemable recovery notes. However, the schools were viewed as having more pressing financial needs. They were also involuntary participants in the county pool. Moreover, there was enough political support for the schools in the state legislature that they could have opted for their own settlement. Some thought the state legislative approval that was needed for this agreement would not have been present without having the schools as participants. Thus, it was also in the best interests of the county government, cities, and special districts to give the schools a higher payout. Most of the pool participants agreed to the settlement that had been negotiated on their behalf in late March. The settlement was approved by the bankruptcy court in early May.

The settlement plan had financial costs for the county government. They would have to find a way to fund the $255 million in recovery notes that they were providing to the schools, cities, and special districts. They needed to borrow the money to pay for the recovery notes right away, since the pool participants were insisting that the recovery notes be redeemable to cash by June. But no investors would lend this amount of money to a bankrupt county. This is where the state government stepped in with legislation that allowed Orange County to finance the pool settlement.

The governor called a special session of the state legislature on February 17 to design the legislation to ease the Orange County financial crisis. It was full of political gamesmanship. Democratic leaders in

TABLE 5-7   STATE LEGISLATION FOR ORANGE COUNTY
INVESTMENT POOL SETTLEMENT

SB 7XX: Authorizes the Orange County Board of Supervisors to sell obligations arising out of delinquent property taxes or assessments

SB 8XX: Establishes a mechanism to intercept county vehicle license fee revenue if other revenues are insufficient to retire refinancing bonds that Orange County issues to honor warrants to local agencies

SB 9XX: Allows the Orange County Board of Supervisors to waive the statutory requirements pertaining to the sale and lease of county-owned property in an effort to expedite the process

SB 12XX: Allows school districts and community college districts in Orange County, under specified conditions, to sell surplus property and use the proceeds for general fund purposes in the district

SB 17XX: Grants Orange County a one-time exemption from the California Environmental Quality Act if the county's ordinance is amended to accept solid waste from out of the county

SB 18XX: Permits Orange County to pledge vehicle license fee revenue as security for certificates of participation or lease revenue bonds issues in 1995 and 1996

SOURCE: Office of Senate Floor Analysis (1995).

the state legislature reveled in the fiscal problems in the home of their conservative Republican colleagues. Still, both sides managed to put aside politics in the end. A series of bills were passed allowing the county to establish separate revenue streams that could be pledged to pay for the recovery notes to the local government investors (see Table 5-7).

Most important was the SB 8XX legislation. This bill allowed the state to intercept the vehicle license fees that normally went to Orange County so that those funds could be specifically used to pay for the recovery notes. This would assure the lenders to this bankrupt county that there would be money set aside to pay the bonds when they came due. As Bruce Bennett, the attorney representing the county government, explained, "The holder of a recovery note, whoever that may turn out to be . . . will have a very, very high degree of confidence in the repayment of that security" (Senate Special Committee on Local Government Investments, 1995c, p. 33). But the county would then have to compensate for the revenues intercepted by the state. The additional funds would be generated by receiving more garbage and thus more revenues from the landfills. Again, ironically, the recovery involved the surrounding counties. The plan was to allow San

TABLE 5-8   ORANGE COUNTY'S OVERALL
FINANCIAL NEEDS

	Amount in Millions
Recovery notes to schools, cities, and special districts	$ 255
Senior claims to cities/special districts	370
County debt deficiency	382
County pool deficiency	305
Outside creditor (vendor) debt	100
Repayment claims	554
Total	$1,966

SOURCE: County of Orange (1995a).

Diego and Los Angeles counties to dump their garbage in the landfills operated by the Orange County government. This expanded use of the landfills to raise revenues would also require new legislation. The state legislature passed SB 17XX to provide an exemption from the California Environmental Quality Act to allow the expanded use of the landfills (*Orange County Register,* 1995b).

The state legislature also passed SB 7XX to allow the county government to raise revenues through long-term borrowing from delinquent property taxes. It passed SB 18XX to provide a borrowing source for the county to fund a sale-leaseback of its landfills after their expansion. The legislature also passed SB 9XX and SB 12XX to make it easier for the county government and school districts to sell property. The governor signed these bills in mid-May. By the end of that month, the cities, schools, and special districts were withdrawing large sums of money from the pool.

The pool settlement was a very important step taken to stabilize the financial crisis. It was accomplished in a relatively short time, compared with the length of proceedings in corporate bankruptcies, largely through the private sector leadership. The inherent weaknesses in the local structure of government, as well as the current level of distrust toward the county government leaders, had been neutralized.

However, the financial nightmare was far from over. Table 5-8 shows that the county government still needed nearly $2 billion to pay its outstanding bills. The recovery notes that would be paid through intercepted funds amounted to only $255 million. There was still almost $1 billion owed to local government investors. The county government was lacking $382 million for debt payments. Also, there was $100 million still owed to vendors. The attorney for the Pool Participants

Committee, Patrick Shea, said "The Settlement Agreement won't end this nightmare. The Agreement will simply turn it into a different kind of beast" (Orange County Investment Pool, 1995c). There was a growing realization that the voters would have to be asked to pay higher local sales taxes.

MEASURE R AND THE PUBLIC RESPONSE

In the last week of March the Board of Supervisors voted to place a sales tax increase measure on the ballot. The vote would be taken in a June 27 special election. The county officials set a short time frame for this election for many reasons. First, the settlement with the pool participants in the Orange County Investment Pool required additional revenues for 100 percent payment. The county officials had to show the pool investors, state legislature, and bankruptcy court that they were making a strong effort to obtain the extra funds they needed. Otherwise, the agreement could unravel. Just as important, there were large amounts of debt coming due in the summer. There had to be a serious good-faith effort to find the funds to pay the bond investors. A default on those bond payments would have serious consequences for future borrowing.

The Board of Supervisors placed the tax increase on the ballot at the urging of the chief executive officer and business leaders. They made this move reluctantly and were very fearful of its political consequences. The Orange County Business Council had urged the supervisors to place the sales tax measure on the ballot in the middle of March. So did William Popejoy, the chief executive officer in county government. The supervisors were concerned that their action in placing a tax increase on a local ballot would be out of character with fiscally conservative politics. So they argued that they were letting the voters decide on the financial recovery of Orange County. The short time frame may have been a financial necessity, but it did pose difficult logistical problems. If the voters initially came out against the tax hike, there would be little time to stage the public debates needed to change their opinions. Also, if the measure was defeated in late June, another recovery plan would have to be quickly devised before the massive bond payments came due in the summer months.

Measure R would raise the sales tax in Orange County by one-half cent for ten years. The revenues it generated would be for general county purposes, such as providing county services and government operating expenses. The new tax funds would be used to finance the county government's debts, such as the money owed to schools, cities, special districts, and bondholders. The supervisors included a citizens' oversight committee for Measure R funds, in the hopes that this would counteract voter suspicions about how the new tax moneys would really be used. Measure R was designed to take Orange County out of fiscal danger in a short time. It would generate the revenues needed for debt payments to enable the county to emerge from bankruptcy.

A public opinion survey was commissioned by the *Los Angeles Times* Orange County edition to gauge initial voter response to the half-cent sales tax increase for bankruptcy recovery. A random telephone survey of 519 Orange County registered voters was conducted from April 6 to 9. This was within a week of when the Board of Supervisors approved Measure R for the June 27 special election. In line with their earlier response to a recovery tax, Orange County voters were against Measure R.

Only about a third of the voters were in favor of paying a half-cent sales tax, while a solid majority said they would vote against the sales tax increase. Fewer than one in ten said they had not made up their minds. About half of the Democrats opposed Measure R, while Republicans were against the sales tax increase by a two-to-one margin. The majority of local voters in every age group said they would vote no on Measure R. The older voters were the most opposed (see Appendix C, Table C-12).

The lack of confidence in the Board of Supervisors at the time was an important factor contributing to the lack of support for Measure R. The voters who provided these county officials with excellent or good ratings in their handling of the financial crisis were likely to support Measure R. However, there were very few voters who gave their county leaders positive ratings. Most voters thought they were doing a fair or poor job during the crisis, and these voters were strongly opposed to raising taxes. There were other indications that the link between the Board of Supervisors and Measure R was limiting public support for the tax increase. More than half of the voters said they disapproved of the supervisors' actions in even placing the sales tax measure on the ballot for the voters to decide (Times Orange County Poll, 1995c).

A follow-up question asked the "no" voters why they had decided to vote against the half-cent sales tax increase. Of the 57 percent who said they would vote no on Measure R, nearly half said that this was because they felt it was unfair to pay for others' mistakes. A quarter of those who said they would vote no reported that they were generally opposed to paying any new taxes. The rest of the "no" voters said they favored taking other actions first, such as having the members of the Board of Supervisors resign or having the county sell off its assets (see Appendix C, Table C-13).

The opposition to Measure R had two sources that added up to a solid majority. As usual, a number of Orange County voters were expressing antipathy toward all taxes. But an even larger group said they were upset about being asked to pay for the mistakes of their county officials. Other results in this survey indicated that confidence in the county's elected leaders was dropping (see Appendix C, Table C-14). Only 13 percent now said that the Board of Supervisors were doing an excellent or good job in managing the financial crisis. A third rated their job performance as only fair, while nearly half said they were doing a poor job. The poor ratings for the Board of Supervisors had climbed fourteen points since the early days of the bankruptcy.

Meanwhile, the voters showed more confidence in appointed CEO Bill Popejoy than in the members of the Board of Supervisors. Three in ten voters said that Popejoy had done an excellent or good job as the chief executive officer in handling the financial crisis. A third gave him fair ratings, while only one in six said that he was doing a poor job. Two in ten voters were not sure. Still, the evaluations of Popejoy are considered good only in comparison with those of the Board of Supervisors. Most voters did not give good ratings to the chief executive officer (Times Orange County Poll, 1995c).

The county leaders who had hoped that the public had become disturbed enough about the financial crisis to support a tax increase were proven wrong. Although the number of voters who were concerned about the bankruptcy had grown in recent months, it was still far short of a majority (see Appendix C, Table C-15). Thirty-two percent said they had heard about local service cuts that would directly affect them or their households this year. Twenty-eight percent believed that the county fund losses would hurt the quality of life in Orange County. Thirty-four percent saw the investment fund losses as harming the quality of education in their local school districts a lot. These findings indicate that public concerns had risen to the point that about a third of the voters were expressing big worries about the bankruptcy. This raised serious doubts as to how a majority of local voters could be convinced to support a tax increase.

Perhaps the threat of a state government takeover of county government, if the financial crisis worsened, could be used as a message to rally these locally oriented voters in favor of a tax increase. However, only slightly more than half of the voters would oppose having a state panel take over and run the county government. About a quarter were in favor of a state government takeover, while one in five were uncertain (see Appendix C, Table C-16). The confidence in local government had sunk to such a low point that nearly half of the voters were either in favor or uncertain about the prospects of a state takeover of Orange County government. Even a state takeover did not appear to affect enough voters to achieve a majority support for a tax increase.

Measure R seemed to be headed for defeat right out of the starting gate. Fewer than four in ten voters said they would support the half-cent sales tax increase for ten years to get their county government out of bankruptcy. There were very few undecided voters. The proponents would have to convince those who were already inclined to vote against the tax to change their minds. This was no easy task given the level of distrust in county government. The voters still appeared to be more angry than worried about the impacts of the bankruptcy. In this political climate, few local politicians would be willing to speak out in favor of the sales tax increase. The Measure R sales tax, which was the centerpiece of the investment pool settlement and critical to the county's efforts to avoid a default on bond payments, was facing a tough uphill battle.

SUMMARY

The county government leaders faced some dark days after they declared bankruptcy. Still, the county government and local governments found ways to overcome some large problems. They worked their way through the fiscal emergency with a series of innovative efforts that helped to solve the immediate problems.

The county government needed someone to manage the Orange County Investment Pool. They called on the former state treasurer. Tom Hayes was able to sell off the risky securities and transform the pool into a safe money-market fund in about a month. This helped to restore confidence on Wall Street and on Main Street. Moreover, the local government investors would now be able to access some of their frozen funds.

The county government did not have the information they needed to make decisions about the agencies that needed funds the most during the crisis. So the Board of Supervisors appointed an Operations Management

Council made up of the sheriff, district attorney, and director of the Health Care Agency. These three county officials gathered the budget facts from all of the county agencies. They reported back to the Board of Supervisors on the immediate funding needs. They also developed the plans for the budget cuts. Their actions allowed the county government to keep functioning.

The Board of Supervisors appointed a chief executive officer to fill the gap in county leadership. The new CEO was instrumental in making the budget and staff cuts that were needed. He removed county officials from office who were tainted by the financial crisis. Bill Popejoy was an outsider to government from inside Orange County whose leadership brought a breath of fresh air during the crisis.

The local governments needed a way to communicate their needs for accessing the funds in the frozen county pool. The U.S. bankruptcy court organized a committee of representatives from the county pool. This committee would review the funding requests of local governments, ask the county government to allow some emergency funds, and avoid any serious disruption in local services. As a result, all of the cities, schools, and local special districts continued to function during the fiscal emergency.

The county government and the local governments who had invested in the county pool were still at an impasse as to how to distribute the remaining funds. Three business executives stepped into the vacuum in county leadership. They helped to negotiate a settlement that all the parties agreed to in a matter of weeks. Their actions allowed the local public agencies to get to the remaining funds, avoided the possibility of bankruptcies, and prevented costly lawsuits between the county and local governments.

The financial emergency had ended, but the bankruptcy was far from over. Large bond payments were coming due. A lot of money was still owed. There were already big cuts in the county budget and no valuable assets that could be sold in a hurry. The state government remained focused on its own fiscal problems and would not be offering a financial bailout. The voters were too angry and distrustful to consider becoming part of the solution. It would seem that these constraints would make it very difficult to exit from bankruptcy. Orange County seemed to be out of miracles.

CHAPTER 6

The Road to Recovery

It was late in the spring of 1995. The pressure was building on county officials. The county government had $1 billion in bond payments coming due in the summer. The cities, schools, and special districts wanted the $800 million plus still owed to them from the failed county pool. The county's vendors were owed about $100 million. County officials had already cut services and laid off workers to balance the budget. The county had exhausted other possibilities for raising enough money to pay its debts.

There was just no other way. The road to the Orange County recovery would have to go through the local voters. A half-cent sales tax for ten years was on the June ballot. It was the centerpiece of the county government's plan to exit bankruptcy and return to normal. There were reasons for county leaders to be very nervous about this prospect. The decision was in the hands of local voters who were notorious for their antitax sentiments and who were angry and cynical toward their county government.

This chapter tells the amazing story of how Orange County was able to recover from the largest municipal bankruptcy in U.S. history in only eighteen months. We analyze the reasons for the defeat of the sales tax measure and look at its political aftershocks. We review the consensus plan that emerged and the state legislation that enabled Orange County to pay its bills without raising taxes or benefiting from a state bailout. We then look at the ongoing story of the postbankruptcy recovery. This

TABLE 6-1   SUPPORT FOR MEASURE R AMONG
ORANGE COUNTY LOCAL OFFICIALS

	City Leaders	School Leaders	All Elected Officials
Yes	18%	54%	37%
No	63	27	44
Don't know	19	19	19

SOURCE: *Los Angeles Times* Orange County Edition (1995g).

story includes legal actions against county officials, lawsuits against the
firms who did business with the county officials, and mounting costs as
a result of the Orange County bankruptcy.

LOCAL ELECTED OFFICIALS
AND THE MEASURE R CAMPAIGN

It was not easy for Orange County elected officials to support a tax increase. For many, such an action went against their political beliefs.
Their support for a tax would also be offensive to many voters who had
placed them in office. A politician would be placing his or her political
future in jeopardy. In the next election, their opponents would destroy
them by bringing up their support for a tax increase. Against this political backdrop, the endorsements of local elected officials were essential to passing the Measure R tax.

The *Los Angeles Times* Orange County edition conducted a telephone survey of local elected officials to gauge their support for
Measure R. County elected officials, city elected officials, and school
board members were contacted between May 10 and May 26. The
newspaper staff received responses from 283 out of the 334 local officials, for a response rate of 85 percent (*Los Angeles Times* Orange
County Edition, 1995g).

Only 18 percent of the city leaders said they supported Measure R;
63 percent were opposed, and 19 percent were undecided (see
Table 6-1). Among the school officials, a slight majority were in favor
of the sales tax increase, while 27 were against it and 19 percent were
not sure. Altogether, 37 percent of the elected officials in cities, school
districts, and county government said they would vote yes on Measure
R, while 44 percent said they would vote against the sales tax. Nineteen
percent were unsure. The level of support among the elected officials in
Orange County was below 40 percent. These results are similar to the

public opinion survey that was taken in April, after the Board of Supervisors voted to place Measure R on the June ballot.

The views of the local elected officials and the voters were also similar in their evaluations of the county's leaders and the financial crisis. Sixteen percent of the local elected officials thought that the members of the Orange County Board of Supervisors were doing an excellent or good job in handling the financial crisis. Twelve percent of Orange County voters gave the Board of Supervisors positive marks in the April survey. Twenty-seven percent of the local elected officials thought that the investment fund losses would hurt the quality of life in Orange County a lot. This was almost identical to the 26 percent of Orange County voters who believed that the bankruptcy and investment fund losses would have a highly negative impact on this region.[1]

The opposition to Measure R was evident among city officials throughout Orange County. Cities as geographically and demographically distinct as Buena Park and Mission Viejo were in agreement over their opposition to the sales tax increase. Some of the cities with the largest amounts on deposit in the investment fund, and thus with the most money still owed to them, also had local elected officials who were opposed to the measure. Four of the five council members in Anaheim said they would vote against Measure R; the remaining member was undecided. Three of the five city council members in Irvine were planning to vote against Measure R; the other two members were as yet undecided. Meanwhile, the school board members were generally in favor of raising the sales tax. These elected officials were expressing the position that they wanted all of the money back for their schools. For the most part, the school officials' views did not seem to be shared by their city leaders and local voters.

Why would city officials oppose the Measure R sales tax for the recovery that would have placed more funds in their city coffers? For one thing, they did not like the idea of raising taxes for the county government. These were locally oriented politicians who would support a tax increase for the region only in special circumstances, such as to improve everyone's roads and infrastructure (Baldassare et al., 1996). Also, the

---

1. Bill Popejoy received higher ratings from the local elected leaders than from the public. Sixty-four percent of officials said he was doing an excellent or good job, 23 percent a fair job, and 5 percent a poor job. Thirty percent of the public had given him excellent or good ratings (*Los Angeles Times* Orange County Edition, 1995g).

crisis of the bankruptcy had diminished in localities when the Measure R campaign was in full swing. Local governments had reached an agreement with the county government on the investment pool settlement. The school districts would receive 90 cents on the dollar, and the cities and special districts would get 80 cents on the dollar. The threat of recalls had passed for most local elected officials. To receive their remaining claims, local leaders could either support a county tax increase or wait for the county to win lawsuits against the Wall Street firms. The latter approach was politically safer than backing a measure that was placed on the ballot by the highly unpopular county supervisors.

The forces of localism and fiscal conservatism were so strong that even the elected officials in the county government were divided on the sales tax increase. Three of the five supervisors—Bergeson, Steiner, and Vasquez—said they would vote for the measure that they had placed on the ballot. Two of them, Stanton and Silva, said they would not support it. The supervisors who opposed Measure R could take comfort in reflecting the views of the local voters in their district, as opposed to supporting what may be in the best interest of the county as a whole. Among the officials who are elected countywide, the sheriff and the district attorney said they would vote yes. John Moorlach, the new county treasurer who had raised the issue of the risky county pool, said he would vote no on the tax increase. The chief executive officer, Bill Popejoy, was a big booster of the tax increase. The other major county officials did not give their views (*Los Angeles Times* Orange County Edition, 1995g).

The opposition to Measure R among county officials and city officials certainly raised questions about the sincerity of the county's efforts to recover from bankruptcy. One of the concerns was that the local elected officials were sending a message to residents that voting against the county's recovery plan was the responsible thing to do. Senator Killea made these observations to her colleagues in legislative testimony: "A public opinion survey by the L.A. Times last month, showed 57 percent of the voters opposed the sales tax, and since that poll came out, not one elected official from the city, county, or schools have joined in supporting the sales tax measure, even Supervisor Jim Silva, who voted to put the measure on the ballot, now opposes it" (Assembly Select Committee on the Insolvency of Orange County, 1995, p. 78). The fact that county officials backed away from the tax increase raised doubts about their political will to do what was necessary to solve the fiscal crisis. Their actions increased calls for a state takeover.

California politicians did understand the difficulty faced by local elected officials in taking a stand in favor of the local tax increase. Assemblyman Richard Katz also noted in testimony, "I appreciate Senator Bergeson, and I know, Mr. Popejoy you've been out there; I know a number of members of the business community has been out there as well, and it's not easy doing that anywhere, particularly in Orange County" (Assembly Select Committee on the Insolvency of Orange County, 1995, p. 89). This observation fits with the reality that moderately conservative Republicans in the business community and in local government might privately support the tax increase for pragmatic reasons, but that many would keep quiet publicly for fear of offending the more conservative leaders in the Republican Party as well as the anti-tax populist groups (Jeffe, 1995). Still, the fact that many local officials were opposed to the major element of the recovery plan, while still others failed to openly support the half-cent sales tax increase, was very unpopular with state leaders and bond investors.

Orange County's local elected leaders' views about the Measure R sales tax mirrored those expressed by the local voters. The political pressures were too strong for them to support a tax increase. Indeed, this was the same political climate that had led so many of them to try to get interest income from the county pool instead of asking voters for higher taxes. The locally oriented officials had defined Measure R as a countywide tax designed to solve a county government problem. State Senator Killea summed up this local attitude in saying, "There doesn't seem to me to be an elected official in Orange County, and I'm not just talking about the supervisors, who is supporting the sales tax measure. It seems to me that is a negative for those communities as well. . . . There is a tendency to assume the problem has nothing to do with them" (Senate Special Committee on Local Government Investments, 1995d, pp. 52–53).

VOTER OPINIONS AND THE MEASURE R CAMPAIGN

Perhaps the voters would have a change of heart about raising their taxes as the election approached. The supporters of Measure R were spending far more for their campaign than were the opponents. The campaign was funded by local companies. Still, a turnaround would be surprising, given the voters' strong rejection of the idea when the Board of Supervisors first announced that they would place Measure R on the ballot.

A random telephone survey of 1,002 Orange County voters was conducted from June 2 to 5 for the *Los Angeles Times* Orange County edition. This was approximately three weeks before the June 27 special election. There was every expectation that this election would have a low turnout. The large sample would allow us to study the likely voters.

The support for the Measure R sales tax increase for the bankruptcy recovery was still at about 40 percent of the voters. For those who were most likely to vote in the upcoming election, only 36 percent said they would vote yes. The likely voter subgroup involved 40 percent of the total sample. We defined the likely voters as those who had voted frequently in the past four years, had expressed a high level of interest in the Measure R election, and had said they were planning to vote on June 27. Their level of support had changed very little from the benchmark survey in early April.

We looked at support for Measure R across demographic categories. No age or income group gave it majority support. Forty-five percent of Democrats, 38 percent of Republicans, and 41 percent of independents would vote yes on Measure R. It seemed unlikely that the sales tax would gain majority support by late June.

After two months of campaigning, the reasons for opposition to the sales tax measure were basically the same as before. Seven in ten said they were opposed to new taxes or they felt it was unfair to pay for others' mistakes. Other survey responses also indicated widespread feelings of distrust and alienation toward county government. Half of the voters believed that the county leaders waste "a lot" of the money that residents pay in taxes. The majority of voters believed that the county government leaders pay very little or no attention to what the people think when they are deciding what policies to adopt. There were no differences between Republicans and Democrats.

The voters who were negative toward county government were the most likely to oppose Measure R. Of those who said the county government wastes a lot of money, 31 percent would support Measure R and 56 percent were opposed. Of those who said their county leaders pay very little or no attention to residents when making decisions, 33 percent would vote yes and 53 percent would vote no on Measure R (see Appendix C, Table C-17). This link also suggested that Measure R's chances were slim to none.

The "Yes on R" campaign had hoped to receive a boost in support from growing anxiety about the impacts of the Orange County bankruptcy. In early June about a third of the voters said they had heard or read about cuts in local services or school programs that would directly affect them during the next year. Fewer than one in four thought that the fund losses would hurt the quality of life in Orange County "a lot." About a quarter also thought that there would be major impact on the quality of education in their schools. In fact, Orange County residents were no more worried about the financial crisis in June than they were before the campaign started in April. This lack of public concern was not good news for the sales tax supporters (see Appendix C, Table C-18).

The "Yes on R" campaign had also hoped to capitalize on a growing pessimism toward the county since the bankruptcy began. In actuality, the voters' outlook toward the quality of life, housing market, and the economy in Orange County had changed very little during the first six months of 1995. These were further signs that the sense of doom and gloom had not grown among Orange County voters during the fiscal crisis.

The supporters of the tax increase had planned a textbook special election campaign for a local ballot measure. They would get their supporters out on election day and hope for a low turnout among the opponents. Their strategy focused on saturating certain households in Orange County with mail about the reasons to support a tax increase. They would mail brochures and letters signed by popular officials, such as Sheriff Gates, that explained why Measure R was necessary to end the bankruptcy quickly, help the schools and police, and prevent a decline in property values and the economy. Later the same voters would be sent an absentee ballot for the June 27 special election. This was the best hope for getting the message out to vote yes on Measure R, since television advertising is not a practical way to reach Orange County voters. (All of the major television stations in this suburban region are based in Los Angeles.)

The Measure R supporters knew that the grassroots groups who opposed the measure would not be able to raise the money that was needed to mount a mail campaign to counter their efforts. The most visible and organized opposition to Measure R was a group called the Committee of Correspondence, which included some of the supporters of Ross Perot from the 1992 presidential election. This was a nonpartisan, anti–big government group with members throughout Orange County. They had a fiscally conservative agenda for local government. They did little fund raising for the Measure R campaign. They relied heavily on volunteers and local newspaper coverage.

At the time of the survey, about half of the Orange County voters said they had received Measure R literature in the mail. A third had received only mail in favor of Measure R, 3 percent had received only mail that was opposed to Measure R, and 18 percent recalled having received mail from both sides. Nearly half of the likely voters had received only mail in favor of Measure R, and those who were older, had higher incomes, or were homeowners were more likely to have received mail. About a third of all voters said they planned to vote by absentee ballot in the special election. More homeowners and higher-income voters said they would cast absentee ballots. The results indicate that the Measure R supporters were successful in their targeting efforts.

Voter interest was a critical dimension in the Measure R campaign. Those who were the most interested would be most likely to go to the polls and decide this special election. About half of the voters were "very interested" in the election. The public's focus on this election was relatively weak, considering the financial stakes for county government and the amount of publicity that the election was generating. Six in ten of the "no" voters were highly interested, compared with fewer than half of the "yes" voters (see Appendix C, Table C-19). So the more motivated voters were on the "no" side.

We also looked at voters' stated intentions to go to the polls for the June 1995 special election. About two-thirds said they intended to vote. This number is always higher than the actual turnout, but it was low compared with the most recent presidential and gubernatorial elections and a 1990 state election in which a local sales tax measure passed. The interest in voting was comparable to that for a 1989 special election in which a tax increase measure failed. The results on intention to vote also gave the advantage to the antitax side in the upcoming election, despite the money spent by the Measure R supporters.

Other findings pointed to a nasty mood among voters at this time. Only one in eight credited the Board of Supervisors with doing an excellent or good job in handling the financial crisis. Half thought they were doing a poor job. One in three said that Chief Executive Officer Bill Popejoy was doing an excellent or good job in managing the financial crisis. One in six thought that he had been doing a poor job. Half thought that Sheriff Gates was doing an excellent or good job in office. Only 8 percent rated his performance as poor (see Appendix C, Table C-20). The fact that the ratings for the chief executive officer and the sheriff were relatively unchanged since the last survey indicated that voters were not thinking less of them because of their support for the sales tax increase. At the same time, the endorsements of these popular figures did not lead to support for Measure R.

In sum, the fiscally conservative voters in Orange County had made up their minds early on. They would oppose a tax increase to bail out their county government. Nothing that occurred between December 1994 and June 1995 seemed to change their views. If anything, the fact that their cities and schools had reached an agreement with the county government on the investment pool seemed to have lessened their worries somewhat. The survey points to an electorate that was not very concerned about the financial crisis and not highly engaged in the Measure R election. The Measure R election had become, for many voters, another opportunity to express their alienation and cynicism toward county government and their current anger toward its leaders.

PLAN B

The Measure R supporters were telling the voters that the half-cent sales tax increase for 10 years was the only way out of the Orange County financial crisis. To say otherwise would be to signal to voters that they did not have to vote for the tax increase. The Measure R opponents claimed there were other ways to avoid default and a long bankruptcy. Supporters vehemently denied the claim that there was a secret "plan B."

However, a "plan B" was in the works. County government was making contingency plans in the likely event that the June 27 sales tax measure failed. On June 2 the county government made an offer to bond investors to roll over the $800 million that was coming due in the summer. If the investors would agree to wait another year for their money, the county government would pay them extra interest on the principal when the bonds came due. The major investors rejected the offer, responding that this plan was the equivalent of a default. They said they wanted their money back on time (see Appendix A, Table A-14). Plan B would be revisited later.

MEASURE R DEFEAT

Orange County voters headed to the polls on June 27 to decide the outcome of the financial plan that would take Orange County out of its financial misery. The half-cent tax would raise the local sales tax from 7.75 percent to 8.25 percent. The sales tax in Orange County would

TABLE 6-2   VOTE ON ORANGE COUNTY
MEASURE R: SALES TAX FOR
BANKRUPTCY RECOVERY

Yes	148,414	38.9%
No	233,113	61.1

34.5% voter turnout on June 27, 1995

SOURCE: Orange County Registrar of Voters (1995).

then be the same as in Los Angeles and four other California counties (Senate Special Committee on Local Government Investments, 1995d, p. 84). The half-cent sales tax would last for 10 years and raise enough money during this time to allow the county to borrow funds to pay off its debts. The county government would be able to exit from bankruptcy in a short amount of time.

On June 27 Measure R was overwhelmingly defeated by Orange County voters. Thirty-nine percent voted for the half-cent sales tax increase, while 61 percent were opposed (see Table 6-2). The "no" side won by a convincing margin of 85,000 votes. About 140,000 who voted did so by mail ballot. This indicated that the Measure R supporters had succeeded in getting absentee ballots into the hands of many voters who might otherwise not have participated in the special election. But the $1.5 million campaign was unsuccessful in convincing the voters to support a tax increase. In fact, many of the voters who were sent absentee ballots may have used them to vote against Measure R.

Special elections in Orange County had had low voter turnouts in recent years. A special election in November 1989 called for the sole purpose of deciding on a sales tax increase for transportation had a 23 percent turnout. That tax measure was defeated. Another special election in May 1991 had one ballot measure to raise the sales tax for local jails and courts, and it had an 18 percent turnout. That tax measure was also overwhelmingly defeated. Only the most dedicated voters tend to participate in these special elections. They tend to be older voters, homeowners, and among the most conservative in the electorate. Despite the arguments of some that the June 1995 election was a unique special election, for most voters this was just another special election about a local tax increase. The result was another low-turnout election resulting in a defeat for new taxes.

About 381,000 of the 1.1 million registered voters in Orange County participated in the special election. The turnout was 34.5 percent, which was relatively high for a special election. But this means that about two-thirds of the registered voters did not turn out for what had been described as a historic countywide election. Apparently, there was considerable apathy about the election. As preelection surveys had indicated, there were many middle-class voters who did not see the county government's crisis as a pressing issue in their lives. The lower-income residents who lost county services, many of them recent immigrants, were less likely to be registered to vote.

The Measure R defeat was also convincing in the consensus across the region. The sales tax passed in only two of the thirty-one cities, Laguna Beach and Newport Beach. Laguna Beach is the most liberal place in Orange County. Newport Beach was home to Bill Popejoy and prominent businessmen who supported the tax measure. However, the measure failed in the other twenty-nine cities. Measure R did not pass in any of the large cities in the county (Orange County Registrar of Voters, 1995). The county leaders and all other interested participants in the financial crisis could only read from these results that the voters were not interested in raising their taxes to recover from the bankruptcy.

In earlier state senate testimony, one of the participants observed, "If the sales tax doesn't pass or even if it does, will we see a further reduction in county services to the residents of Orange County . . . is there any incentive in terms of direct services to residents that county residents have to pass the sales tax? What do they get out of it?" (Senate Special Committee on Local Government Investments, 1995d, p. 12). The Measure R campaign had clearly failed in its efforts to convince voters that there would be benefits to the sales tax increase and dire consequences to its defeat. Many still believed that spending could be maintained by cutting government waste. Orange County residents were about to learn firsthand of the impacts of the ballot choice they made.

POLITICAL FALLOUT

The June 27 election had immediate political fallout. A few days after the election, the Board of Supervisors met with the chief executive officer in private. The outspoken county government critic and tax supporter was no longer needed. They informed Popejoy that he would no longer be setting policy for the county government. They wanted to take back some of the power they delegated to Popejoy during the crisis. Popejoy announced his resignation within two weeks of that meeting. The Board of Supervisors moved quickly to appoint Jan Mittermeier, a long-time county employee with fiscal experience and head of the county airport agency, to be their interim chief executive officer. Soon after, Mittermeier was permanently named to that position.[2]

In early August Supervisor Gaddi Vasquez, who was the current chair of the board, announced that he would resign from elected office in late September. Among his reasons for stepping down he cited the stresses of the past few months and the anger directed at him by the voters. Supervisor Vasquez would be replaced by an appointee of Governor Wilson. Donald Saltarelli, a mayor from the City of Tustin, which had withdrawn its money from the county pool a year earlier, was appointed to the Board of Supervisors. The newly appointed supervisor made a commitment not to seek election. The difficult decisions he made would thus not be dependent on his political aspirations. The voters were to receive what they wanted, which was a resignation from the Board of Supervisors. The governor was, at the same time, able to take a step that had the outward appearance of the state exerting more influence over the county's actions.

The defeat of Measure R would lead to increased calls for a state takeover. Many of the state officials had assumed that the measure would be defeated, based on the preelection polls and the lack of campaigning by local elected officials, so these discussions had been ongoing. One of the immediate worries concerned the $800 million in bond payments that were due in the summer. An executive in Moody's Investors Service had warned in state senate testimony, "Should the county default on its debt due . . . then the constraints and limitations preventing the county from acting will forever be viewed as systemic weakness to prevent California localities from appropriate responding to adversity" (Senate Special Committee on Local Government Investments, 1995d, p. 39). The Orange County bankruptcy had already shocked the investment firms by breaking the promise of a municipality to back its obligations with its "full faith and credit." The Wall Street firms gave their warning that the state government should act to avoid the statewide implications of a huge bond default.

The increased talk of the need for a state takeover came from a variety of sources. The current bond investors wanted their money re-

---

2. Jan Mittermeier had been favored over outside candidates because of her success in managing the county's airport and her knowledge of the county budget and financial issues through her previous positions in county government.

turned. The potential bond investors wanted to be sure that their money would be safe. The officials from cities, counties, schools, and special districts throughout the state did not want the financial crisis to affect their ability to borrow. State officials did not want the Orange County problem to affect their lending rates. Some in the state legislature envisioned the appointment of a state trustee to run the financial affairs of the county. Other legislators thought that the state government should guarantee the county's debt through a joint state and local agency. No one wanted to have the state pay for what were viewed as the mistakes of Orange County.

Senator Killea proposed legislation for a state takeover. "I do not support a bail out. This measure would say, Default is not an option. It says to Orange County, if you don't fix the problem yourself, the state will be forced to fix it for you, using your resources, perhaps your property taxes, perhaps worse cuts, perhaps other fees you won't like, possibly all of the above, but we will not allow you to walk away from your obligations because of the tremendous effect on everybody else in the state" (Assembly Select Committee on the Insolvency of Orange County, 1995, p. 79).

The governor seemed to follow the same model that he had throughout the financial crisis. He would send top financial experts to assist county officials. The governor would promise no state aid, but he would look favorably toward state legislation that would help the county out of its troubles. He would also closely watch the crisis and threaten a state takeover if the county officials seemed to be making no progress.

The governor had support for his position. The state legislature did not want a bailout. The local governments also opposed a state takeover. A representative of the California State Association of Counties said, "I believe that an extraordinary amount of oversight in the case of Orange County is appropriate. What I am suggesting is that you bring that up short of establishing a trustee. . . . I just think that a trustee or governing board or whatever that is not elected by the people of Orange County is the wrong way to go" (Assembly Select Committee on the Insolvency of Orange County, 1995, p. 87).

In sum, that the county officials would reluctantly propose a sales tax and that the voters would overwhelming defeat it were widely anticipated events. Why did county officials go through this exercise? Perhaps the county government was merely going through the motions. This was a way to send a message to the bond investors and the pool

TABLE 6-3   ORANGE COUNTY'S OBLIGATIONS
AND ALLOWED CLAIMS

Amount in Millions		
Recovery bonds	$ 236	Only interest budgeted; principal begins in 2001
Secured claims	342	9 cents on the dollar for nonschool participants
County debt shortfall	423	Reduced to $356 million with delinquent property tax bonds
County nondebt shortfall	360	County's investment pool loss
Vendor debt	100	Money owed to contractors
Repayment claims	513	Subordinated claims to pool investors
Total	$1,974	

SOURCE: County of Orange (1995b).

investors that the county government was making a good-faith effort to
pay its debts. But the defeat of the sales tax had many negative consequences. Orange County received even less sympathetic reviews from
its critics in the national media and around the state. The voters were
described as wealthy "deadbeats" who refused to pay their bills. The
Wall Street investors had their first real experience with California voters intervening between the contract and promises that are made for
"full faith and credit" between investment firms and local governments.
The state government would now put more pressure on Orange County
to find a workable recovery plan or lose its autonomy.

THE BANKRUPTCY RECOVERY PLAN

The defeat of Measure R set into motion a frantic search for other solutions to the financial crisis. It was back to "plan B." One important
ingredient of the plan was to have the bond investors agree to roll over
for a year the $800 million that was coming due in the summer. The
idea of paying interest to extend the bonds another year had been rejected in early June. This plan was reluctantly approved by the investors
a week after the defeat of Measure R.

The county still had a staggering level of debt. There were nearly $2
billion in obligations and allowed claims (see Table 6-3). There was
also the county budget shortfall and the money that was lost in the
county pool. There was $100 million owed to the vendors. There were

also the claims to pool investors. These were debts that were faced in a county that had declared bankruptcy and had limited borrowing capacity.

In July there were several failed attempts at resolving the bankruptcy. There was a "family of governments" proposal by local governments to transfer the John Wayne Airport to the Orange County Transportation Authority and the landfills to the Orange County Sanitation District, all in exchange for $800 million of the pool investors' claims against the county (Orange County Investment Pool, 1995c). The county government rejected this proposal, since it would have taken away the county's most valuable assets. The state legislature approved a diversion of $70 million in sales tax revenues each year from the Orange County Transportation Agency to pay for the bankruptcy debt.[3] The funds had been earmarked for public buses. The governor vetoed this legislation, citing, among the reasons, that it was tied to support for a tax diversion for public health care in Los Angeles County, which he opposed (*New York Times*, 1995c). At the time, Los Angeles was facing a budget deficit of $1.2 billion and was also seeking to divert transportation tax funds to solve its fiscal problems.

On August 3 Governor Wilson issued a challenge to elected officials in Orange County. They must come up with a plan for recovery from bankruptcy before the state legislature returned from its summer recess on August 21. Otherwise, the state would most surely take the problem into its own hands. Orange County's plan could include requests for legislation, but there would be no financial bailout. Within two weeks the county government sent a menu of options for the state legislature to choose from, including the diversion of tax revenues from the transportation agency, cities, and local special districts. State legislators rejected the idea of choosing from a menu. Instead, county leaders were asked to submit a full recovery plan (*Orange County Register*, 1995b).

Once again, leaders from the private sector were called in to facilitate the difficult negotiations between the county government and the cities, schools, and special districts in Orange County. The chair of the board of the Orange County Business Council explained in state senate testimony on August 22, "We were asked by both sides if we would spend some time

---

3. There had been considerable talk about tapping some of the so-called Measure M funds, which were the sales tax dollars approved by voters to be dedicated specifically to transportation funds. Such a direct diversion of the earmarked tax funds would certainly have had political repercussions with the local voters.

in a role of bringing folks together so that as of this week we could honestly and realistically talk to you about a true consensus response where
Orange County deals with its problems" (Senate Special Committee on
Local Government Investments, 1995e, pp. 3–4). There was no shortage
of proposals from the county, cities, transportation agency, and special districts at this time. The role of the Orange County Business Council was, in
the chair's words, "to see where the golden threads in those suggestions
were found and how we can tie those together to make some sense"
(Senate Special Committee on Local Government Investments, 1995e, p. 4).

A "consensus plan" was negotiated before the state's deadline. It had
the support of representatives of the county government and all of the
other local government units in Orange County. It contained four main
components that would allow the county government to meet its debts,
recover from the financial crisis, and escape bankruptcy.

First, the pool participants would no longer hold the county responsible for their $861 million claim from the investment pool settlement.
They would remove this debt from the county and wait for their funds
to be paid through lawsuits. Second, the general fund for the county
government would receive $240 million from property tax revenues that
would otherwise be deposited with three county agencies. The flood
control district, the development agency, and the agency responsible for
harbors, beaches, and parks would each have $4 million diverted to the
county for twenty years. Third, the general fund for the county government would receive $570 million from sales tax revenues that would
otherwise have been deposited with the transportation agency. This
would be done through a diversion of $38 million in sales tax revenues
for fifteen years from the Orange County Transportation Agency.
Fourth, the county government would agree to transfer $360 million of
its motor vehicle fuel tax revenues to the Orange County Transportation
Agency. These funds for county roads would partially compensate for
the revenues lost by the county transportation agency. In sum, the plan
called for a combination of removal of debt and diversion of tax revenues to the general fund to allow the county to pay its outstanding bills
and meet its debt obligations though a large bond offering (Senate
Special Committee on Local Government Investments, 1995e, pp. 7–8).

The forgiving of debt by the pool investors was a key element of the
recovery plan. This was not an easy task because of the rocky past between the county government and the local government investors.
Patrick Shea, the attorney for the Orange County Investment Pool, summarized the agreement in saying, "The component of this plan that we

are required to shoulder is essentially to remove from the books of the County of Orange as an obligation to the County of Orange which must be met from its general revenues over time the sum of $861 million, and to take that entire amount and, make it nonrecourse to the county and contingent only upon recoveries from third-party litigation" (Senate Special Committee on Local Government Investments, 1995e, p. 43). This was a major compromise that came about, once again, through the "reality checks" and group facilitation provided by the business leaders.

Chief Executive Officer Jan Mittermeier explained the consensus plan to the state senate hearing: "We believe now that we have a plan that is going to work for everyone" (Senate Special Committee on Local Government Investments, 1995e, p. 7). This plan would require state legislation to allow the funds to be diverted from other local public agencies to the county's general fund. The request for state legislation had some complications. For one, Los Angeles County had a $1.2 billion budget gap and wanted legislation to divert transportation funds to pay for public health (Office of Senate Floor Analysis, 1995). The state legislators from Los Angeles County would demand that the Orange County recovery bills be linked to help for Los Angeles County. The governor had already stated his opposition to the Los Angeles County fund diversions when he vetoed the earlier plan for Orange County to divert its public transit funds.

There was also the problem of an unstable assembly leadership. The Democrats had lost control of the assembly. The long-time Speaker, Willie Brown, had relinquished his post. An Orange County Republican, Doris Allen, had been named Speaker in June with the votes of all of the Democrats plus herself. Another Orange County Republican, Curt Pringle, had become the Republican assembly leader and was a party in an effort to recall Doris Allen. Orange County had Republican legislators in high places when the legislation was needed. Unfortunately, this was not a cohesive group that was fully focused on the recovery plan (Scott, 1995a, 1995b). It was thus not a given that the state legislature would deliver the package of recovery bills.

On September 15 the state legislature passed the bills that made it possible for the county consensus plan to be implemented (see Table 6-4). Bill SB 863 allowed the county to take property taxes for twenty years in the amount of $4 million from the County Flood Control District; $4 million from the Harbors, Beaches, and Parks fund; and $4 million from the Orange County Development Agency. These revenues would be diverted to the general fund to pay its bankruptcy-related bills. Bill AB 1664 allowed the State Board of Equalization to take $38

TABLE 6-4   STATE LEGISLATION FOR
ORANGE COUNTY DEBT PAYMENTS

AB 1664: Allows Orange County to modify its contract with the State Board of Equalization to require that $3,166,667 of the Bradley-Burns sales tax revenue that would otherwise be deposited in the local transportation fund be deposited in the Orange County general fund each month (double-joined with SB 727, SB 863, and SB 1276)

SB 863: Requires that property tax allocations to the Orange County Flood Control District be reduced by $4,000,000 and that allocations to the Harbors, Beaches, and Parks fund be reduced by $4,000,000 and allocated to the county; starting on July 1, 1996, and for a period of twenty years, the Orange County Development Agency must transfer $4,000,000 to the county general fund (becomes operative only if SB 727, SB 1276, and AB 1664 become operative)

SB 1276: Allows the governor to appoint a trustee if the Orange County Board of Supervisors has not filed a plan of adjustment with the bankruptcy court by January 1, 1996; requires the County of Orange to pay the Orange County Transportation Authority $1,916,667 of the county's motor vehicle fuel tax receipts each month from July 1997 to June 2013 (double-joined with SB 727, SB 863, and AB 1664)

SB 727: Allows the Los Angeles County Board of Supervisors to divert to the county general fund up to $150 million on the local transaction and use tax revenues that would otherwise have been allocated to the Los Angeles County Metropolitan Transit Authority

SOURCE: Office of Senate Floor Analysis (1995).

million a year of Bradley-Burns sales tax revenue from the Orange County Transportation Authority and deposit it in the county's general fund for fifteen years to pay for bonds to relieve the county of some of its bankruptcy-related debt. Bill SB 1276 required the county government to deposit from its motor vehicle fuel tax the amount of $24 million a year for fifteen years to the Orange County Transportation Authority. These funds, which were used by the county for road projects, were to help partially compensate for the revenue losses of the transportation authority. The three Orange County bills would not become laws unless the state legislature and the governor also approved a relief package for fiscally stressed Los Angeles County. Bill SB 727 would allow county government in Los Angeles to take up to $150 million from the Los Angeles Metropolitan Transit Authority for its general fund. The governor signed these bills into law on October 9.

The state legislation that was passed included a provision to ensure that the county government would move in a speedy manner to implement the consensus plan for the fiscal recovery. Bill SB 1276 would allow Governor Wilson to appoint a state trustee if the Orange County

Board of Supervisors had not filed a plan of adjustment with the U.S. bankruptcy court by January 1, 1996. The bankruptcy escape plan was filed in court on December 21, 1995. This was one year and two weeks after the county had declared bankruptcy. The county government would still need the approval of its creditors, but most were expected to approve the bankruptcy plan. The county would still have to sell nearly $900 million in bonds to pay its current bondholders and pay the vendors that were still owed money in order to emerge from bankruptcy by the end of June 1996 (*New York Times,* 1995c).

The county government sold $880 million in thirty-year bonds on June 5, 1996. The funds borrowed allowed the county to pay $359 million to bondholders in principal and interest, $110 million to refinance pension bonds, $44 million to vendors, $60 million to refinance existing debt, $50 million for a debt service reserve, $50 million for litigation services, $50 million for third-party accounts administered by the county such as trust assets, $35 million for employees' salaries, and $25 million for consulting and legal fees related to the bankruptcy. The remaining funds went to bond costs and other creditors. The bonds sold because they were insured and paid a higher yield to compensate investors for the risks (*Los Angeles Times* Orange County Edition, 1996f).

On June 12, 1996, at 9:50 A.M., the county government officially emerged from U.S. bankruptcy court protection. The bondholders and other outstanding debts had been paid with the $880 million of new debt. The bankruptcy ended eighteen months after it had begun (*Los Angeles Times* Orange County Edition, 1996a). No one had expected in the dark days of December 1994 that the bankruptcy would end in such a short time.

LINKING ORANGE COUNTY AND LOS ANGELES COUNTY

It is a great irony that the fate of the state legislation for the Orange County recovery was dependent on Los Angeles County. A century ago the state had created Orange County out of southern Los Angeles County. For decades Orange County had prided itself on being a suburban metropolitan region that was separate from and better than the more urbanized county to the north. Their fates had become intertwined once again.

Both Los Angeles and Orange counties had fallen on financial hard times in the early 1990s. Los Angeles County saw its spending exceed its revenues by a wide margin. When the 1995–1996 county budget was proposed, a $1.2 billion deficit was estimated. This was a result of

the shift in property taxes from the county back to the state and a reduction in federal support for health care. At the same time, the need
for health services was growing (Legislative Analyst, 1995b, p. 1).
Orange County also saw a major drop in its property tax funds from
the state at this time. The county's response was to seek more revenues
from the risky investments in the county pool.

The $1.6 billion loss in the Orange County pool and the $1.2 billion
deficit in Los Angeles had some similarities in their causes. Both would
need the attention of state government. An official from the California
State Association of Counties said, "What brought Orange County to
the edge of the cliff were the same forces that brought LA . . . to the
edge. The underlying circumstances are identical. . . . None of the fundamental relationships have changed with these patchwork solutions"
(Lazarovici, 1995, p. 32).

Both Orange County and Los Angeles County sought and received
permission from the state to divert transportation funds to pay other
kinds of bills. This was a controversial proposal for a fiscally conservative state in which voters had grown accustomed to earmarking new
tax dollars for their favorite programs, which included transportation
projects. The legislative analyst (1995c, p. 7) raised concerns about the
appropriateness of these tax transfers. Lawsuits have been filed to challenge the constitutionality of the legislation that diverted the county
funds to solve the Orange County bankruptcy and the Los Angeles crisis (*Orange County Register,* 1996c). The controversy over these fund
diversions points to the fragile nature of the recovery plan.

LAWSUITS AGAINST OUTSIDE FIRMS

The county government has filed several waves of lawsuits seeking billions of dollars in compensation from outside firms. The civil litigation
is an important piece of unfinished business on the road to recovery.
The costs of the bankruptcy cannot be determined until it is known
how much the local governments will gain from the lawsuits. The
amount of time it will take the county to pay its debts and return to
normal budgeting depends on its winning the lawsuits. The attempt to
seek local revenues through litigation is another Orange County fiscal
strategy. Since the county pool is no longer generating high yields,
county leaders have turned to the courtroom for money.

A lawsuit against KPMG Peat Marwick was submitted within days
of the county's filing its plan with the U.S. bankruptcy court in late

December 1995. The county sued this private firm for $3 billion. This firm acted as the outside auditor for the county from 1992 to 1993 and for part of 1994. The county claims that KPMG Peat Marwick had been specifically asked to review the Orange County Investment Pool because the internal auditors did not have the necessary financial expertise. The outside audits made no mention of the fact that Bob Citron had been involved in massive leveraging that, according to the county, violated the state constitution by exceeding the debt limit. But KPMG Peat Marwick claimed that its only role as consultant was to make sure that the county's financial statements met with general accounting principles. The firm found that they did. They denied any wrongdoing, saying they were not asked to be financial advisors for the Orange County Investment Pool (*New York Times*, 1995b).

On January 12, 1995, the county government sued Merrill Lynch for $2 billion. At that time this was the amount determined to be the total loss in the county pool. In the *County of Orange v. Merrill Lynch* filing, the county claimed that the firm "wantonly and callously" encouraged Bob Citron's investment practices of exceeding the debt limit, and the attorney representing the county later said, "The county's position is that Citron could not have acted in a vacuum" (Hector, 1995, p. 38).

Merrill Lynch was targeted because it had sold the county about two-thirds of the securities in the pool. The county claimed that the treasurer had exceeded the debt limit set by the state constitution when he purchased the billions of dollars of reverse repurchase agreements. Since Citron had no right to enter into those agreements, the county argued, the taxpayers should not be accountable for those financial transactions. Therefore, Merrill Lynch would be responsible for any losses. The county also claimed that Merrill Lynch had sold securities that were inappropriate for a local government investment pool and had offered investment advice that led to the financial losses. Merrill Lynch has countered by saying that the debt provision does not cover reverse repurchase agreements. They also claimed that Bob Citron was in full control of the county pool, and that they had warned the treasurer against his risky strategy. In addition, Citron rejected their offer to buy back some of the more volatile securities. Moreover, they claimed they acted as a broker, rather than a financial manager, for the county pool.

The county government won a round in its legal battles with the investment firm in June 1997. Merrill Lynch agreed to pay $30 million to the Orange County district attorney in exchange for dropping the criminal investigation of the brokerage house's relationship with the county

TABLE 6-5   ORANGE COUNTY'S LAWSUITS AGAINST
FINANCIAL INSTITUTIONS

Firm	Amount	Responsibilities
Merrill Lynch	$2 billion	Sold 68% of pool securities
KPMG Peat Marwick	$3 billion	County's outside auditor
Student Loan Marketing Association	$58.7 million	Sold the pool risky securities
Fuji Securities	$120 million	Sold the pool risky securities
Standard & Poor's	Unspecified	County's ratings agency
LeBoeuf, Lamb, Greene and MacRae	Unspecified	County's bond counsel
Rauscher Pierce Refsnes	Unspecified	County's financial advisor
Morgan Stanley	Unspecified	Sold the county risky securities

SOURCE: *New York Times* (1995b); *Los Angeles Times* Orange County Edition (1996b, 1996d).

government. This was a civil settlement in which Merrill Lynch did not admit to any criminal wrongdoing, and it has no impact on the $2 billion suit that the county government has filed against the company (Merrill Lynch, 1997).

Five major lawsuits were filed only days before the county officially emerged from bankruptcy in June 1996. These lawsuits were filed against a broad range of participants in the financial affairs of the county government (see Table 6-5). The county went after two of its past financial advisors in this legal round. LeBoeuf, Lamb, Greene and MacRae, which was a bond counsel in 1994, was accused of "deceptive and incompetent services" by failing to disclose risks in the investment pool. Rauscher Pierce Refsnes, which participated in writing the statements for a 1994 bond offering, was accused of a "breach of contract and professional negligence" for not warning of the risks in the pool (*Los Angeles Times* Orange County Edition, 1996b).[4]

4. Other suits were considered at this time against the investment firms that liquidated the collateral for reverse repurchase agreements after the bankruptcy. The county has claimed that they should not have done so because of the Chapter 9 protection and has left open the possibility of litigation against several firms at a later date.

Perhaps the most unusual legal move in this round involved the lawsuit against Standard & Poor's for an "erroneous evaluation." This is the bond rating agency that had reviewed the county's debt offerings in the months before the bankruptcy filing. At that time, they gave the county bonds, which were for the sole purpose of borrowing money to invest in the county pool, a high rating. The county government claims that the rating agency should have uncovered the problems with the county pool. Instead, the county officials and bond investors were misled by the high ratings given to the Orange County bonds (*New York Times*, 1996). Standard & Poor's has argued that it was given bad information about the investment pool by county officials.

Several investment firms were sued because of the types of securities they sold to the county. The Student Loan Marketing Association was sued for selling risky securities that were "unsuitable" for a local government investment pool. Moreover, the county claims that the association had not disclosed that Merrill Lynch would be compensated for the sale of these securities. The county also filed litigation against Morgan Stanley for selling risky securities and for engaging in reverse repurchase agreements that were beyond the debt level authorized by the state. A few months later, the county also sued Fuji Securities for $120 million over the same issue, which was the sale of unsuitable securities to the investment pool (*Los Angeles Times* Orange County Edition, 1995d).

In retrospect, the county leaders may have had other motives for pursuing these lawsuits. They would demonstrate to the pool participants and the U.S. bankruptcy court that the county was serious about returning the money that was lost in the investment pool. The timing of several lawsuits did, after all, coincide with some critical stages in the crisis.

The lawsuits against outside firms also provided a political opportunity for the county leaders to try to diffuse the blame for the financial crisis. In the beginning of the crisis Bob Citron told the state legislators that he made his risky investment decisions on the advice of Merrill Lynch and its representatives. Members of the Orange County Board of Supervisors have blamed other investment firms for not offering them any warnings about the financial crisis (*Orange County Register*, 1995b). There is no evidence that these efforts by county officials to shift the blame have met with any political success. The county supervisors have consistently received low ratings for their handling of the financial crisis. As a result of their engaging in lengthy litigation, the debate about who is to blame will continue. The lawsuits may remind voters of the failures of the county leaders.

LEGAL ACTIONS AGAINST COUNTY OFFICIALS

An important part of the Orange County recovery is the legal actions taken against county officials. Most of the voters believed that their elected officials had somehow failed them and should be held accountable for the county's bankruptcy. The local governments that deposited funds in the county pool have also held the county officials responsible for not safeguarding their money. State legislators complained about the lapse of supervision by county officials that led to the fiscal crisis. There were legal questions that needed to be answered before county government could return to normal. The voters, local government officials, state leaders, and financial institutions all demanded that any criminal wrongdoing by county officials be punished.

Three criminal indictments have occurred as a result of the Orange County financial crisis (see Appendix A, Table A-5). The defendants include former treasurer Bob Citron, former assistant treasurer Matthew Raabe, and former county budget director Ronald Rubino. These county officials were not charged with massive leveraging of the investment pool, buying risky securities, or losing $1.64 billion in local government funds. These were highly damaging actions that caused the collapse, but they were allowed by state law. They did not represent criminal activities. Nor were the officials accused of stealing money for personal gain. There is no evidence that any county leader had profited from the securities transactions in the county pool. The three county officials were charged with falsifying financial records, misappropriating profits and losses in the county pool, and making misrepresentations to the pool investors.

The California state auditor had noted the misallocation of investment pool funds in a March 1995 report to the governor and state legislative leaders. The report specifically notes this most disturbing discovery from their audit: "The treasurer's office altered accounting records, which allowed the county's general fund to receive approximately $93 million more in interest earnings than it was entitled to receive, to the detriment of the other participants" (California State Auditor, 1995). The county general fund should have received $26 million between April 1993 and June 1994. In actuality, $118.9 million of interest earnings was deposited in the county's general fund at that time. A separate illegal act was the transfer of $15.4 million from the commingled investment pool fund to a special fund that was designated specifically for the treasurer's office. There was also the transfer of securities that had lost $271 million in value from a specific account of the county's general fund to the commingled pool. Fifty-four securities were transferred for no other reason than to charge these large financial losses to all pool participants instead of only to the county government. Finally, the treasurer made promises of risk-free investment to five pool participants, and thus the other pool members were charged with their loss of $27 million. The Newport-Mesa Unified School District and North Orange County Community College District were given written guarantees, while the City of Laguna Beach, the Irvine Unified School District, and the Orange County Board of Education were each made promises. The treasurer had been treating some pool members differently, when they all should have been subject to the same conditions. He provided no-risk guarantees to five pool members, clearly at the expense of all of the other investors (California State Auditor, 1995, pp. 25–34).

Bob Citron pleaded guilty to six felony counts in April 1995. He faced up to fourteen years in prison and $7 million in fines. Citron was ultimately sentenced to one year in jail and a $100,000 fine. He actually served an eight-month sentence with a day job in the Orange County sheriff's department, which allowed him to return home at night. The facts that he is in frail health, has mental problems, and is seventy-one years old were considered in the sentencing.

Matthew Raabe was charged with five felony counts and faced a similar sentence and fine. Raabe pleaded not guilty. The county paid $1 million for his attorney fees after he successfully argued that he did not have the money to pay for his own defense. Citron testified against his former colleague at the trial. He said that Raabe was the one who recommended the interest diversion scheme. He told Raabe to "go and do what he recommended." In explaining this decision, Citron said, "I didn't believe I was doing anything illegal or unethical" (Los Angeles Times Orange County Edition, 1997e). The defense argued, to no avail, that the county treasurer's office had routinely set interest rates for pool investors and had the right to redistribute the earnings. Raabe was found guilty on five counts and was sentenced to three years in prison.

Ronald Rubino was criminally charged with assisting Bob Citron in his efforts to illegally divert interest earnings from the investment pool to the county fund. The trial ended in a hung jury. Rubino later agreed to plead guilty to a misdemeanor offense of falsifying public documents. He must perform 100 hours of community service during a period of unsupervised probation. Rubino can have his guilty plea changed to not guilty after one year and clear his name of these charges (*Los Angeles Times* Orange County Edition, 1996a, 1996c, 1996g, 1997b, 1997c; *Orange County Register*, 1996d, 1997).

There have been three civil actions as a result of the bankruptcy. In December 1995 the Orange County grand jury accused Supervisor Roger Stanton and Supervisor William Steiner of "willful misconduct" for failing to "safeguard the financial health of the county." The charge was that the five-member Board of Supervisors had failed to adequately oversee and supervise the actions of the county treasurer in the months leading up to the bankruptcy in December 1994. The other three supervisors were not named. Two members had since retired, and one had already resigned from office. The punishment is removal from office, so charges were not pursued once these supervisors left office. A year later a state appeals court dismissed the civil charges against the two supervisors in office. They ruled in November 1996 that "something more than neglect is necessary to constitute willful conduct" and that removal from office required proof of a criminal or purposeful failure (*Los Angeles Times* Orange County Edition, 1996a, 1996c). The Orange County district attorney had argued that they failed to carry out their duties. In the opinion of the court, the local voters should be the ones to decide if they should be removed from office for reasons such as acts of incompetence. Supervisor Roger Stanton left office when his term ended in 1996. Supervisor William Steiner remains as the only one of the five board members who was present in 1994.

The Orange County grand jury also made a civil charge of "willful misconduct" against Auditor-Controller Steve Lewis. The claim was that he failed to provide the county with an accurate assessment of the financial situation and that he encouraged the county to borrow $750 million in the summer of 1994 when he should have known that the county would not be able to pay these debts. In fact, the chief executive officer at that time, Bill Popejoy, had asked the auditor-controller to resign from office over similar concerns. This elected official refused to resign, and the CEO did not have the authority to remove him from elected office. If the auditor-controller was found guilty, he would be removed from office. On December 6 the attorney general's office recommended dropping the pending case against Lewis (*Los Angeles Times* Orange County Edition, 1996a, 1996c, 1997g). No other civil charges of "willful misconduct" were filed against county officials. Of the remaining county leaders with major roles in the financial crisis, the county counsel has resigned and the county administrative officer was fired.

The U.S. Securities and Exchange Commission conducted its own investigation of the financial crisis and issued its report on January 24, 1996. The SEC filed a complaint in court against Bob Citron and Matthew Raabe and instituted a cease-and-desist order against the Board of Supervisors. The officials were charged with violating the antifraud provisions of the federal securities laws. The report found that the official statements of $2.1 billion in bond offerings in 1993 and 1994 had misrepresented or failed to disclose information to potential buyers concerning the Orange County Investment Pool's strategy and risks. The county should have also noted in these official statements that interest income was the largest source of income from the county's discretionary budget. The report also mentioned that the treasurer's office had misrepresented the bond offerings to the ratings agencies. The Board of Supervisors had not fulfilled their obligations when they authorized the bond offerings and then approved official statements that did not disclose information about the county's financial condition. The county officials consented to the entry of these judgments without admitting or denying these complaints (*Government Finance Review*, 1996).

In sum, there have been few legal actions against the county officials who were involved in the Orange County financial crisis. The treasurer, assistant treasurer, and budget director have all been punished, though to varying degrees. The court dismissed the charges of "willful misconduct" against the supervisors and has yet to decide the case of the auditor-controller. The Securities and Exchange Commission filed a damaging report on the county treasurer, assistant treasurer, and the Board of Supervisors. Those thirsting for harsh punishment for the county officials caught up in the crisis may have been disappointed by these outcomes. But there is no question that the bankruptcy has made "toast" of their political careers. One out of five members of the Board of Supervisors has remained in office since the bankruptcy filing to the present. Not one board member who served during the crisis has sought reelection.

COSTS OF THE BANKRUPTCY

The end of the bankruptcy does not mean that the fiscal pain has ended. The recovery plan came with a high price tag. The county had to divert

TABLE 6-6   DIRECT COSTS OF THE BANKRUPTCY

Cities, schools, and special districts	Lost $865 million in the investment pool
County government	Lost $360 million in the investment pool
Public infrastructure	$50 million a year less for flood control, harbors, beaches, parks, redevelopment projects, buses, and transportation projects; funds diverted to pay for recovery
County budget cuts	About 2,000 county government jobs eliminated
County's poor	Many job losses in the Social Services Agency; cuts in mental health, homeless, child abuse prevention, and medical services; cuts in bus service
Increased user fees	Higher landfill dumping fees, planning and permit fees; higher parking charges at county beaches and parks; higher library fines

SOURCE: County of Orange (1995a); *Orange County Register* (1996b); *Los Angeles Times* Orange County Edition (1996c, 1996e); *New York Times* (1996).

county funds from other purposes, eliminate county programs, and lay off county employees. Some county residents, notably the poor, have been harmed more than others by the budget cuts. Local governments had to cope with monetary losses when they gave up their claims on the county pool. Here we attempt to tally up the costs of the financial crisis and its aftermath, including the indirect cost of being labeled a "deadbeat" county.

An exact dollar amount cannot be placed on the bankruptcy cost. Some of the expenses are ongoing; other costs may surface later. Table 6-6 reviews some of the direct expenses that have occurred so far and their consequences. First, there were the financial losses for the participants of the Orange County Investment Pool. The cities, local schools, and special districts lost about $865 million. The county government lost about $360 million. There is no accounting of how these funds would have otherwise been spent for local programs, services, and construction projects. We do know that many local officials decided to invest as much money as they could in the county fund—and, in some cases, borrowed more for that purpose—so that they could increase spending for their local budgets. The legislative analyst (1995c, p. 10) concluded, "If the litigation is not successful, cities and special districts are likely to reduce future capital expenditures for roads and other public facilities." It is safe to assume that residents will have some program reductions as a result of these losses.

As a result of the county revenues that have been diverted to pay for the bankruptcy-related debts, there will be $50 million a year less to pay for public infrastructure projects for more than a decade. The funds are being taken out of flood control, harbors, beaches, parks, redevelopment projects, and transportation programs. Many of these projects may not be missed immediately, but there may be hidden costs of not maintaining the regional infrastructure. There may be long-term effects of these losses on the county's economic development and the quality of life for residents. For instance, the legislative analyst (1995c, pp. 10–12) expects a reduction in public bus service, a delay in local road projects, impacts on capital improvements and maintenance for flood control, reduced park maintenance, and elimination of new park land acquisition.

The county also had to reduce its general fund budget because of the loss of interest income. As a result, the county has 2,000 fewer employees today than it did before the financial crisis began. There has been considerable suffering among those who lost their jobs, and the remaining staff has had to make do with less support. The county's residents, meanwhile, can expect a longer wait when they seek county services.

The county's poor have suffered disproportionately from the budget cuts for several reasons. They are more dependent on county government programs and, thus, a budget reduction is most likely to affect them. Moreover, there were very large budget cuts and staff reductions in the Social Service Agency, which serves the poor. Four of the agency's neighborhood offices were closed, making it more difficult for the poor to access the services they need (*Orange County Register*, 1996b). A program geared toward child abuse prevention was cut in half, a program for the homeless was eliminated, a prenatal health clinic shut its doors, and fifteen clinics for children were closed (*New York Times*, 1995e). In the meantime, the head of the Orange County Transportation Authority said in testimony, "I believe you'll have reductions in bus service because of this program" (Senate Special Committee on Local Government Investments, 1995e, p. 50). The legislative analyst (1995c) reached the same conclusion about the impacts. The cuts in bus service would also hurt the poor the most.

Some of the other costs of the bankruptcy involve higher user fees for county services. The landfill dumping fees increased because the county had to generate more revenues for the recovery plan. Planning and permit fees also increased for businesses. Users were also asked

TABLE 6-7   INDIRECT COSTS OF THE BANKRUPTCY

Increased cost of borrowing for county bonds now and in the future

Ongoing attorney and consultant fees because of the bankruptcy

Ongoing legal fees for criminal charges and civil claims against the county officials

Thirty-year bonds of $800 million to pay for the bankruptcy will limit other spending

Permanent loss of interest income as a significant revenue source

Economic losses caused by the uncertainty of the bankruptcy (e.g., job growth, consumer spending, and housing market) from December 1994 to December 1995

Potential for loss of new businesses and new residents because of the image problem from the bankruptcy and financial crisis from December 1994 to present

SOURCE: County of Orange (1995a); *Orange County Register* (1996b); *Los Angeles Times* Orange County Edition (1996c, 1996e); *New York Times* (1996).

to pay higher parking charges at the county parks and beaches, and higher fines for overdue books in the county library system. These are the relatively small financial impacts that are felt by most county residents.

Other costs of the bankruptcy are ongoing and indirect. Some of these expenses, which are even more difficult to measure than those just discussed, are presented in Table 6-7. For instance, Orange County will have to pay more for the money it borrows now and in the future. There were extra costs in the $800 million in bonds that were sold to allow Orange County to pay its debts and leave bankruptcy in June 1996 (*Los Angeles Times* Orange County Edition, 1996f). The second bond offering in January 1997 also came with a higher yield and with the cost of bond insurance (*Wall Street Journal*, 1997). The county will have to pay more for its borrowing because it has lost its stellar bond rating, which may take years to recover.

There are also the fees for the attorneys and financial consultants who work on behalf of the county government. These were the outside professionals who advised the county as it entered bankruptcy, liquidated the investment pool, and developed recovery plans that were ultimately approved by the U.S. bankruptcy court. The county estimates that bills for lawyers and consultants totaled about $50 million by the time the bankruptcy ended (*New York Times*, 1995e). This cost did not include any of the attorneys and financial advisors who had to be retained by the cities, schools, and special districts that had invested their money in the county pool. There are also ongoing legal costs for the billions of dollars in lawsuits against the Wall Street firms.

Additional costs are associated with legal claims against the county officials who were part of the financial crisis. The county government paid over $2 million for defense attorneys for the five county officials who were indicted on civil or criminal charges. Then another $2.5 million was spent by the Orange County district attorney for investigations (*Los Angeles Times* Orange County Edition, 1996c, 1997b). However, the defense and prosecution costs are ongoing since there are cases still pending.

The recovery plan required that the county borrow $800 million over thirty years in order to pay its bond investors and outside vendors. The interest payments on this large amount of debt will limit the county's ability to meet emergency budget needs as they arise. Already the county has had to put on hold its plans to expand the jails, courts, and shelters for abused children (*Los Angeles Times* Orange County Edition, 1997f). This amount of debt also limits the county's ability to borrow money for other purposes. The bankruptcy-related debt will be a major constraint on the county budget. The legislative analyst (1995c, p. 10) concludes, "From 10 percent to 15 percent of County tax revenues will be earmarked for debt service on the recovery program.... These factors will further squeeze county resources in the future.... It will have limited flexibility to deal with unanticipated events which may arise in the years ahead."

The county's general fund has also permanently lost its major source of discretionary revenue. The interest income from the county pool in the future will be minimal as a result of the restrictions on the investment strategy, and so will the return. While the county can be assured that the principal is safe, the excesses of the former treasurer have taken away the prospects of earning somewhat higher interest by taking modest risks with the local government funds. County leaders do not have a plan for replacing the lost interest income, except to win the lawsuits against the financial firms that did business with the county. They face the prospects of either permanent budget cuts or asking the voters to pay higher taxes. In this fiscally conservative county, the strong likelihood is for lower expenditures in the county's general fund.

There were also economic losses in Orange County as a result of the financial crisis. The bankruptcy came at a time when Orange County was beginning to recover from the recession. There was a great deal of uncertainty about the economic impacts of the bankruptcy between

December 1994 and December 1995. One reason is that no one had experienced such a large municipal bankruptcy, and its possible effects were thus unknown. This uncertainty had the effect of damaging consumer confidence and, as a result, probably had some negative repercussions on the housing market, consumer spending, and job growth. Orange County still has the potential of losing new businesses and residents that it might otherwise attract because of the stigma of bankruptcy and the negative publicity it has received in the national media.

There have been many costs associated with the bankruptcy, and there are more to come. Still, some have argued that local governments enjoyed high interest income for years on the county pool. They say that this extra income should compensate for their losses. However, there was a lot of variation in gains and losses among the 194 investors. Some made more than others before the pool collapse, and some did better than others in the settlement. Also, local governments were prevented from developing a better approach to managing their revenues and expenditures because of their dependence on interest income. They may have, for instance, found ways to raise more revenues or save money. A better path, for instance, may have been to consolidate local services and rely on new technology as a cost-cutting measure. Also, the local governments have not received the interest income from their lost funds since the county pool was frozen in December 1994. Further, they no longer get higher returns on their investments because of the excesses of the county pool in the early 1990s. These two factors have offset some of the higher returns they received in earlier years. The short-term gains of the interest income also need to be weighted against the long-term effects of being tainted by this crisis. County government can expect to pay more for its borrowing for many years as a result of losing its stellar bond rating. In all, the county pool was not a good investment.

SUMMARY

The road to recovery took some unusual twists and turns. But the end came remarkably quickly considering the size of the bankruptcy. The sales tax measure was overwhelmingly defeated by voters in June 1995. The state then placed enormous pressures on the county officials to resolve their problems by the end of the year. They responded with a plan that was accepted by the governor and state legislature.

There were several false starts toward a recovery plan in July 1995. Once again, local business leaders were called upon to facilitate the negotiations. A consensus plan for the bankruptcy recovery was approved by all units of local government in August. The plan called for the diversion of infrastructure funds to pay for the county's debts, while the pool investors would also end their claims against the county. The consensus plan would require state legislation. The bills passed only after they were linked to similar legislation to help Los Angeles County out of its financial troubles.

Orange County filed a plan with the U.S. bankruptcy court in December 1995. This was within about a year of its declaring the biggest municipal bankruptcy. After a successful offering of $880 million in thirty-year bonds to pay its outstanding debts, the county government was able to emerge from municipal bankruptcy in June 1996.

The county has paid a big price for the bankruptcy. The total cost is not yet known and may never be determined. A full recovery will depend on the county winning billions of dollars in its lawsuits against Wall Street firms, since the voters would not foot the bill. In the meantime, there has been a major loss of funds that could have been devoted to local services today and a better county infrastructure for the future. Most of the middle-class residents may not have noticed any major impacts of the bankruptcy; all they have seen are increases in some user fees. However, the safety net that county services provided for the Orange County poor has been damaged by the financial crisis.

CHAPTER 7

Reforms after the Crisis

There were many people calling for local government reforms in response to the Orange County bankruptcy. Their ideas were drawn from
perceptions of the causes of the fiscal crisis, complaints about county
officials' responses to the fiscal emergency, and a recognition of the fiscal limitations occurring after the bankruptcy. Some saw a lack of oversight as the major contributing factor in the county pool losses. Others
noted that the local governments were unable to respond as well as they
should have during the fiscal emergency. Some thought that a more efficient local government was needed to cope with the lean budgets demanded by the recovery plan. A few also saw the Orange County
bankruptcy as a golden opportunity to float their favorite, and often
radical, ideas for local government restructuring. They hoped that their
bold proposals would be carried forward by the winds of political
change.

Although there were some reforms in local government after the fiscal crisis, they could hardly be described as sweeping changes. Many of
the ambitious proposals were ultimately rejected. This chapter examines some of the more significant changes that took place in county government and other local governments in Orange County. These include
statewide reforms of the county treasurer's operations, the first stages
of a restructuring of Orange County government, term limits for the
Board of Supervisors, and a council of governments. We also look at
the reform efforts that failed—notably, a county charter and several

dramatic proposals to reshape the relationships between the state, the county, and local governments.

THE PUBLIC MOOD FOR CHANGE

The opinions of local residents are an important component in the process of reforming local government. Public pressures on local elected officials would influence the proposals, if any, presented for change. Good ideas that are not politically acceptable may never even be recommended. And for certain reforms, such as a county charter, it is the voters who decide if they are adopted.

At the end of June Orange County voters had defeated the sales tax measure that was supposed to be the only way out of the bankruptcy. Within a matter of weeks the county and other local governments were in agreement on a recovery plan that involved no new taxes. They would redirect existing taxes. This plan would seem to confirm the belief by voters that the local governments had plenty of money and that there really was no need to raise taxes. In the late summer of 1995 we examined the Orange County public's views of their local government system. This was when the worrisome elements of the bankruptcy were winding down and the recovery plan was being unveiled. We wanted to determine what local government reforms, if any, the residents wanted.

The public's confidence in local government was badly shaken by the financial crisis. Fifty-one percent of Orange County residents described the current system of county and city governments in sharing responsibility for solving problems as ineffective. Forty-one percent said the local system was effective, which was a fifteen-point decline from a decade earlier. The loss of public confidence appears to have increased the already strong desire for the cities to have more power and the county government to have less influence. Two in three said they would prefer their city governments to have more authority over local affairs. Fewer than one in four would give the county more authority. There was little support for a regional government, even as local governments struggled with fiscal limits. One in four favored a consolidation of city and county governments, while two in three were opposed (see Appendix B, Table B-6).

Orange County residents looked favorably at a number of proposals to change their county government. Most of the reforms, however, focused on limiting the powers of the Board of Supervisors. Fifty-nine percent favored appointing a chief executive officer to run county government and changing the Board of Supervisors from full-time to part-time positions. Eighty-three percent also supported term limits for the members of the Board of Supervisors. The support for these two concepts points to a strong desire to weaken the powers of the current board members. On the other hand, 71 percent opposed the idea of increasing the size of the five-member Board of Supervisors. This was a proposal that had been discussed to increase representation. Instead, it was viewed as expanding a government body that was not highly regarded. The public also expressed considerable interest in reducing the size of the county government bureaucracy. Sixty-eight percent were in favor of authorizing county government to contract out with private companies to provide public services. The concept of privatization as a way to reduce county government costs, and the number of the county government employees, had been discussed during the crisis. This idea had a lot of supporters in this fiscally conservative county (Baldassare and Katz, 1995).

A proposal that did not resonate well with local residents was the idea of changing some of the countywide elected officials to appointed officials. One of the reforms that had been discussed after the investment fund losses by Bob Citron was to turn the treasurer's position into an appointed post. The county treasurer could then be hired on the basis of specific credentials, would be supervised on a daily basis, and could be fired by county officials for failing to carry out duties. Only 41 percent were in favor of changing the county treasurer, auditor, and clerk from elected to appointed positions; 53 percent were opposed. Apparently, residents did not want to give up the ability to elect the county officials. Perhaps voters were also reluctant to give this decision to the Board of Supervisors, who were not held in high esteem at this time.

The public mood raises questions about the residents' resolve for change. They saw the bankruptcy as a major problem for the county government, but not one that affected their lives. Seven in ten residents viewed the financial crisis and bankruptcy as a "big problem" for Orange County. When asked to name the top problem facing Orange County, however, 26 percent named the bankruptcy. Others mentioned crime, immigration, the economy, public schools, transportation, housing, and population growth. One in four said they or someone in their family had been affected in some way by the spending cuts resulting from the county investment fund losses in the past year. A similar number said that they were "very fearful" that they would be affected by the investment fund losses, either financially or in terms of cuts in local services (Baldassare and Katz, 1995).

In sum, county residents had a definite perspective on local government reform after the bankruptcy. Their solution to political fragmentation was to increase the amount of power given to their city governments. They wanted to limit the powers of the Board of Supervisors and reduce the size of the county government bureaucracy. They were not willing to give up the power to elect officials such as the county treasurer, even after their bad experience with Bob Citron. The local government reforms favored by the public reflected their distrust of government and localism. These attitudes would set the parameters for the government restructuring in Orange County.

COUNTY TREASURER REFORMS

The $1.64 billion loss in the Orange County Investment Pool by Bob Citron was certain to bring about reforms. When the investment policies of the former county treasurer were uncovered, they were found to include massive leveraging through reverse repurchase agreements, the purchase of exotic securities with high risks, and a money-market portfolio for local government investors that included too many long-term securities. The treasurer had also pleaded guilty to improperly allocating the profits and losses to local government investors. There was clearly a lack of oversight of the treasurer by other county officials. There were also insufficient financial reports to the local governments that invested in the county pool. It was easy to diagnose the problems and determine that the solution was to change the current state laws.

A series of state laws were passed after Proposition 13 that redefined the financial activities permitted of county treasurers. Certainly, the state legislation was not intended to be put to all the uses that Bob Citron had devised in Orange County. The risk taking with county funds that gained notoriety after the bankruptcy may have been foolish and inappropriate for local governments, but at the time it was legal. The voters, local government investors, and state officials demanded reforms in the county treasurers' offices throughout the state to prevent future financial collapses. During the financial crisis state officials had raised alarms that the creditworthiness and solvency of state and local governments had been hurt by the pool losses and bankruptcy. It would take state legislation to undo the flawed system for county pool investments that had evolved over the past two decades.

TABLE 7-1   STATE LEGISLATION FOR
COUNTY TREASURER REFORM

SB 866: Specifies that the objectives of investing public funds are, first, safety of the principal, then the liquidity needs of the depositor, and, finally, achieving a return on the funds. Limits the amount that can be invested in reverse repurchase agreements; prohibits investments in inverse floaters and other exotic securities; limits the length of term of investments on borrowed funds. Requires the Board of Supervisors to establish a county treasurer oversight committee; establishes educational qualifications for the county treasurer. Specifies rules for local agencies to enter and exit from county investment pools; requires that local governments give adequate notice of withdrawals.

SB 564: Places requirements on local treasurers to provide the local governing boards and their oversight committees with an annual statement of investment policy, and to provide quarterly reports containing specified financial information.

SOURCE: Office of Senate Floor Analysis (1995).

The governor signed legislation to reform the county treasurer's office in the state on October 12, 1995 (see Appendix A, Table A-6). This was the same time that the state bills passed allowing Orange County to implement the consensus plan for the financial recovery. Many of the new requirements went into effect by January 1, 1996.

The county treasurer reforms were sweeping. The SB 866 legislation was a comprehensive effort authored by state senators Craven, Hayden, and Killea that ended most of the practices and abuses that were associated with the financial collapse of the Orange County Investment Pool (see Table 7-1). The state government would radically shift its direction from its earlier goals of deregulation. The state legislators justified these new restrictions on local government by stating, "The Legislature hereby finds that the solvency and creditworthiness of the local agency can impact the solvency and creditworthiness of the state and other local agencies within the state. Therefore, to protect the solvency and creditworthiness of the state and all of its political subdivisions, the Legislature hereby declares that the deposit and investment of public funds by local officials and local agencies is an issue of statewide concern" (Office of Senate Floor Analysis, 1995, SB 866 Sec. 16.53630.1).

One major provision of SB 866 was to set guidelines for investing the local government funds on deposit. The bill specifies that the three investment objectives of the county pool are, first and foremost, to safeguard the principal, then to meet the liquidity needs of the investors, and, last of all, to achieve a return on the funds. This bill restricts the use of reverse repurchase agreements to 20 percent of the portfolio and thus eliminates the possibility of having a highly leveraged county pool. There are also prohibitions against buying "inverse floaters" and certain other exotic securities. This means that the county pools would not suffer heavy losses if interest rates were to suddenly increase. There were also limits on the terms of investments, so that short-term borrowing would not be used to purchase long-term investments.

The state bill permits local governments to invest their surplus funds in the county pool, but it also asks the county government to observe specific rules for depositing and withdrawing these funds. The local governments who choose to invest their funds, in turn, must give the county proper notice of intent to withdraw their funds. This notice was designed to prevent a liquidity crisis from a run on the pool.

Another element of SB 866 was to demand more involvement and accountability from the county government officials. The Board of Supervisors is required to appoint a county treasury oversight committee to review the investment pool policy and to conduct an annual audit of the county pool. The oversight committee would include the county treasurer, a financial officer in the county, a representative of the Board of Supervisors, a representative from the local schools, a representative of the local public agencies that have voluntarily invested in the county pool, and members of the public.

The state legislation also established some educational requirements for the elected office of county treasurer. County treasurers in office after January 1, 1996, are required to take continuing education courses in public finance and to provide a certificate that they have successfully completed forty-eight hours of training over a four-year period. For those seeking election for terms beginning January 1, 1998, or later, a candidate must have either a college degree, certificate of training, or several years of service as a senior financial officer in a public agency to be eligible for county treasurer. Finally, the bill establishes that the county treasurer is a trustee and a fiduciary who is subject to acting with skill, care, prudence, and diligence with the purpose of safeguarding the principal and maintaining the liquidity needs of the pool participants. As a result, there are now legal consequences for reckless investing.

One other state law that reformed the county treasurer's office passed at the same time. Bill SB 564 requires that the county treasurer submit to the Board of Supervisors and the oversight committee an annual statement of the investment pool policy. It also requires a quarterly financial report about the county pool. This legislation was needed specifically to reverse the trend that was started by the state government in the early 1990s, which was the elimination of report requirements as a way of saving time and money for the local governments. Bob Citron had provided very little information about the state of the county pool. The annual and quarterly reports would provide for more oversight of the county treasurer's investments.

In Orange County, efforts to reform the county treasurer's office went beyond what was required by state law. This is because of the serious lack of confidence of the public, county officials, and local government investors in the county investment pool after the financial crisis. This was also largely a result of the efforts of the acting treasurer, John Moorlach, who ran as a reform candidate against the incumbent Bob Citron. He had vowed to change the county treasurer's office. He was to get his chance.

The new county treasurer began to make changes as soon as he was appointed to that office. A major emphasis was placed on increasing the level of oversight. A treasurer's oversight committee had been established in March 1995, even before it was required by the new state law. This group was disbanded and then recreated on January 1, 1996, when the new state law took effect. The members of the oversight committee include the chief executive officer, the auditor-controller, the treasurer, the superintendent of schools, and a member of the public. The county treasurer formed a second oversight group, called the Technical Oversight Committee. This group includes outside financial experts from the private sector, other financial professionals, and some pool participants. The Board of Supervisors also established an audit committee. In stark contrast with the past, the treasurer now meets every three weeks with the chair of the Board of Supervisors to discuss the county treasurer's operations (Moorlach, 1996).

The county pool has also been transformed to a money-market fund. The detailed investment policy statement forbids the use of reverse repurchase agreements. No derivatives are allowed in the investment portfolio. The average maturity date of the securities purchased is about 30 days; it can be no greater than 90 days. The treasurer also has a management team that meets weekly to monitor closely the risk in the portfolio and review the decisions on securities purchases. The investment pool had also been managed by an investment firm after the pool losses, but the Board of Supervisors gradually returned control to the county treasurer's office.

The county pool has now shrunk to about $2 billion. The county government and school districts are the only pool participants. Moreover, the schools have a separate fund as additional security for their deposits. There are no voluntary participants in the funds to date, such as cities or special districts. Among the reasons for this is that there is no incentive of receiving higher yields in a money-market pool. The county fund has an AAA rating from Fitch Investors Service (*Los Angeles Times* Orange County Edition, 1997a).

The Orange County financial crisis changed the way that the county treasurer's office operates throughout the state. The investments are highly regulated, and there is considerable oversight and reporting. In Orange County even more steps were taken to ensure the safety of principal and increase the oversight of the county treasurer. The statewide and local changes focused on the problems that led to the pool collapse; they did not address the fiscal stress that led local governments to risk their funds. For instance, the state government did not return the property tax money it took from the counties, cities, and special districts beginning in the early 1990s. Perhaps the fiscal austerity of the state government prevented this type of local reform. The treasurer's reforms will reduce the revenues that local governments will receive from interest income, but they do not replace this income with other revenue sources.

DRAMATIC REFORM PROPOSALS

For some, the Orange County bankruptcy was a once-in-a-lifetime opportunity to try to "reinvent" local government. Proposals were offered calling for radical changes in the ways the county government went about its business. Some called for limiting the powers of the Board of Supervisors. Others asked the county government to turn some of its responsibilities over to the cities. Still others said the solution was to have the private sector do more of the tasks of local governments. This section reviews four of the more dramatic proposals for reforming local government.

The earliest proposal was offered in a study by the Reason Foundation called "Rescuing Orange County" in February 1995. This study was commissioned by the Howard Jarvis Taxpayers Association and the Lincoln Club of Orange County. The latter is a conservative Republican group. The purpose of the study was to devise a plan for the county government to replace its $1.64 billion loss in the county investment pool and the annual $160 million in interest income. The author of the report saw the Orange County financial crisis as "an opportunity to rethink, redesign and rightsize County government for the 21st century" (Poole, 1995, p. 1). The suggestion was for the county government to sell its assets, reduce its workforce, and privatize services.

The county government would receive $1 billion to $1.5 billion from asset sales. This would include sale and leaseback of office buildings and sale of the airport, landfills, properties leased to others, correctional facilities, and surplus lands. The study also called on the special districts to sell their assets. Another $2.5 billion could be raised if the largest water systems, county sanitation districts, and wastewater systems were sold. The asset sales would not only provide much-needed cash; they would also generate property tax revenues as the government holdings went into private hands.

The study estimated that there could be as much as $50 million in new property tax revenues, which would help to offset the loss of interest income from the county pool. The county government would also save $91 million a year with a 10 percent reduction of its workforce and $82 million a year by reducing employee pay and benefits by 10 percent for the remaining workforce. Finally, about $60 million a year would be saved by outsourcing several county services, including animal control, fleet maintenance, jail operations, paramedics, and fire protection.

The suggestions offered in the Reason Foundation study were self-described as "a new paradigm for streamlined, more efficient and more effective government which could be emulated across the country" (Poole, 1995, p. 1). However, these radical ideas proved to be too conservative even for Orange County. They failed to get the support that was needed from the Board of Supervisors and the county's business community.

Another proposal to shake up the status quo was offered from a most unexpected source. It came from a member of the Board of Supervisors. The "Orange County 2001" report was issued by Supervisor Marian Bergeson in July 1995. This elected official had joined the Board of Supervisors after the bankruptcy had begun. Bergeson had previously served in the state legislature and had many years of experience with local government issues. Bergeson (1995, p. 5) operated on the assumption that the county system was outdated and that "supervisors' days as land barons and as full-time governors of the unincorporated area are long gone." The proposal sought to realign the relationships between the state, county, and city governments. The objective was to find efficiencies given the new fiscal realities of more limited resources.

The first and perhaps most controversial step would be to eliminate the five-member Board of Supervisors. They would be replaced with an elected county mayor. An eight-member Board of Commissioners would be elected by district, serve part-time, and be paid on a per diem basis for attending bimonthly meetings. The county government would focus on providing regional services. It would establish an "Orange Regional Services Authority," which included health and human services, public facilities, public protection, and transportation. The city governments would take over some of the local services that had been performed by county government. This would include law enforcement and police services, local planning and land use, low- and moderate-income housing, and library administration. The county government would contract out with the state government to perform the functions of election supervision and voter registration, the county treasury and investment oversight, the administration of property taxes, and the duties of the courts and marshal. So that the county government could become further removed from providing local services, the remaining unincorporated areas would either be annexed by adjacent cities or become incorporated into new cities. Less than 10 percent of Orange County's population now live in unincorporated areas.

The Bergeson plan received some favorable reviews by the local government experts in the state government. The proposal had its supporters because it would reduce the political fragmentation in suburban metropolitan governance and limit the size and costs of county government. However, "Orange County 2001" would require a county charter. Thus, the Board of Supervisors would need to place such a measure on the ballot. The other members of the Board of Supervisors were not keen on becoming part-time employees and giving their powers to a county mayor. In fact, Supervisor Bergeson's ideas were met with public hostility and ridicule by one of her colleagues. The Charter Commission appointed by the Board of Supervisors never adopted any of these proposals as part of their recommendations for local government reforms.

The Orange County Business Council presented its plan for local government restructuring in August 1995. This business group was very involved in the negotiations for the pool settlement and the recovery plan. As a result, they had some firsthand knowledge of the problems in governmental structure that had led to the financial crisis. They also had ideas about changes in the local political system that would be needed as the county government prepared for an era of fiscal limits. The guiding principle in their suggestions about restructuring is summed up in their report: "For an enterprise (government or private) to be successful it must first have an operating culture that aligns authority, responsibility and accountability" (Orange County Business Council, 1995, p. 3).

The Orange County Business Council report presents a restructuring plan with two phases. The first phase calls for changes in county government. An appointed chief executive officer would run the day-to-day operations of the county government, with all department heads reporting to that person. The Board of Supervisors would continue to be elected by district and be expanded to an eleven-member panel with part-time duties and minimal pay. They also called for eliminating all countywide elected positions, except for the sheriff, assessor, and district attorney, each of whom is required by the state constitution. Their proposal also called for a realignment of local services; the county would provide only regional services, and local services would be provided by cities. They also suggested more contracting out for local services to the private sector, whenever contracting out was proven to be the most cost-effective method.

The second phase of the Orange County Business Council's restructuring plan focused on the other local governments. The group called for the consolidation of local special districts, such as water, sewer, and transportation, into regional agencies in order to reduce duplication of administrative efforts and reduce the costs of local government. They also recommended the creation of a council of governments. This would give the county government, cities, and special districts a forum for regional planning and policy. This council would develop a long-term vision for government in Orange County.

The recommendations of the local business group would require the creation of a charter county. This would depend on the endorsement of the Board of Supervisors, who, once again, were being asked to go along with reforms that would severely limit their powers. Some of these proposals became part of the recommendations of the Charter Commission, which was appointed by the Board of Supervisors. Notably, proposals included the appointment of a chief executive officer and increased use of privatization and contracting out. Larger-scale reforms did not survive. For their part, the Orange County Business

Council focused on solving the immediate problem of the bankruptcy, which they saw as jeopardizing the economy and business community, rather than making a major effort to promote their ideas for local government reform. They handed their proposals to others rather than taking them directly to the elected officials.

Finally, the Government Practices Oversight Committee was appointed by the Board of Supervisors soon after the bankruptcy was announced. This was separate from the Charter Commission, which was created to write a county charter. This twenty-five-member volunteer group was given the task of developing a "factbook" on local government based on extensive research and then making recommendations for changes in local government. The chair of this group noted in its final report issued in August 1996, "It is this Committee's belief that Orange County can emerge from the bankruptcy as a model of good government" (Government Practices Oversight Committee, 1996, p. 7).

The report made a number of very specific management suggestions, rather than calling for a drastic overhaul of the local government structure. For instance, the committee wanted the county government to develop a business plan and measure the performance of the programs that were being funded. They called for better definitions of the roles and responsibilities of the Board of Supervisors. They wanted better use of the internal audit division. They wanted to combine some county departments, eliminate certain services, and change the award process for county contracts. They also recommended that the cities take over some of the county-run services. As part of their final report, they created a very detailed organization chart of the county services that could be shifted to the state or cities, eliminated, privatized, or consolidated.

Their recommendations were submitted to the Board of Supervisors. However, they have yet to be integrated into the chief executive officer's ongoing plans for local government restructuring, which were formally endorsed by the Board of Supervisors. Some feel that the efforts of this committee have been ignored. They claim that the county government has focused on internally generated plans for its structural reform.

In all, there were several far-reaching proposals that would have drastically changed the organizational structure of local government in Orange County. Most of these ideas would require a county charter. They would need the strong backing of reform-minded local elected officials. However, these ideas lacked the support of the political establishment in Orange County, which wanted less drastic changes to the status quo. As the financial crisis eased, so did the pressures for major reforms in local government.

COUNTY CHARTER

There were legal limits to how much the county government could reform itself. Orange County is a general-law county, and, as such, its organizational structure is determined by the state laws. For instance, the number of supervisors, their election by local district, and their four-year terms are set. So are the positions of countywide elected offices. The Board of Supervisors could not decide on their own to change the county treasurer's position from an elected office to an appointed office. Nor could they decide that there should be more members on the Board of Supervisors. In order for the county government to make big changes, it would need to become a charter county.

Supervisor Roger Stanton noted in a memo to board members a month after the bankruptcy, "The best efforts to restructure county government will probably require the establishment of a Charter County status" (Stanton, 1995). The process of establishing a charter is not one that is designed for achieving an instant makeover of county government, as some in Orange County may have wanted after the bankruptcy. A commission is appointed by the Board of Supervisors to gather facts and testimony about the structural changes. Then the Board of Supervisors receives the charter recommendations from the commission. The board can then decide whether or not to place the charter proposal on a countywide ballot. A majority of the voters in an election must approve the charter for it to become law. This is not an impossible task. Most of the urban counties in the state are governed by charters. Supervisor Stanton called on his colleagues to begin the process so that voters could be presented with a charter to restructure their county government.

The Board of Supervisors appointed the Charter Commission in March 1995. The commission held meetings throughout the year. It was chaired by Bruce Sumner, a local retired judge and a Democrat. Sumner had also been the chair of the California Constitutional Revision Commission, whose work resulted in the last overhaul of the state constitution in the mid-sixties. The Board of Supervisors voted unanimously on November 28, 1995, to place the county charter measure on the ballot. The voters would be asked to approve the charter measure as part of the March 26, 1996, primary.

The county charter proposal was designed to correct some of the structural problems that led to the financial crisis, while also giving the county leaders more flexibility in the postbankruptcy era of limited revenues. It had five separate parts. It would create a stronger position of chief executive officer to be appointed by the Board of Supervisors. This person would manage the day-to-day county operations and supervise the department heads. The charter would change the Orange County treasurer, clerk, and auditor from elected positions to appointed positions responsible to the chief executive officer. It would limit members of the Board of Supervisors to no more than two consecutive four-year terms in office. The charter would also authorize the county government to contract out with private companies to provide county services. These four proposals were included in Measure T on the March 1996 ballot. The voters would also be asked to consider as part of the charter an increase in the number of members of the Board of Supervisors from five to nine. This proposal was part of Measure U on the March 1996 ballot. If Measure T passed, then the voters could also decide through Measure U if they wanted nine county supervisors.

There would be a four-month campaign to educate the voters about the charter. The hope was that there would be financial support from the business community. The Orange County Business Council asked the Board of Supervisors to place the charter proposal on the ballot. The council had some of its reform proposals in the charter.

There were opponents to the county charter proposed by the commission even before it was placed on the ballot. The Committee of Correspondence, the grassroots group that had opposed the Measure R sales tax, opposed the charter measure. They asked the Board of Supervisors to place another county reform measure on the ballot, one that had been drafted by their group. The Board of Supervisors refused to do so, since the alternative proposal had not gone through the formal process of public meetings and hearings to develop the restructuring proposals. The Committee of Correspondence was thus able to define the charter election as a vote to support a proposal that had the endorsement of the Board of Supervisors. An author of the alternative charter proposal said of the charter election, "This is deja vu in terms of Measure R. . . . You have the same players on both sides" (*Los Angeles Times* Orange County Edition, 1996h). The supporters of the charter measure would have to overcome this early labeling in an abbreviated four-month campaign.

In an Orange County voter survey taken three weeks before the election, 41 percent said they would vote in favor of the county charter proposals in Measure T. Three in ten were opposed, and three in ten were undecided. Forty percent were also in favor of Measure U, which would increase the number of members of the Board of Supervisors. More than half were opposed, while fewer than 10 percent were undecided. Likely voters had the same response to these ballot measures for the charter proposals. Democrats and Republicans gave the same level of support to the charter. There was no age, income, or geographic group that gave more than 50 percent support.

The specific proposals that were part of the county charter received a mixed response (see Appendix C, Table C-21). Term limits for supervisors had strong support, with eight in ten voters favoring this idea. Two-thirds of the voters wanted to give the county government more financial flexibility with respect to contracting out for services. A slight majority were in favor of having a more powerful chief executive officer who is appointed by the Board of Supervisors. However, only one of three voters wanted to change the treasurer and other countywide elected officials to appointed positions. The Democrats and Republicans were in agreement on these individual proposals, although the Republicans expressed a higher level of support for privatization of county services.

The lack of voter support for the county charter seemed to have two sources. One was the public's misgivings about specific elements of the proposed charter. The other was the continued dismal ratings of the Board of Supervisors. Even after the recovery plan had been approved and the official bankruptcy was drawing to a close, there was still plenty of anger being vented at the county leaders. Only one in six voters gave the Board of Supervisors excellent or good ratings for their handling of the county's financial crisis, while 43 percent thought they were doing a poor job. Two in three voters wanted the two supervisors who were in office when the bankruptcy occurred to resign before their terms were completed. Three in four said that the county government should not pay for the legal defense of the two supervisors who were facing civil charges for their failure to oversee the county fund. Democrats and Republicans had similar responses to these survey questions (see Appendix C, Table C-22).

The charter proposal was in trouble for other reasons. Measure T was placed on the ballot by the Board of Supervisors, and it would extend the powers of the supervisors by allowing them to appoint a

TABLE 7-2   VOTES ON ORANGE COUNTY
MEASURES T AND U FOR THE COUNTY CHARTER

Measure T (Restructure County Government)

Yes	168,545	39.4%
No	258,961	60.6

Measure U (Increase Board)

Yes	111,279	24.7%
No	339,256	75.3

43.3% voter turnout on March 26, 1996

SOURCE: Orange County Registrar of Voters (1996a).

strong chief executive officer and currently elected officials, such as the county treasurer. Moreover, Measure U called for the election of more members at a time when few voters had anything positive to say about the five supervisors they now had. The charter proposal also did not turn the Board of Supervisors into part-time elected officials, a reform that was favored by the voters.

There seemed to be a ceiling on the level of voter support that the county charter would achieve at the ballot box. This is because some charter elements were highly popular, while others were not. The total package added up to less than a majority support. In all, only 40 percent of the voters thought that passing Measure T would make county government leaders more likely to spend taxpayer money wisely. Similarly, only four in ten voters thought that passing the Measure T charter proposal would make county government leaders more likely to represent the needs of residents.

The March 1996 election did turn out to be a "deja vu of Measure R," as the opponents predicted (see Table 7-2). The county charter measures were overwhelmingly defeated in what was a low-turnout election. Measure T, which included the four proposals to restructure county government, lost by a 61 to 39 percent margin. This measure was defeated by almost 100,000 votes. Measure U, which would have increased the number of supervisors had the county charter been passed, was defeated by a 75 percent to 25 percent margin. This measure lost by more than 200,000 votes.

The vote against the charter proposal was overwhelming in both its margin and the consensus that was achieved across the county.

Measure T passed in only two cities, Laguna Beach and San Juan Capistrano, and only narrowly in these two small localities. Once again, the
liberal leanings of Laguna Beach distinguished it from the rest of
Orange County. Measure T lost in twenty-nine of the thirty-one cities
and the unincorporated areas. The defeat was so convincing that there
has been no talk since of a county charter proposal.

The charter proposal was defeated in an election that attracted only
43 percent of the registered voters. Measures T and U appeared on a ballot for a presidential primary that had been moved from June to late
March. But at the time there were no longer serious challengers on the
Republican or the Democratic presidential ticket, resulting in a record
low turnout for this presidential primary. Had the charter measures been
placed on the ballot for the November presidential election, which had
a higher turnout, at least more voters would have had the opportunity
to decide on this proposal to restructure county government. There
would also have been more time to discuss the pros and cons of the
charter than was possible in a four-month campaign.

Measures T and U were not even the most closely watched local ballot measures in March. Measure S was a citizens' initiative placed on
the ballot by south Orange County voters to turn back Measure A,
which required that the El Toro Marine Air Base would be converted
to a civilian airport. This measure had narrowly won in November
1994 through the financing of business leader George Argyros, who
had assisted with the investment pool negotiations. Measure S was a
highly contentious issue that split the voters in the north and south,
business leaders and local residents, and the Board of Supervisors.
Measure S was defeated by a wide margin through a well-organized
countywide campaign. The El Toro Marine Air Base issue siphoned off
campaign funds and energy from the business community and the interest of the local newspapers, which might otherwise have been directed at the county charter. Measure S also pitted the local elected
officials from the north against those in the south, near the El Toro
base, making it impossible for there to be united support for a county
charter.

Orange County took the steps needed to become a charter county,
but the support for these reforms did not materialize. The commission
appointed by the Board of Supervisors recommended only modest
changes. Some of their proposals were highly popular; others were not.
The supervisors' endorsement of the county charter did not help it gain
support. For many, true reform could only come out of a more public

process. The business community did not put much effort into the campaign. Since the voters soundly rejected the ballot measure, the local government reforms would have to take place without the legal authority of a county charter.

COUNTY GOVERNMENT RESTRUCTURING

The overwhelming defeat of the county charter left the supervisors in a difficult position. They knew the voters wanted changes in their county government. On the other hand, the voters distrusted their elected officials too much to support a county charter that was endorsed by the Board of Supervisors. The supervisors were aware that reforms were needed, if for no other reason, for their own political survival. Two weeks after the March 26 defeat of measures T and U, the Board of Supervisors turned to their chief executive officer. Jan Mittermeier was asked to develop a plan to restructure county government for the board's approval that would not involve a county charter.

The chief executive officer submitted the restructuring plan on June 20, 1996. This was within a week of the county government's official exit from bankruptcy. The plan begins with a redefinition of county government, presented in a mission statement that says, "The County of Orange is a regional service provider and planning agency representing all residents of Orange County. Our core businesses are: public safety, public health, environmental protection, regional planning, public assistance, social services, and aviation" (County of Orange, 1996a, p. 2). The goals laid out for the restructuring revolve around improving accountability and cost efficiency. These were the obvious challenges that the county government was facing as a result of the treasurer's losses in the investment pool and the severe budget constraints demanded by the recovery plan. The restructuring was divided into three phases, with the first two including two stages of internal restructuring and the final phase involving an external restructuring of the county government's relationships with other local governments.

The first phase of the internal restructuring involves the County Executive Office, the General Services Agency, and the Environmental Management Agency. The County Executive Office would be expanded to include five assistant chief executive officers. There would be a chief financial officer and human resources, information and technology, public affairs, and strategic affairs officers. Perhaps most important, the chief financial officer would chair a finance cabinet including the county auditor-controller and treasurer/tax collector. This would increase accountability and coordination of the county's fiscal management. The public affairs position was also an outgrowth of the bankruptcy experience. As noted in the restructuring plan, "As we learned in the days and months following the declaration of bankruptcy, the County currently has neither the structure nor the resources to provide accurate and timely information regarding the county, its responsibilities and its actions to the public or the media" (County of Orange, 1996a, p. 12). The strategic affairs official would focus on regional planning issues and intergovernmental relations. This position also is a response to the problems with political fragmentation between the county and city governments and special districts throughout the financial crisis. In addition, the county government would need more local cooperation in this era of tight budgets. New positions in human resources and information and technology point to the fact that the county executive office would have control over the typical kinds of government operations.

The other stage involves the elimination of two large departments. This decision was not directly related to the bankruptcy. It was part of an effort to reduce costs through staff layoffs as a way of coping with the frugal county budgets resulting from the debt payments. The General Services Agency and the Environmental Management Agency would be dissolved. The General Services Agency was described as having "inefficient splintering and duplication of staff support functions" (County of Orange, 1996b, p. 14). The agency's resources and responsibilities would be shifted to the county executive's office or to the individual departments, which would then handle their own administrative services. In reviewing the Environmental Management Agency, Mittermeier noted a large number of diverse functions and said, "I am unable to identify either synergies or cost savings associated with combining such diverse services" (County of Orange, 1996a, p. 13). In the place of this superagency, there would be two smaller departments: Planning and Development Services and Public Works. The latter was renamed Public Facilities and Resources, and Housing and Community Development was added as a third separate department when the business plan for the county government restructuring was approved in November 1996. The elimination of the two county departments was designed to achieve $11 million in cost savings with the loss of 241 jobs.

The next phase of county government restructuring will be a much more challenging task. The chief executive officer will seek to increase accountability and efficiency among the line departments with appointed heads, such as the Community Services Agency, Health Care Agency, and Social Services Agency. Many of their services are state mandated, so the county government will have less flexibility in cutting expenses beyond the cuts made after the financial crisis. This phase also touches on the departments that are managed by countywide elected officials, including the auditor-controller, treasurer, sheriff, and district attorney (County of Orange, 1996b). These department heads have had considerable autonomy in the past. Some have voter support and powerful local allies. There is likely to be resistance to the efforts of the chief executive officer to exercise greater control of their operations.

The third phase of the county government restructuring plan will be even more difficult. This would require having the county government enter into negotiations with other local governments concerning the delivery of local public services. A main goal is to develop more cost-effective arrangements for providing services to local residents. This could involve restructuring county and city responsibilities in unincorporated areas, as well as shifting some of the county services to the city governments. The county government would also take a lead role in seeking special district consolidations, such as for water districts and sanitation districts, to reduce administrative redundancies and overhead costs. The issue of seeking more cooperation in regional transportation planning, which is currently handled by several public agencies, would also be addressed (County of Orange, 1996b). The county government will face difficulties in these discussions. County officials will be meeting with cities and special districts that lost money in the county pool, and that recently forgave the county for about $850 million in debt. The county government is eager to begin these discussions as a way of shifting the costs of some county services. Local governments may not see this as being in their interest. The external restructuring efforts will face resistance by the many city officials and voters who favor localism over regional cooperation.

The chief executive officer has limited powers in implementing a plan for the county government restructuring. The CEO position was created by the Board of Supervisors, and it is not protected by a county charter. Thus, the position could be eliminated or redefined. One member of the Board of Supervisors has suggested that the title be changed to "chief operations officer" and that the powers be reduced accordingly. Other board members have called for the board to reassert itself and be more involved in making decisions (*Orange County Register,*

1996d). The members of the Board of Supervisors could decide, as they did before the bankruptcy, to consider themselves as "the plural CEO" as the crisis passes from memory and the public pressures for reform and structural change diminish. Without a county charter, the current approach to county government restructuring is highly vulnerable to internal political pressures.

To date, county government restructuring has largely focused on the chief executive officer bringing more financial accountability to county departments. This will help the county government avoid a repeat of the recent financial crisis. Small cost efficiencies have resulted from the restructuring, which will also help the county government in its efforts to live within its more modest means. The restructuring plan stated, "What the bankruptcy did was make us focus on the deficiencies of an outdated governance and service delivery system" (County of Orange, 1996b, p. 1). This system is still largely in place today. The internal restructuring is at a very early stage. It is much too soon to say whether or not the restructuring is working or is cost-efficient.

COUNCIL OF GOVERNMENTS

The financial crisis exposed the fragmentation of local governments. The thirty-one cities in Orange County were not a cohesive group. Moreover, they had a contentious relationship with the county government. One of the lessons learned from the bankruptcy was that local governments should have a mechanism for communicating their current efforts to each other and coordinating their plans for the future. This realization led to an effort to develop a council of governments in Orange County.

At the time of the bankruptcy, Orange County governments were voluntary members of the Southern California Association of Governments. This organization served as the council of governments and metropolitan planning organization for a six-county area with 16 million residents. Some Orange County officials were reluctant to support this organization because it included Los Angeles. It represented a regional government or "another layer of government bureaucracy." These were unpopular concepts with local voters. The Orange County Transportation Authority had wanted to take over the responsibility of being the metropolitan planning organization for Orange County, so that it could determine the use of federal transportation funds. Thus, it had a very strained relationship with the Southern California Association of Governments.

For several years city and county governments had talked about the possibility of establishing a council of governments in Orange County. This would be a voluntary organization that would give the local governments a forum for discussing regional planning issues. These talks had always ended in a stalemate. Many cities had a strong interest in this organization, but the county government appeared to be reluctant to join anything that would rival its current authority over regional planning and policy. The result was the formation of intergovernmental committees, councils, and working groups over the years. But there was no council of governments (Huston, 1995).

The financial crisis led to a renewal of discussions about the new kinds of local government structures that might be needed. In May 1995 a group of city managers met and recommended the establishment of a council of governments. Their reasoning was that the cities, county, and special districts needed a forum where they could meet regularly to exchange information and ideas and coordinate a broad range of regional activities. They wanted the local governments to remain in the Southern California Association of Governments but argued for the creation of a separate council of governments for Orange County. Another rationale was that the new organization would provide a strong and unified voice for representing Orange County's interests in the Southern California Association of Governments and the state legislature.

The recommendations of the city managers were developed into a proposal for a council of governments in the fall of 1995. The Orange County Division of the League of California Cities approved the proposal. This organization also took the lead role in promoting this concept to the county government, cities, and local special districts. The idea for a council of governments in Orange County gained sufficient support to become a reality in June 1996, which was the time that the county government emerged from bankruptcy. Twenty-nine of the thirty-one cities agreed to join the council of governments, as did the sanitation districts and the Orange County toll road agency.

The nonmembers included two of the largest cities, Anaheim and Garden Grove. A majority of the members of the Board of Supervisors did not support this effort, and the chief executive officer had decided not to take a position for or against the council of governments. So the county government did not join this organization. Two of the most significant single-purpose agencies, the Orange County Transportation Authority and the Orange County Water District, have also not joined.

The Orange County Transportation Authority still has as its overriding interest to become the sole metropolitan planning organization for the county. So this large and powerful regional transportation agency also did not join the new organization.

What the council of governments has done is to take over some regional planning functions. These include developing demographic data, performing regional housing needs assessments, and monitoring the air quality management plan. The council of governments would be a liaison between Orange County governments, the Southern California Association of Governments, and the South Coast Air Quality Management District. The ultimate goal was to develop a countywide consensus on issues so that Orange County could make recommendations and advocate them to the regional governments and the state legislature (County of Orange, 1996a; Huston, 1995). This would be a formidable task without the participation of the county government, two large cities, and the regional transportation and water agencies.

Orange County did take an important step in creating a council of governments after the bankruptcy. The purpose was to increase cooperation among local governments and communication with the regional agencies and state government. This effort can only be viewed as a limited success. Several of the major local governments refuse to participate. Even after the various governments had gone through a crisis together, localism and fragmentation continue to be stumbling blocks to regional cooperation.

TERM LIMITS AND TAX LIMITS

The November 1996 election would provide a test of voter attitudes after the financial crisis. The voters had rejected the county charter reforms in March. The county was officially out of bankruptcy in June. The chief executive officer was rearranging county government. Would voters still want to impose term limits on the supervisors? Given the tight local budgets, would they want to impose further limits on local taxes?

A measure to limit the terms of members of the Orange County Board of Supervisors to two consecutive four-year terms was on the countywide ballot. Seven cities had similar term limits measures for their city council members. On the state ballot there was a citizens' initiative to limit the ability of local governments to raise local taxes and fees without majority approval of the voters. This was Proposition 218, which had the effect of extending the Proposition 13 restrictions on raising local revenues.

TABLE 7-3   VOTE ON ORANGE COUNTY
MEASURE A: TERM LIMITS FOR
COUNTY SUPERVISORS

Yes	534,915	79.1%
No	141,148	20.9

61.9% voter turnout on November 5, 1996

SOURCE: Orange County Registrar of Voters (1996b).

Measure A, stipulating term limits for the Board of Supervisors, was overwhelmingly supported in surveys before the vote. Two weeks before the November election 75 percent said they would vote yes on Measure A. Eight in ten likely voters said they would support the measure. Seventy-two percent of the Democrats and 79 percent of the Republicans supported these term limits. This measure had been placed on the local ballot by the members of the Board of Supervisors, most of whom saw this as a way to meet public demands for restoring confidence in this office. Several of the board members had already announced that they would not seek reelection. The surveys before the charter election indicated a similar level of support for term limits.

The supervisors were still receiving few positive grades from the voters (see Appendix C, Table C-23). Only about one in nine voters said that the Board of Supervisors was doing an excellent or good job in providing overall leadership. Four in ten rated their overall leadership as poor. Only about one in eight gave the Board of Supervisors an excellent or good rating for representing the views of local residents. One in three said they did a poor job of representing local residents. Only about one in nine said the Board of Supervisors was doing an excellent or good job in managing the county budget. Half said they did a poor job in managing the county's budget. The supervisors, who had mediocre ratings before the financial crisis, had ratings that were even worse after the bankruptcy. This would increase support for term limits.

In the November 5, 1996, election, the measure requiring term limits for county supervisors won an overwhelming victory. Seventy-nine percent of the voters supported Measure A, while only 21 percent opposed it. More than 500,000 voters supported the term limits measure, and it won by nearly a 400,000-vote margin (Table 7-3). This was an election in which 62 percent of the registered voters participated. The high turnout provided assurances that this was a county government reform that was supported by most of the Orange County voters, and not only those who cast ballots in low-turnout elections.

In seven of the thirty-one Orange County cities, measures for term limits were on the November 1996 ballot.[1] These included Buena Park, Costa Mesa, Dana Point, La Palma, Laguna Niguel, Orange, and Yorba Linda. These cities were from the north and south parts of the county and varied considerably in population size, affluence, and ethnic and racial composition. One element common to all of these cities was that they had all voluntarily participated in the Orange County Investment Pool. Term limits overwhelmingly passed in all seven cities. The level of support ranged from about 69 percent to 83 percent. In all, 104,286 voted for term limits while 28,065 were opposed. The overall result was that 79 percent voted in favor of city term limits while 21 percent were opposed. The overwhelming support for term limits for the seven city councils matched the county vote for term limits for the Board of Supervisors (see Table 7-4).

Orange County voters also overwhelming approved Proposition 218 on the state ballot in November 1996. Sixty-two percent supported the tax-limiting measure, while 38 percent were opposed. Proposition 218 received approval by over 450,000 Orange County voters and won by nearly a 200,000-vote margin in this high-turnout election (see Table 7-5). This measure was supported by 56 percent of the California voters, while 44 percent were opposed. Orange County thus passed Proposition 218 by a wider margin than the rest of the state. This is typical for this fiscally conservative region.

The main purpose of Proposition 218 was to change the state laws so that voter approval would be needed for all new taxes and most new charges to property owners. Proposition 13 had restricted increases in local property taxes and required the voters' approval for special taxes and general taxes. However, there were other revenue sources such as assessments, utility user taxes, hotel taxes, and property-related fees that were not included. Proposition 218 thus extended the tax limitations on local governments by requiring voter approval in more instances (Legislative Analyst, 1996b). This proposition raises new fiscal concerns for cities, counties, and special districts. It would place severe constraints on their already limited abilities to raise new revenues.

---

1. There were two term limits measures on the Yorba Linda ballot. Measure S was for a three-term limit and Measure T for a two-term limit. Measure S received 69 percent of the vote to win over Measure T, which had 61 percent of the vote. Thus, we report the results of Measure S in Table 7-4.

TABLE 7-4   VOTES ON TERM LIMITS FOR CITY
COUNCIL MEMBERS IN ORANGE COUNTY

Buena Park, Measure E

Yes	12,759	81.2%
No	2,961	18.8

Costa Mesa, Measure F

Yes	20,804	79.5%
No	5,365	20.5

Dana Point, Measure H

Yes	10,163	83.1%
No	2,074	16.9

La Palma, Measure O

Yes	3,705	79.4%
No	962	20.6

Laguna Niguel, Measure N

Yes	15,358	77.8%
No	4,388	22.2

Orange, Measure R

Yes	27,731	82.1%
No	6,037	17.9

Yorba Linda, Measure S

Yes	13,766	68.7%
No	6,278	31.3

61.9% Orange County voter turnout on November 5, 1996

TABLE 7-5   ORANGE COUNTY'S VOTE ON
PROPOSITION 218: MAJORITY VOTE
FOR LOCAL TAXES

Yes	457,355	62.3%
No	276,294	37.7

61.9% voter turnout on November 5, 1996

SOURCE: Orange County Registrar of Voters (1996b).

Orange County voters seemed to like the package of local government reforms presented to them in the November 1996 election. Unlike the county charter, this was not an integrated effort toward local government restructuring. The term limits measures were proposed by county and city officials for the Orange County voters. Proposition 218 was a statewide initiative, and thus the impetus for reform was not from Orange County. Yet these ballot measures all change the way that local governments will operate. These measures were overwhelmingly approved. Orange County voters expressed their lack of confidence toward city and county officials by limiting their stay in office and their control over raising new revenues. If there were voter concerns about how local governments would cope with revenue restrictions, given the tight budgets after the bankruptcy, they were nowhere in evidence. Two years after the county pool collapse, the stage was again set for local officials to scramble for nontax revenues.

PUBLIC OPTIMISM AFTER THE BANKRUPTCY

Orange County residents had expressed fairly pessimistic attitudes about their county and its local leadership throughout the eighteen-month financial crisis. With the end of the bankruptcy in June 1996, a positive change in their perceptions of the county as a place to live offers evidence that Orange County had, at least in their minds, returned to normalcy after some turbulent times. However, public confidence in the local governments, and especially the county government, was not yet on the mend.

Orange County residents' evaluations of the county economy had improved dramatically now that the bankruptcy was behind them. These were the findings in the 1996 Orange County annual survey conducted in the late summer of 1996. It was the first clear sign that the doom and gloom surrounding the bankruptcy had lifted. Forty-four percent believed the Orange County economy was in excellent or good shape, while only 10 percent said it was in poor shape. The positive ratings had improved twenty-five points since the 1995 survey, while the negative ratings had declined by twenty points. In 1996 the perceptions of the county economy were at their highest point so far during the 1990s.

Ratings of the quality of life in Orange County had also increased sharply from a year earlier. Eighty-two percent said they believed that things were going well in terms of the quality of life in Orange County. Only 18 percent said that things were going badly. Compared with a year ago, there was a fourteen-point increase in the number who said the quality of life in the county was going well. The positive scores in 1996 were a significant improvement over the quality-of-life ratings at earlier times in the 1990s.

Optimism about Orange County housing as an investment also rebounded from a year earlier (see Appendix B, Table B-7). Six in ten homeowners said that buying a home was an excellent or good investment, and only 8 percent said that housing in the county is a poor investment. The number believing that an Orange County home was a favorable investment had increased by ten points since 1995, while the number who said it was a poor investment had dropped by ten points. Homeowners were now as optimistic about Orange County housing as they were before the financial crisis.[2]

Orange County residents also had a better outlook on their own finances than they had during the bankruptcy. Forty-six percent of county residents said they were financially better off than they were a year ago, while 21 percent felt they were worse off. The number with positive views was up eight points from 1995. Fifty percent expected to be financially better off the following year, while only 6 percent thought they would be worse off. This was a five-point improvement from a year earlier. Sixty-five percent reported that now was a good time for major purchases, while 18 percent saw it as a bad time to buy big consumer items. There was a six-point drop in the view that now was a bad time to make purchases (Baldassare and Katz, 1996).

Worries about the county government's fiscal crisis had faded into the background. When residents were asked to name the most important problem facing the county, crime was mentioned by 27 percent, immigration by 15 percent, schools by 13 percent, and jobs and the economy, growth, and traffic were each mentioned by 11 percent. Only 7 percent named the county's financial crisis as the top public policy issue facing Orange County; this was a nineteen-point decline from a year earlier. Crime was considered the top county problem among all income, race, and ethnic groups. The financial crisis was not the top issue for any demographic group.

2. Among renters, 45 percent called the local housing market an excellent or good investment, 34 percent said it is fair, and 17 percent called it poor. The number who consider buying a house in Orange County to be an excellent or good investment had risen four points, while the number who consider it a bad one was down eight points. Renters' confidence in the housing market is at about the level it was in 1994.

The public's ratings of local services showed no decline after the financial crisis. Most residents gave positive ratings to the local services they were receiving. In fact, some ratings had improved since the early 1990s. More than seven in ten ranked their police protection and parks and public recreation services as excellent or good, while about six in ten gave high rankings to public libraries and streets and roads. Fewer than one in ten rated any of these local public services as poor. Forty-two percent gave positive ratings to their local public schools, while 14 percent gave poor ratings (see Appendix B, Table B-8).

The positive ratings for police protection and public schools had actually improved since the early 1990s. The ratings of parks and public recreation, and streets and roads were unchanged; public libraries were not previously asked about. There was no evidence that lower-income residents and ethnic and racial minorities had especially negative ratings of local public services (Baldassare and Katz, 1996).[3]

However, it was also apparent that trust in county leaders had not rebounded after the crisis. Many residents continued to express little confidence in county government. One in four said the county government does an excellent or good job at solving problems in their community (see Appendix B, Table B-9). By comparison, four in ten gave their city governments positive grades for solving problems. The city governments had also received positive evaluations by four in ten residents in a 1991 survey. This indicates that the city's ratings were unchanged after the bankruptcy. Unfortunately, we did not ask the public for ratings of the county government in the 1991 survey.

Most residents did not see their county leaders as very responsive. Fewer than one in ten said the county government leaders pay "a lot" of attention to what the people think when they decide what policies to adopt. About half of the residents saw their county leaders as paying only some attention, while four in ten perceived them as paying very little or no attention to what the people think before they make county policies. The ratings had shown improvement since the Measure R sales tax vote in June 1995. At that time, 53 percent said that the county leaders paid very little or no attention to what the people think during the bankruptcy, compared with 38 percent in September 1996. Most of

---

3. Compared to the 1982 survey, however, the 1996 surveys indicate that the ratings of police protection and public schools were about the same and that ratings of parks and streets had declined (Baldassare and Katz, 1996).

this change was due to an increase in those saying that the county government paid "some" attention to the people's wishes before they make policies. In both surveys, few said that their county leaders paid a lot of attention to residents.

Local residents tended to view their city government leaders as more responsive than the county government. Fourteen percent said city leaders paid "a lot" of attention to what the people think before they make policy decisions. Fifty-three percent said they paid only some attention, and 30 percent said they paid little or no attention to what the people think. However, very few residents viewed either their county or their city government as highly responsive to local residents (Baldassare and Katz, 1996).

Even after the county government made severe budget cuts following the financial crisis and bankruptcy, many residents still described their county leaders as wasting taxpayer money. Four in ten said that those who run county government waste a lot of the money people pay in taxes. Almost half said that they waste some of the tax money they receive, while only about one in ten saw their county government leaders as wasting very little or no tax money. However, attitudes had improved somewhat since before the Measure R vote. In June 1995, 51 percent had said that the county government wastes "a lot" of tax money during the bankruptcy, compared with 39 percent in the post-bankruptcy survey. There was a small increase in those saying they waste only "some" money and a small increase in those saying they waste "very little" or "none." Still, many residents in both surveys perceived that the people who run county government waste a great deal of taxpayer money.

The perception of the city government with regard to fiscal issues was more favorable. Twenty-nine percent thought their city government leaders wasted a lot of taxpayer money, 44 percent thought they wasted some money, and 20 percent said they wasted very little or none of the money paid to them in taxes. However, many residents saw both units of local government as highly wasteful. Three in ten thought their city governments wasted a lot of money, and four in ten believed the county government did not spend taxpayer money wisely (Baldassare and Katz, 1996).

At last, the public's shock about the Orange County financial crisis seemed to have worn off by the fall of 1996. Their ratings of the economy, quality of life, public services, and their own finances were all good. There was a growing sense in the public that things were now

returning to normal. No doubt, the improvements in the state economy contributed to the return to optimism. Job growth, consumer
spending, and housing sales were increasing in the county at this time.
The residents were no longer naming the county's financial crisis as the
top public policy issue. They were back to focusing on concerns about
crime, immigration, traffic, schools, jobs, and growth.

The lingering effects of the bankruptcy are found in the ratings of
county government. Few are confident in the county government's ability to solve problems or believe that their county leaders pay a lot of attention to what the people think before they make decisions. Many still
think the county government wastes taxpayer money, even after the severe budget cuts. City government is viewed more favorably relative to
the county government. However, fewer than half of the residents give
their cities positive ratings for solving problems, and many report that
their city leaders are not highly responsive to residents and do not
spend taxpayer money wisely.

There is no evidence from the public opinion survey to suggest that
the less affluent have had a more difficult time after the bankruptcy.
This is not to say that the poor population and recent foreign immigrants have not been affected by the budget cuts in county health and
social services. Certainly, there have been layoffs and program reductions that affect the poor. However, such groups are often hard to reach
in public opinion surveys of the general public. Large-scale surveys of
the poor population may very well find that the bankruptcy has had
longer-lasting effects on their lives.

SUMMARY

This chapter examined the local government reforms that have occurred as a result of the Orange County financial crisis. Many people
had said that the investment pool losses pointed to the need for structural changes, and the fiscal constraints of the financial recovery plan
would require a new era of local government cooperation. To what extent have things changed now that the bankruptcy is over?

The most dramatic changes have taken place in the county treasurer's office. The state legislature took away most of the flexibility it
had given to these local officials after Proposition 13. There are strict
limits on leveraging, and many of the risky securities are once again
outlawed. There is also more oversight of the treasurer's activities and
new requirements for reporting on investment activities. The abuses in

Orange County have changed the nature of local government investing throughout the state. However, the state legislature did not seek to reform the fiscal policies that led many of the local governments into more risky investments that paid higher yields. There was no effort to return the property tax money that the state had taken from the counties, cities, and special districts since the early 1990s. Nor has the state government found new revenues to replace the loss of interest income as a result of the new rules.

Outside the county treasurer's office, there have been only small changes in the politically fragmented structure of local government. The county government is in the first stage of a restructuring effort. A number of assistants have been added to the county executive office, with the largest impact of this change being increased financial accountability. A number of county departments have been eliminated, mostly in an effort to reduce costs to cope with a smaller budget. The next stages will involve the departments that are managed by elected officials, where changes may be much more difficult to implement. The other local governments have formed a council of governments. A major limitation of this regional effort is that the county government and the regional transportation agency are not members of this voluntary association.

The public's attitudes about reforms are shaped by their distrust of government and their local orientation. Citizens overwhelmingly defeated a county charter that would have restructured county government. It was endorsed by the Board of Supervisors and would have increased their powers. Later, residents voted to extend Proposition 13 and to limit the terms of the supervisors. Their desire for government reforms that restrict tax increases and limit the powers of elected officials is unshaken by the bankruptcy.

The public's mood after the county government emerged from bankruptcy showed a remarkable recovery from the doom and gloom of the previous eighteen months. The only remnant of the financial crisis was a lack of confidence in the county government. However, the growing satisfaction with life in Orange County will make it difficult to maintain the momentum for change. The resistance to regional cooperation by local officials also raises doubts about the future of local government reforms.

CHAPTER 8

Lessons Learned from the Bankruptcy

The biggest municipal bankruptcy in U.S. history is now over. There remain some nagging questions about what we can learn from Orange County's mistakes. Can it happen again in another big city or suburban region? Why did the financial crisis occur in Orange County rather than somewhere else? Can we identify the conditions of a financial disaster in the making that will help us to avoid future problems? Or are we powerless to prevent an official with poor judgment, such as County Treasurer Bob Citron, from causing big trouble at any time and any place? A main purpose of this chapter is to inform policymakers and scholars about the lessons to be learned from Orange County in order to limit the chances of repeating this fiscal crisis.

I will first examine the reasons for the relevancy of Orange County, and then I will determine the reasons the financial crisis occurred in Orange County at a certain time. Following that, I will make some judgments about the parties that are most responsible for this fiscal crisis and its resolution. Then I will examine the possibility of similar financial problems taking place elsewhere and the likelihood that an event like the Orange County bankruptcy can be prevented in the future.

ORANGE COUNTY IS RELEVANT

When the surprising losses in the Orange County Investment Pool were discovered in December 1994, many seemed to think that this strange event could only occur in this unusual suburban county. Since Orange County emerged from bankruptcy in June 1996, there has been a tendency to think that this kind of financial disaster will never happen again. However, I have provided empirical evidence that Orange County is not a peculiar place. This county has much in common with the suburban regions where most Americans live and work. I have also demonstrated that the defining characteristics of the Orange County bankruptcy were political fragmentation, voter distrust, and state fiscal austerity. There is every reason to believe that these three conditions are present in many locales. Orange County happened to have these necessary conditions in large quantities before the problem surfaced in 1994. For this reason, I conclude that its severe financial problem could be repeated elsewhere.

Others have agreed that the Orange County bankruptcy has relevance to the future. An official from Moody's Investors Service, David Brodsly, placed this episode in perspective, saying, "This has been a huge event: It is really huge. It's the kind of thing like New York's default. . . . It will form the market and market practices for the rest of time as we know it" (California Debt Advisory Commission, 1995, p. 24). An event of this magnitude can offer policymakers and scholars the opportunity to learn from the mistakes, and the recovery from disaster, that occurred in Orange County. It is thus important to summarize what has been learned from this financial crisis so that other municipalities can avoid the problems experienced by Orange County.

The Orange County financial crisis is most applicable to three types of bodies that today include a large number of local governments. They are the large central cities, suburban metropolitan regions, and California counties. The fact that many large central cities are struggling with fiscal strain, as their tax base has eroded and their expenditures for health and welfare have grown, has been studied by many urban experts. However, no large municipality had ever used the option of bankruptcy. Thus, the experiences in Orange County offer some valuable insights.

The Orange County financial crisis is also the first major episode of fiscal strain in a suburban region. This event sends a warning to other suburban governments that they are not immune to such problems. It provides them with an opportunity to compare their current conditions to what was found in Orange County.

Finally, all of the counties throughout California face similar fiscal circumstances because of Proposition 13. As their property tax revenues have declined, they have become more dependent on state funding for providing county services. In the 1990s the state government's fiscal austerity has meant that all of the counties have also had to find new sources of revenue to replace the property tax funds that the state took back. Orange County's troubled investments can be partly blamed on county government's efforts to overcome the loss of state funds. This episode also provides an example of how the state government will respond when a county government is in serious fiscal trouble and faces its own budgetary problems. The Orange County bankruptcy crisis thus sheds new light on state and local government relations.

MAJOR FACTORS AT WORK

A municipal bankruptcy in Orange County was unexpected for many reasons. Fiscal crises had occurred in large central cities, but they had never been observed in suburban regions. Orange County was supposed to be a wealthy suburb, and the predominance of affluent residents was supposed to shield its county government from problems with revenues, spending, and debts. This county was also known for having Republican officials who were elected by conservative voters, and this political combination should have resulted in tight fiscal management. Nevertheless, a fiscal problem of immense proportions emerged in Orange County. At the end of 1994 the county government became the largest municipal bankruptcy in U.S. history.

The discussion about why the fiscal crisis took place in Orange County should begin with the county treasurer. In fact, previous speculation about why the financial meltdown occurred in Orange County has focused almost entirely on Bob Citron. This long-time county treasurer had earned a state and national reputation as the guru of local government investing. The county pool he managed had achieved higher yields for local governments than any other. The interest earnings had lured most of the local governments in Orange County, and even some public agencies from afar, into the investment pool he managed. His strategy of leveraging funds to borrow risky and long-term securities had succeeded during the 1980s and early 1990s. He then made a series of large, wrong-way bets on interest rates that led Orange County into financial disaster in 1994. Citron was forced to resign in disgrace by the same county officials who had recently supported his reelection and praised his financial performance. It is hard to imagine how financial problems of such an immense magnitude could take place without Bob Citron. The media's portrayal of the county treasurer as a soft-spoken loner who wore turquoise jewelry and consulted psychics about the county's investment decisions has certainly added to his image as the gambling man who brought down Orange County. However, his personality alone does not fully tell us why Orange County went bankrupt. There were factors in Orange County and in California that explain how the excesses of Bob Citron could go unnoticed and why so many of his actions were tolerated, legally allowed, and even encouraged.

Any analysis of why the financial crisis occurred in Orange County should also consider the Wall Street firms that lent money to the county government. The county treasurer was able to borrow $14 billion through reverse repurchase agreements for the purpose of buying risky securities to invest in the county pool. It was the fact that these loans could not be paid back in a timely fashion that ultimately led to the bankruptcy. Up until this point, borrowing large sums of money was easy for Orange County. The county government was considered a safe bet and, moreover, a very attractive client from the lenders' perspective. Credit rating agencies gave it one of the highest bond ratings of any county government. In fact, a county bond offering in mid-1994 received one of the highest ratings in the state, even as the investment pool was rapidly deteriorating. They perceived the residents as wealthy and did not see any evidence that a middle-class migration would result in a loss of tax revenues. The taxes, spending, and debt outlined in the county budget also seemed to be in order. The county government appeared to be managed by Republicans and conservatives who had a high regard for careful fiscal management. The kinds of attributes outlined here are generally what large investors prefer. They are also what differentiate suburban regions from the New York model of fiscal crisis. The fact that Orange County had a healthier credit rating than most large municipalities has to be viewed as an important reason why this kind of financial crisis could take place. Not every municipality could borrow the large sums of money that were needed to get into the amount of financial trouble faced by Orange County. What is important is that the fiscal problems of Orange County were hidden, and perhaps to some extent concealed, and they went unnoticed for some time by highly sophisticated financiers. The Wall Street investment firms also failed to recognize that there are other financial risks involved in lending to suburban regions, as well as to large municipalities in California today. As a result, most of the nation's municipal investment experts had overestimated the county government's ability and the voters' willingness to pay the debts.

I have taken the position that Bob Citron and the Wall Street investors that lent him money were not the sole causes of the Orange County financial crisis. Bob Citron was the catalyst for this event. The bankruptcy was made possible by the political, organizational, and fiscal context in which these actors were operating during the 1990s— specifically, the political fragmentation of local government, voter distrust of local government officials, and fiscal austerity in the state government. The Orange County financial crisis took place because all three of these factors were present in large degree in Orange County in 1994. However, although these are the necessary conditions, they are not sufficient in themselves. Bob Citron did the damage.

Political fragmentation refers to the structure of local government in this suburban metropolitan region. The area is characterized by numerous local governments and no central political authority within the suburban county. The government entities typically have overlapping geographic boundaries and a duplication of service responsibilities. There is no one local public entity that coordinates all of these different local government activities. The decentralization of political power results in each local government setting its own course for fiscal policies, land use, and the provision of public services and local programs. At times, these local governments compete with one another for new residents and businesses and the tax dollars they can bring to their localities. The end result of this political fragmentation is a local government with a structure that emphasizes local policies and is lacking in regional cooperation.

The evidence presented in this book indicates that Orange County prior to the bankruptcy had layers upon layers of political fragmentation. The county government itself was politically fragmented in several ways. There were five supervisors elected by district to reflect the wishes of their local residents and not the county. There was no mayor representing all of the county's voters. The county departments did not report to a chief executive officer with direct authority over their actions. Several of the departments were headed by countywide elected officials, such as the county treasurer, who could operate in a fairly autonomous fashion. Outside of the county government, there was the traditional form of suburban political fragmentation. There were thirty-one municipal governments, several single-purpose regional agencies, about two dozen local school districts, and many local special districts. The efforts of the county, cities, school districts, and special districts were not coordinated. Moreover, there was a long history of distrust toward the county leaders by other local governments. The relations took a turn for the worse when the investment pool suffered losses and the county froze the funds that were on deposit from the cities, schools, and special districts.

The lack of a central authority within county government is a major reason for the Orange County financial crisis. There was a lack of oversight of the county treasurer by the other county officials. The lines of authority were fuzzy, and the countywide-elected treasurer was not really accountable to either the Board of Supervisors or the county administrative officer. Since the other county officials could not keep track of what the treasurer was doing, they did not have up-to-date information on the county's finances. They were also not in a position to dictate the treasurer's investment decisions. In the meantime, the cities, schools, and special districts invested their funds in the county pool with a single focus on what the investments would mean to their own localities. Their political fragmentation was so deep that they did not consult with each other about their decisions to invest their locality's funds in the county pool. Had the local leaders been in communication with one another about their similar county investment pool decisions, they may have noticed that they were all being made the same promises by the county treasurer of safety, liquidity, and high yield. It would have been evident that the individual promises could not all be kept, given the number of local governments that were in the pool.

The political fragmentation also explains the ways in which Orange County's government chose to respond to the fiscal emergency. The Board of Supervisors created the position of chief executive officer and a crisis management team of three agency heads to assist a county government that, at the time, lacked a central authority or any internal cohesion. It also explains why the Orange County business leaders had to be called upon to mediate the financial disputes among local governments, and between the local officials and the county officials. There was a basic lack of trust and no open lines of communication between the local public entities.

After the bankruptcy, the plan for fiscal recovery was dictated by the limits of political fragmentation. The local governments could only agree on a plan to divert county tax funds that were supposed to pay for regional infrastructure. The future funding for local public services provided by local special districts, schools, and cities would be spared. The local governments were paid back most of the funds they had invested in the county pool. The cities, schools, and special districts would receive the rest of their money if the county government won its lawsuits against the investment firms.

The resilience of the political fragmentation is seen in the local government reforms that were a product of the bankruptcy. The main focus of the reforms in county government was to increase oversight of the county treasurer and prohibit risky investments in the county pool. A chief executive officer was appointed by the Board of Supervisors and thus far has focused on improving fiscal accounting within county government. Otherwise, there has been little in the way of county government restructuring. Most of the cities joined a council of governments to improve their communication. However, the county government and regional transportation agency are not part of this effort. The relations between the local governments and county government are still strained.

Voter distrust is also a dominant feature that helps to explain why a specific kind of financial crisis took place in Orange County. Many middle-class voters have become distrustful of their elected officials and lack confidence in the way they handle the taxpayers' money. As a result, they are reluctant to raise their taxes except in special circumstances. For instance, they might have supported a tax increase for a specific public service that they perceived as deficient, such as transportation, if the tax funds were earmarked specifically for that service. These voters also do not want government to interfere with personal decisions. Thus, their profile tends to be one of fiscal conservatism and liberalism on social issues. These political attitudes are common in the suburbs and are found among a large cross-section of Democrats, Republicans, and independents. These fiscally conservative voters have elected "New Fiscal Populist" leaders who are charged with representing their constituents' wishes on tax and spending issues. In order to please their supporters, the elected officials need to maintain or decrease local taxes, but not at the cost of cutting local programs. At the same time, the voters want their elected officials to maintain or increase the public services provided to middle-class residents like themselves. The only area of local government spending that they favor reducing are welfare programs and the local public services designed for the poor. Ideally, these middle-class voters want their elected officials to produce the same or a higher level of middle-class service with a reduction in taxes.

One of the main reasons the fiscal crisis occurred in Orange County is that the elected leaders were under intense pressure from voters to find new revenues so that they could maintain or increase services without raising taxes. They endorsed the county treasurer's schemes to increase interest income through the county pool because it offered them a new source of revenue that was not from taxes. When the state took back some of the county's property tax funds, these officials went along with the county treasurer's idea to increase the risk level in the county pool in order to earn even more interest income. The alternative would be to cut services or ask the voters for a tax increase to maintain current service levels. These were unacceptable political risks in this fiscally conservative county. Other local government officials, such as the city and special district leaders, faced similar fiscal and political pressures. They also gave their funds to the county treasurer in the hopes of raising their revenues.

This political climate also explains the responses to the fiscal emergency. From the moment the bankruptcy was announced, the voters were more likely to express anger at their elected officials than fear toward the loss of county funds. Many Orange County residents simply did not believe that the fiscal problem was that serious since it was not felt from their perspective. Many thought that the problem could be solved by cutting waste in government, which they perceived as plentiful, and thus there would be no need to raise taxes or reduce county services. The New Fiscal Populist leaders at the county and city levels were reluctant to suggest a tax increase to pay off the debts.

Fiscal conservatism also guided the recovery plan for the bankruptcy. The voters overwhelmingly rejected a tax increase. Many local elected officials, including members of the Board of Supervisors, went along with the voters and opposed the tax measure. The county leaders also focused spending cuts on government operations and programs for the poor. These were moves that were designed to please the middle-class voters. County tax funds were diverted from long-term projects for the regional infrastructure in the hopes that no one would notice their absence. Local services were maintained at current levels for the middle-class taxpayers, many of whom scarcely noticed that a bankruptcy had taken place. Also, a nontax revenue source is now being sought as a way to pay back the county, cities, schools, and special districts for their losses in the county pool. There are lawsuits pending that seek billions of dollars from the investment firms that did business with the county. This revenue effort should please the fiscal conservatives, although the lawsuits will cost millions of dollars to pursue.

The local government reforms that have been supported after the Orange County bankruptcy also derive from the environment of voter distrust. The voters rejected a county charter largely because it would have strengthened the powers of the Board of Supervisors and denied them the power to elect the county treasurer. They may have approved a different charter that strengthened the chief executive officer and limited the authority of the Board of Supervisors. For now, the voters apparently want the power to elect county officials such as Bob Citron, even if they did made a mistake. An alternative explanation is that they expect even worse choices from their county leaders. Voters also overwhelmingly approved term limits for members of the Board of Supervisors. In seven cities term limits passed by a wide margin. The voters also strongly approved a state ballot measure, Proposition 218, requiring that the voters be asked for permission to raise local taxes and fees that were not covered by Proposition 13. Thus, Orange County voters did achieve some reforms after the crisis. Whether or not these changes will reduce the level of voter distrust is not yet known.

The third factor that is important to consider is the presence of state fiscal austerity. The phenomenal growth of suburban regions from the 1950s to the 1970s was highly dependent on generous funding from the federal and state governments. The federal government has been faced with large budget deficits since the 1980s, when expenses rose dramatically and taxes were sharply reduced, and it has been turning over financial responsibilities to the states and local governments. In 1978 Proposition 13 passed in California, and that has affected the ways in which the local governments have become dependent on state funding. Proposition 13 drastically reduced local revenues from property taxes and restricted the abilities of local governments to raise new taxes. For most of the 1980s the California economy was good and the state government provided funds for the cities and county governments to make up for the property tax dollars they lost. In the early 1990s the state government was faced with a high deficit. There were high costs associated with foreign immigration and declining revenues because of job losses during a serious recession. Fiscal austerity forced the state officials to withhold billions of dollars that they had previously given to counties, cities, and special districts. This state action placed local governments in difficulty, since their options were to cut local spending and services or find new revenue sources. Most could not expect their voters to support new taxes or accept the fact that their services would have to be reduced.

Orange County is a suburban region that experienced the impacts of state fiscal austerity. After Proposition 13 the state government's formula for allocating property tax relief provided less support for Orange County on a per capita basis compared with other large counties, such as Los Angeles and Alameda. In the early 1990s the state government took away some of the property tax revenues that had been allocated for the county government, as they did elsewhere in California. The cities, local special districts, and county government all had their state funding allocations reduced.

At the time state funding was shifting, there were demographic and economic changes under way in Orange County that called for increased spending. The population grew rapidly in the 1980s, largely a result of a dramatic increase in foreign immigrants. By 1992 Orange County had among the highest numbers of Asian and Hispanic residents and a large poor population. After a decade of strong job growth, Orange County had fallen into a serious economic recession in the early 1990s. These trends resulted in the need for more revenues to pay for services at just the time that the state government was reducing its financial support to county governments.

It is clear that state fiscal austerity is a factor in why the fiscal crisis occurred in Orange County. The county government was forced to look for alternatives to state funding after the early 1980s. It was receiving a smaller per capita share of the state's distribution of property taxes compared with other large counties. It was at this time that Bob Citron began to dabble in leveraging and exotic securities as a means to increase interest income in the county investment pool. The state government encouraged these kinds of activities by loosening the restrictions on investments and reporting by the local treasurers. This is perhaps because state government officials knew they could not provide the tax revenues that local governments would need for all of their services. When the state government took back the county's funds in the early 1990s, the county government responded by seeking more interest income from risky investments in the county pool. Cities and local special districts in Orange County followed the same fiscal strategy to overcome their loss of funding from the state. Their elected officials turned to investing extra funds in the county pool.

The fiscal austerity also resulted in a new precedent for state governments when it came to responding to Orange County's fiscal emergency. The state government did not intervene in the credit markets, as was the case when other large municipalities, such as New York or Cleveland, faced serious debt problems. The county government instead was allowed to go bankrupt. The state had serious budget problems itself, and any form of a financial bailout was ruled out. The role of the state government in the early days of this municipal fiscal disaster was limited to offering financial expertise, such as arranging for a former state treasurer to take charge of the county pool and sending the state auditor to assess the damages that had been done. The state legislature threatened a state takeover however; it also kept at a safe distance from this local government fiscal crisis.

Fiscal austerity also had an impact on the plan for fiscal recovery that was implemented in Orange County. The state government did not lend any money to this bankrupt county government or to any of the local governments that had lost money in the county pool. It did not guarantee loans for the county to reorganize its finances, as was the case when other large municipalities in recent years had faced similar debt problems. The state government passed the legislation that was needed to allow the county government to divert county taxes for bonds that would pay off the outstanding debts. Although there was a threat of the state government stepping in if the local governments failed to develop a plan, the state was clearly reluctant to get involved in providing the funding or credit that was needed.

Local government reforms were also constrained by the fiscal conditions of state government. The state officials tightened the rules that governed investments and reporting by local treasurers.[1] They turned back the clock to the days before Proposition 13 and took away the chance for local governments to make additional interest income to replace the property taxes they lost. It is important to note that the state government steered away from any efforts to reform the system of local and state government finance that had contributed to the Orange County financial crisis and made it more difficult to resolve. They did not give back the property tax funds they took from local governments before the recession began, even though the state's recession was over. The state government did not resolve the issue of how the counties would be able to raise new revenues. The state government, perhaps reflecting its weakened financial condition, also avoided discussions about the realignment of state and county government programs or paying more for the state-mandated services offered by the counties.

1. These changes were enacted in state bills SB 866 and SB 564. See Table 7-1.

WHO IS RESPONSIBLE?

There has been a lot of public posturing about who is responsible for the Orange County fiscal disaster almost from the beginning of the crisis. Bob Citron blamed Merrill Lynch and later turned on his former assistant treasurer. The Board of Supervisors blamed Bob Citron and other high-level county officials. State legislators blamed the Board of Supervisors for not supervising. The local officials blamed the county officials. These accusations were often blatantly self-serving. They were from people trying to deflect public criticism, save their political careers, avoid legal sanctions, or win lawsuits. The assignment of responsibility can be an important step in learning why the bankruptcy took place and how it was resolved. With that goal in mind, we look at the evidence collected in this book on the roles that various actors played in this event.

Bob Citron is certainly responsible for the financial collapse of the Orange County Investment Pool. There are many signs of hubris in his annual reports that were submitted to the Board of Supervisors in the 1990s. He bragged about "perfecting the reverse repo procedure to new levels" and earning more than the state treasurer. He took high risks with public funds, presumably to benefit his political career and public standing, that went way beyond the intentions of the state law. His lack of openness with elected officials and the press was inexcusable for a public official. Citron lured many local officials into the county fund with an irresistible sales pitch that was dishonest. That is, he assured them safety and liquidity of funds and a high yield. In 1994 a stubborn reliance on an investment strategy that was no longer working led to bigger bets and huge losses in the county pool. Citron's actions typify the "woodenheadedness" that government officials have shown in times of tragic failure (Tuchman, 1984).

The members of the Orange County Board of Supervisors also showed a lack of respect for the public offices they held. They were willing to accept vague annual reports from the county treasurer about his investment activities. They praised Citron for helping the county budget with extra interest income without asking how he got the money. They became defensive when there were criticisms of the county treasurer during a heated campaign instead of investigating these allegations. When the county fund collapsed, they pleaded ignorance about derivatives and reverse repurchase agreements, as if this were an excuse for why they approved the borrowing that fueled the risky investment policy. During the crisis the Board of Supervisors did place others in charge who were able to maintain order in county government. They also attempted to deflect public criticism by having the newly appointed chief executive officer take the heat on the controversial issues of budget cuts and layoffs. Some of them avoided unpopular stands, such as supporting a tax increase, to extend their political careers. The chair of the Board of Supervisors announced his resignation even while the county government struggled to develop a recovery plan. The Board of Supervisors failed the public on three accounts: proper oversight of county affairs, leadership during the crisis, and willingness to take responsibility for their collective mistakes.

Other county officials also failed in their duties to monitor and report the activities in the county treasurer's office. The auditor-controller and the county administrative officer were in positions that should have given them keen knowledge of the county treasurer's operations. The budget director and assistant treasurer have also pleaded ignorance to the details. The fact that Bob Citron did not share all of the information about the county pool was irrelevant, since the interest earnings alone should have been enough of a red flag for these budget experts. They may have lacked the powers to control the county treasurer, but they could have made a stronger demand to the Board of Supervisors, or to the public or media, to investigate his practices.[2] For these officials, steering clear of Citron's risks was the way to play it safe in a county structure that had become addicted to high interest earnings from the county pool.

The investment brokers and financial advisers who worked with the county seemed to have overlooked the fact that their client was a public agency. Merrill Lynch had issued warnings to Citron about the risky nature of his investment strategy and even offered to buy back some of the securities he had purchased. Later they sold him more risky securities when market conditions were even worse. The outside auditor, KPMG Peat Marwick, led the county officials to believe that their finances were sound. The firms that prepared the statements for the county's bond offerings did not mention the fact that the county pool was a high-risk investment. Standard & Poor's gave a high credit rating to the county government's debts only months before the bankruptcy. While some did issue warnings, the private firms seemed intent

---

2. The reforms to the Orange County treasurer's office are outlined in Chapter 7.

on keeping the county officials they worked with happy while making their commissions. The companies that did business with the county government forgot to put the public before their profits.

The local elected officials in cities, schools, and special districts claimed that they were the innocent victims of the Orange County bankruptcy. To some extent this was true, since they were misinformed by the county treasurer. But there were also actions that showed irresponsibility by these public servants. The cities and special districts voluntarily placed their public funds into the county pool. Some of the school districts, which were required to deposit excess funds, went out and borrowed money to invest in the pool. These local elected officials did not ask probing questions when they became willing participants in the county treasurer's scheme to earn higher yields. No one was asking how the money was made; these officials only wanted to know how much was being made. It does not seem sufficient for the public officials to say that they trusted the county treasurer. If they were following the rules of prudent investing for taxpayer money, they should have been requiring proof on a regular basis that their funds were safe and could be withdrawn. These were politicians drawn to a revenue source that they saw as a quick fix for fiscal problems. During the fiscal emergency, local officials focused on having their funds returned and showed little commitment to solving countywide problems. To their credit, though, they did forgive the county government of debts and they agreed to wait for lawsuits to be paid in full, which was a key ingredient to ending the bankruptcy.

State officials also need to be held accountable for the financial crisis and the ways in which it was resolved. In the early 1990s the governor and state legislature took back some of the property tax revenues that had gone to counties, cities, and special districts. Then they turned their backs on Orange County, Los Angeles County, and other local governments that ran into financial trouble. The Orange County bankruptcy represented a new low for state involvement in the fiscal rescue of an ailing large municipality. The governor watched intently and dispatched experts to the scene, but he did not offer financial assistance or assurances to shaken residents. State legislative leaders seemed mostly intent on using the financial crisis as an opportunity for political gamesmanship and getting back at Orange County legislators for past partisan battles. The state legislature did, at least, have leaders who saw their way to pass the laws that allowed Orange County to borrow its way out of the bankruptcy. Even here, though, the recovery package was held up by partisan bickering over a Los Angeles rescue plan. This was not the finest hour for state leaders, and perhaps it reveals what can be expected when state fiscal austerity leads to such indifference toward local government crises.

The Orange County news media failed to carry out their duties as the "fourth estate" in the months before the bankruptcy. John Moorlach had made very serious allegations about the investment strategies of Bob Citron during the campaign for county treasurer in the spring of 1994. He had claimed that the county fund was being managed in a fashion that was far too risky for government agencies. Later he said that the county fund had a paper loss of over a billion dollars. The county treasurer denied these charges and pointed to past performance as an indicator of his professional expertise. The *Los Angeles Times* Orange County edition, the *Orange County Register,* and the *Orange County Business Journal* were all aware of these allegations. They all prided themselves in offering comprehensive coverage of Orange County issues. They each had reporters on staff who covered business and finance issues, such as derivatives and reverse repurchase agreements. They each had sources in the Wall Street investment firms and county government. Yet not one of them systematically examined Moorlach's claims to see if they were merely election rhetoric or based on facts. Their defense was that Moorlach's claims were too complicated for their readers to comprehend or fell between the cracks between the business and government news desks. Later in the year the media would have to explain the meaning of municipal bankruptcy. If an objective local source, such as any one of these news organizations, had brought Bob Citron's practices into daylight in early 1994, there may never have been a fiscal meltdown in December. These local news organizations did not live up to their role as watchdog for the public.[3]

The Orange County voters, who expressed so much anger at their county leaders for letting them down, cannot themselves escape blame for the financial disaster. They voted for the county treasurer who gambled with the taxpayer's funds. They elected the members of the Board of Supervisors who failed to provide oversight and showed themselves lacking in leadership during the fiscal crisis. They presented their local elected officials in the county government, cities, schools, and special

---

3. Paterno (1995) provides a critique of the media's coverage of the Orange County treasurer's race.

districts with the impossible task of providing more and better services with no new taxes. They did, in fact, pressure their local officials into providing them with "something for nothing" and ended up with a fiscal strategy that relied on interest income from risky investments. The local voters also showed a great indifference to the people who ran their county government and the necessary functions that it performed for local residents. Moreover, after the bankruptcy, the local voters showed no interest in reforming county government other than by imposing term limits and tax limits. Ultimately, a local focus coupled with a public apathy toward regional governance led to a dysfunctional county government that was described by an insider as "an accident waiting to happen."

As mentioned in earlier chapters, the Orange County business community played an important role at critical junctures during the financial crisis. The team of three business leaders was critical in facilitating the negotiations between the local government investors and the county government that led to the investment pool settlement. The Orange County Business Council sent its leaders to hammer out the details of a recovery plan that could be agreed upon by the county government, cities, schools, and special districts. Still, compared to the potential for leadership before and after the crisis, the activities of the business community were very limited in scope. Several of the business leaders said there were rumors on Wall Street about the Orange County Investment Pool in early 1994. No one called the county government to ask if there was a problem. Later on, John Moorlach made comments about the amount of interest being earned from the county pool. This should have raised concerns among the savvy investors in Orange County. No one in the business community demanded a full investigation of the county treasurer. During the bankruptcy, the Orange County Business Council submitted proposals for local government reforms. However, the business community was remarkably quiet on the issue of the county charter, and soon after that business leaders dropped their calls for the need for local government restructuring. In sum, business leaders deserve praise for responding to the fiscal emergency, but their actions also show that they lack a sustained commitment to ensuring good government.

There are many others who can claim responsibility for making a positive contribution to the Orange County financial crisis. These are the people who acted in ways that minimized the crisis, speeded the recovery, and initiated much-needed local government reforms. Orange County Sheriff Brad Gates took the lead role in making sure that county agencies had the funds they needed to serve the residents. Orange County District Attorney Mike Capizzi went after the county officials for their alleged criminal and civil misdeeds without regard to the implications for his own political career. Chief executive officer Bill Popejoy took on the task of being the point person in the crisis, without pay, and steered the county into its new fiscal reality. Former State Treasurer Tom Hayes restored calm both inside and outside county government when he sold off the risky assets and stabilized the sinking county pool during the weeks after the bankruptcy. The attorneys for the county government and the local government investors, Bruce Bennett and Patrick Shea, worked together to make sure that their clients did not engage in lengthy and costly litigation that would be harmful to local residents. Then there were the skilled financial advisers, such as Chris Varelas, who came up with ideas for ways to fund the bankruptcy recovery without money from the voters or the state. County Treasurer John Moorlach brought back a sensible investment strategy and a reasonable approach to public queries to an office that was in disgrace. Donald Saltarelli answered the call of duty from Governor Wilson and took on the thankless task of acting supervisor when the chair of the board resigned. There was the team of business leaders and consultants who worked closely with Gary Hunt, George Argyros, and Tom Sutton for weeks to make sure that the county government and local governments would reach agreement on a pool settlement. There were also the armies of local volunteers who provided advice on public finance and government restructuring. Orange County was, through their efforts, able to fill the void when government failed.

HOW MANY MORE ORANGE COUNTIES?

After the New York fiscal crisis, Terry Clark (1976) published a paper titled "How Many More New York's?" In the late 1970s there was great concern that the serious financial distress that had occurred in New York could befall other American cities. A similar question should be asked about the likelihood of replicating the Orange County bankruptcy. It is important to know if this new kind of fiscal disaster could happen again. As mentioned earlier, some view the Orange County bankruptcy as an unusual event that could not be repeated elsewhere. I will present some of the reasons why there may be more "Orange Counties" in the future.

First, Orange County is not the only local government that has been involved in a risky investment strategy to raise income. Moody's Investors Service conducted a study in December 1994 and found that fourteen counties in California had been using leveraging or derivatives. They singled out six counties that had engaged in significantly riskier uses of these investment vehicles. These were Monterey, Placer, San Bernardino, San Diego, Solano, and Sonoma counties. The county government in San Diego perhaps came closest to replicating the problems in Orange County. Their $3.3 billion had lost 11 percent of its value in December 1994. They informed their investors that they would share in the losses if they withdrew funds, and they were thus able to avoid the more serious crisis that took place in Orange County (*New York Times,* 1994a, 1994c). A national survey of 1,450 local governments by Moody's concluded that Orange County stood out in the amount of money at risk in December 1994. But there were plenty of instances in 1994 of local governments having paper and real losses from investing in risky securities. Cuyahoga County, Ohio, had to absorb the losses of other local government investors and cut its budget by $11 million. A Texas state investment fund faced $70 million in losses because of declining values of derivatives. Financial problems were also noted in small towns in Maine and Minnesota and colleges in Chicago and Texas (*New York Times,* 1994d).

The concerns about local governments losing money through risky investments seem to have subsided since Orange County declared bankruptcy in December 1994. However, this is because interest rates have been stable or slightly declining in recent years. When the Federal Reserve Board again raises interest rates significantly, then, it is likely that a number of local governments throughout the United States could be exposed to significant losses. We could once again hear about investment losses that result in budget cuts for local governments.

New legislation in California has restricted local treasurers from taking the kinds of risks that led to the fiscal collapse in Orange County. However, the use of leveraging and derivatives are still allowed in some other states. One also cannot assume that that laws governing investments in California are permanent. The state government changed course on local government investing in the mid-1980s, after San Jose experienced losses from risky investments that were constructed in much the same fashion as in Orange County. By the early 1990s the state legislature was back to loosening restrictions on local government investments and reporting. If the Orange County bankruptcy is seen as an unusual case that will not be repeated, then the state legislature could again decide to allow more flexibility with risky investments.

Also, it is likely that fiscal problems are more widespread because there were other California counties experiencing deep fiscal problems in 1994. These counties point to significant effects of their recent losses in state funding. Eight small counties were on the verge of financial collapse and had to ask the state legislature for $15 million in relief. The state government turned down their request for a bailout, much as it dismissed the possibility of getting involved in Orange County (*New York Times,* 1994a). Los Angeles County faced a $1.2 billion deficit and was considering the prospect of closing its public hospitals because it could no longer pay its bills (Lazarovici, 1995). The state legislature then passed a bill that allowed Los Angeles County to raid its county transit funds, much in the same way as it handled the Orange County bankruptcy. Since the Los Angeles County and Orange County crises, there has been little talk of California counties in fiscal trouble. However, the credit for the financial turnaround belongs entirely to the state's economic recovery.

The basic problem that could cause a repeat of the Orange County fiscal crisis is the system of state and local government finance in California that has evolved since Proposition 13. The state government can provide the funds that local governments need in good economic times, but it is not a dependable source of local revenues in bad economic times. The problems faced by the small counties and big counties such as Los Angeles, San Diego, and Orange are really the same. The state government pulled funds away from these counties during the severe recession. For many local governments, that is when they needed outside funding the most. The next recession may push other counties to the financial brink, if the post–Proposition 13 system of state and local funding is still in place. The fiscal situation for counties has become even worse since the voters passed Proposition 98. This means that even during the good times most of the excess funds go to schools.

An additional reason that events such as those in Orange County could happen again is that many places share the suburban characteristics that contributed to the crisis. For instance, many county governments have a Board of Supervisors whose members are elected in local districts and a county treasurer who is elected countywide. In addition, few county governments have a chief executive officer who has authority over the department heads. It is thus possible that the politically fragmented and decentralized leadership styles that are common in suburban regions would be accompanied by a lack in fiscal oversight and accountability. Middle-class voters who demand that local services should be improved without an increase in taxes can also be found in many other suburban regions. Such political pressures on locally elected officials could end in desperate attempts to raise new revenues without asking the voters, as was the case in Orange County. Also, as Steinberg and Lyon have noted, urban counties and large municipalities throughout the nation have been forced by federal and state governments to take on more responsibilities without increases in their financial capabilities (Steinberg, Lyon, and Vaiana, 1992, pp. 2, 3). Many local governments will have even more difficulty making ends meet in the next few years as state governments and federal agencies seek to balance their budgets by turning over the responsibilities for welfare and other services.

Much has been said about how unusual it was that the Orange County voters refused to raise taxes to help their municipality recover from the bankruptcy. Some have argued that voters in other municipalities would have acted differently when faced with bond defaults and the prospects of service cuts. However, at no other time has a fiscal recovery plan for a municipality in fiscal stress been placed in the hands of the voters, as in the case of the Orange County ballot measure for a sales tax increase. There is thus no evidence to support the claim that local voters elsewhere faced with bankruptcy would raise their taxes. It is possible that voter distrust is also high in other suburban regions. Voters may assume, as in Orange County, that the fiscal problem could be resolved with existing funds by cutting what they view as excessive waste in government spending. Thus, it may be misleading to assume that the experience of the Orange County voters rejecting a recovery tax would not be repeated elsewhere.

Finally, the surprising nature of the Orange County fiscal crisis is another reason for believing that a fiscal disaster of this magnitude could happen again in local governments. In other words, there could be financial problems that are well hidden. An official from Moody's Investors Service, David Brodsly, said, "What brought Orange County down was debt that wasn't even on the books. It was these reverse repurchase agreements. . . . That won't happen again perhaps, but what other kinds of liabilities aren't being measured and aren't being recognized that could bring distress? Unfunded pension liabilities? Tort liabilities? Environmental liabilities? Deferred maintenance? Deferred expenditures?" (California Debt Advisory Commission, 1995, p. 23).

The Orange County episode suggests that the present way of thinking about the causes of fiscal strain in local government, which generally focuses on the economic characteristics of the municipality and its ability to pay debts, is too narrow for today's fiscal world. We now know that many other local fiscal problems can surface.

CAN WE AVOID FINANCIAL DISASTERS?

A major question that policymakers have asked is whether or not anything can be done to prevent financial disasters such as the Orange County bankruptcy. On one side are those who believe that "bad things happen" and there is nothing that can be done to prevent such calamities from occurring again. Bob Citron would be viewed by this camp as the kind of abnormal personality who, from time to time, wreaks havoc in an institutional setting. On the other side are those who argue that there were some fundamental conditions present that permitted Citron to take the unusual actions that led to the financial collapse of the county pool. This places the emphasis on the structure of decision making and other areas in government that can be improved.

The point of view one adopts on this topic has importance for the public policy implications of the Orange County bankruptcy. Those who are more fatalistic say that it is not worthwhile to set up a system to constrain all public servants because of the inevitability of uncontrollable abnormal activities. Those who believe the fault lies with the institutional conditions in which the individuals operate look to making changes based on the lessons learned. I have taken the position that we cannot prevent another Orange County bankruptcy. However, there are many things that can be done to reduce its likelihood in the future.

One way to gain perspective on this issue is to look at other human disasters for common threads with the Orange County bankruptcy. Barbara Tuchman (1984) demonstrates how many serious miscalculations by governments, from Troy to Vietnam, have in common a trait she describes as "woodenheadness." This shortcoming is defined as "assessing a situation in terms of preconceived fixed notions while ignoring or rejecting any contrary signs" (Tuchman, 1984, p. 7). There are times when powerful government leaders fail to remain open-minded about how well their past decisions fit with current conditions. Thus, they ignore warnings and information that would point to a need for new policies. Powerful positions can sometimes insulate people from the reality that they are in error and, without checks and balances, can lead to decisions that are no longer in the public interest. There are many parallels between the "folly" that has occurred in governments at other times in history and the actions that led to the Orange County fiscal collapse. Bob Citron continued to pursue a risky strategy that he thought he had "perfected" when the market had shifted against him. No one in county government was in a position to stop him from making terrible mistakes.

Two human disasters come to mind, one in finance and the other in government, that have strong parallels with the Orange County bankruptcy. The Barings Bank collapse in February 1995 was caused by an employee named Nick Leeson who generated $1.2 billion in company losses from making big bets in derivatives (see Leeson, 1996; Fay, 1996; Rawnsley, 1995; Zhang, 1995). The NASA *Challenger* space shuttle accident in January 1986 occurred when government officials approved a launch after being warned about a likely O-ring failure by Thiokol engineers (see McConnell, 1987; Presidential Commission on the Space Shuttle *Challenger* Accident, 1986; Brody, 1986). The Barings collapse and the *Challenger* accident led to debates about whether one can stop disasters of such magnitude in the future. Since then recommendations have been issued on how to prevent a "rogue trader" from destroying a financial company. New procedures have been developed by NASA to make sure that government officials heed warnings about danger before a launch. The conclusion that was reached from these two disasters is that we can learn from our mistakes and make improvements.

One common thread in all three cases is that they raise questions about the ethics of people who wield power. There was no personal financial gain at stake in the decisions that were made, but career gains came into play. Nick Leeson gambled with his company's money to make up for past losses and to show his superiors that he was still their "wonder boy." NASA officials risked the lives of seven astronauts for the sake of avoiding a delay of the space shuttle launch that would place this program in a bad light. In Orange County Citron misappropriated earnings from local governments to the county fund to meet his commitment to the Board of Supervisors to help with their budget problems. These acts revealed individuals in power, left to their own devices, who were trying to achieve personal success and win approval from others.

A large element of hubris led to an unwillingness to heed warnings in all three instances. Future success was assumed based on past experience. Bob Citron ignored the advice of Merrill Lynch and moved deeper into his risky strategies. After all, he had always outperformed the market in the past. NASA officials did not listen to the Thiokol engineers who warned that an O-ring problem could occur with low-temperature launches. The launches that succeeded in the past had become an indication of space shuttle safety to NASA officials. Nick Leeson assumed that he could beat the futures market even while he realized that his own actions were affecting prices because they were so closely followed by other traders. He was thinking of the large sums of money that he had made for his company in the past.

The institutions surrounding the actors in these three events failed by not following through on the warnings they received and stopping these disasters from happening. Thiokol engineers pointed out the problems with the O-rings, but the top officials succumbed to client pressures and signaled their approval of the infamous launch. One NASA official had complained, "My God, Thiokol, when do you want me to launch? Next April?" (McConnell, 1987, p. 196). Merrill Lynch acted with similar ambivalence as the broker for Bob Citron. First, a top executive warned about the risks of the county pool and agreed to buy back the risky securities. Later the company continued to sell Bob Citron the kinds of risky securities it had advised against. A civil trial is pending on the actions of Merrill Lynch toward the treasurer.

The news media also fell short in their efforts to provide the public with knowledge about the impending problems in all three cases. A Pulitzer prize–winning journalist noted about the *Challenger* accident, "The press was somewhat lulled by the many successes of NASA. . . . The press somehow came to believe that NASA was pretty-nigh infallible" (McConnell, 1987, p. 82). On the Barings collapse, a British trade publication said, "The whole thing might have been avoided had we published last autumn a hair-raising tale of the antics of Mr. Leeson" (Rawnsley, 1995, p. 160). It was mentioned earlier in this chapter how the Orange County news media failed to investigate the serious allegations raised against Bob Citron. We can observe from these facts that the news media may be exposed to institutional problems, but they cannot always be relied on to investigate and report the problems in a timely fashion.

The Barings collapse, the *Challenger* accident, and the Orange County bankruptcy are all characterized by problems in communication with the top leaders and a lack of adequate oversight of the lower levels of authority. The President's Commission concluded that the decision-making process that resulted in the *Challenger* launch was "seriously flawed." In their view, a better system would have highlighted the problems with the O-rings and the higher authorities would have canceled the launch (Presidential Commission on the Space Shuttle *Challenger* Accident, 1986). As for the Barings Bank collapse, Zhang (1995, p. 156) observes, "Many participants in the derivatives industry believe that the crisis was more a managerial problem than a system or trading problem." He goes on to describe how the management in London was largely unaware of the trading that Nick Leeson was doing in Singapore. In the case of Orange County, the former chief administrative officer had described the system of reporting from county departments to the Board of Supervisors as "an accident waiting to happen." The county treasurer was buying reverse repurchase agreements and inverse floaters for the county pool with little oversight or financial control by top officials in the county government.

In closing, the Orange County bankruptcy provides another glaring example of a government leader whose "woodenheadedness" got in the way of reason and actions designed for the public good. The communications and oversight problems that allowed the Orange County Investment Pool to collapse are similar to the conditions that led to the *Challenger* space shuttle accident and the collapse of the Barings Bank. There were changes made as a result of the two other disasters. After the Barings collapse, financial institutions tightened controls on the trading of derivatives, and to date there has been no repeat of the "rogue trader" incident. NASA instituted a new system for launch approvals and, at this time, there have been no more space shuttle accidents. The reforms resulting from the Orange County bankruptcy have been limited to new restrictions on local treasurers. The soul-searching analysis that occurred after the other financial and government disasters has yet to be seen. It is essential to identify the broad range of policy changes suggested by the Orange County financial crisis. It is the first step in reducing the likelihood that it will be repeated in the future.

CHAPTER 9

Recommendations
for the Future

We need concrete proposals for change if we want to avoid repeating
past mistakes. Many good reforms were instituted after the Orange
County financial crisis, but they have not gone far enough in dealing
with the bigger issues. In this chapter I present ten policy recommendations resulting from the lessons learned from the Orange County
bankruptcy. Along with each proposal I offer a brief discussion of why
it is a significant issue for policymakers. The recommendations are
based on the analysis presented in earlier chapters on the causes, response to the fiscal emergency, recovery plans, and local government reforms. Finally, I look at the broader issue of the need to "reinvent" state
and local government relations. The Orange County crisis exposed the
complex system of revenue distribution and service delivery that has
evolved in California. The broader issues will take on greater importance throughout the United States when the federal government transfers welfare and other responsibilities to state and local governments.

*1. Local governments need to maintain high standards for fiscal over-
sight and accountability.*
One of the main reasons that the Orange County Investment Pool suffered huge losses was that Bob Citron was fully in control of this public fund. The county treasurer made an annual report to the Board of
Supervisors, which offered little detail besides the investment yield.
Occasionally, he made requests for bond offerings that were solely for
the purpose of investing borrowed money in the county pool, but these

were not closely scrutinized because of his track record of providing high interest income for the county budget. Otherwise, his investment activities were largely out of view of the Board of Supervisors. Citron was not required to report on the current performance of the fund to any other county official, such as the county administrative officer or the county auditor. The county treasurer did not have a board of trustees or an outside group of professionals to offer timely investment advice and periodically review the pool's portfolio.

This lack of oversight and financial accountability was what gave Bob Citron the freedom to leverage the local government funds into a $20 billion pool that had large positions in risky securities. The fact that the Board of Supervisors and the county administrative officer were not fully informed about the county pool meant that they had little warning that a financial crisis was brewing in the fall of 1994. These county officials, then, had very little time to develop a strategy to avert the bankruptcy. When they forced the county treasurer to resign, moreover, there was no one in county government that knew as much as he did about the investments and the lenders. When Bob Citron left, the Wall Street investment firms seized the securities that were being held as collateral for the county's reverse repurchase agreements. They correctly assessed the situation and saw that there was no one in control of the county fund.

In a state senate hearing after the bankruptcy, Eli Broad, who is the head of a financial institution in California, said to Bob Citron during questioning, "It seems to me that you really achieved pretty close to absolute power in investing this money. . . . What we have here is, in effect, a failure of a basic American principle in government, and by that I mean a system of checks and balances. In substance, the fund was totally unregulated as compared to banks, insurance companies, pension funds, mutual funds." Bob Citron responded by saying, "In retrospect, I would presume that a fund such as ours could have a small board of advisors or people qualified by training and education to advise on what type of investments should be made or on investment policy" (Senate Special Committee on Local Government Investments, 1995a, p. 30).

The need for oversight and fiscal accountability is a theme that was also stressed by state officials after the Orange County bankruptcy. The state auditor's report recommended that several steps be taken to make sure that local funds are kept safe and liquid. These include having the Board of Supervisors adopt and approve the county's investment fund

policies, appointing an independent advisory committee to oversee investment decisions, requiring more frequent and detailed investment reports from the county treasurer, and establishing stricter rules for
selecting brokers and investment advisors (California State Auditor,
1995, pp. S2–S3, 51–54). The state treasurer (1995) also issued a series
of recommendations, which included a statement of investment policy
delivered to the Board of Supervisors and quarterly investment reports.

The state legislature passed two bills after the Orange County bankruptcy as part of the recovery plan. They restricted the amount of leveraging and purchasing of risky securities. As another part of this effort
to increase the safety of principal, they required the establishment of an
oversight board and reporting requirements for the county treasurer.
The new Orange County treasurer implemented more restrictions on
investing, and the chief executive officer has moved toward a financial
team approach in order to involve more county officials in the investment decisions.

Local officials should see the Orange County bankruptcy as a warning. New state regulations are a good start, but their vigilance is
needed. They should adjust their government structures to make sure
they have proper financial controls in place at all times. One observer
noted to county officials after the bankruptcy, "Responsibility for investment policy should never rest solely with one person" (Shields,
1995, p. 30).

*2. Local elected officials need more financial expertise and objective
professional advice so that they can make sound fiscal policy decisions
in the complex world of municipal finance.*
The Orange County bankruptcy revealed a basic lack of knowledge and
sophistication about investing at many levels of local government. Bob
Citron followed an aggressive strategy of using reverse repurchase
agreements to buy risky securities that went against the advice of many
of the professional experts at the time, including even those that sell
these kinds of instruments. After a series of interest rate hikes, the
county treasurer operated under the naive assumption that interest
rates would again decline soon, perhaps because this was the only financial scenario he had experienced in the past. Clearly, this local official, who had little formal schooling and a very narrow range of
experience in bond investments, was in way over his head when he was
faced with managing $20 billion of local government assets in a rapidly
changing interest rate environment.

Other county officials had failed to look beyond the returns they achieved through the Orange County Investment Pool. The Board of Supervisors approved bond offerings that would be put to use in a speculative fashion in the county pool. They did not think to ask about how the money would be invested and what the risk would be to the borrowed principal. Then they acted dumbfounded when they learned of the losses that the pool had suffered. Some county leaders pleaded ignorance, saying they did not understand what a derivative was or how a reverse repurchase agreement worked, when the county treasurer presented his annual report. The supervisors were forced to learn about the complex world of municipal finance during a fiscal emergency. With only a little knowledge, they made important decisions about how to handle these complex investments after asking for the resignation of Bob Citron.

The local officials from the cities, schools, and local special districts that had deposited money in the county pool were unsophisticated investors for the most part. They also claimed not to know what Bob Citron was doing with their money. Many did not understand how inverse floaters and other derivative securities worked or why leveraging funds was a risky strategy when interest rates were on the rise. Most did not bother to learn, leaving the worrying about such matters to the county treasurer who held their funds. All of the local officials in the Orange County Investment Pool failed to comprehend one of the most basic rules of investing, which is that higher returns on one's money are achieved only through taking greater risks. They have claimed that the county treasurer's office misled them about the safety of their principal. Still, they should have made more of an effort to protect the public's money.

In a report that was issued after the bankruptcy, the state treasurer focused on the importance of increasing knowledge about financial investments. One of the recommendations was that state associations develop continuing education programs for local officials who are charged with investment responsibilities so that they can be more knowledgeable about the financial markets and securities. As part of the state bill that reformed the local treasurer's operations, there are now education qualifications and continuing education requirements for county treasurers. The county charter in Orange County sought stricter criteria for officeholders by changing the county treasurer from an elected to an appointed position, but the voters rejected the county charter. The Orange County treasurer who was appointed by the Board of Supervisors after Bob Citron resigned, and was later elected by the voters, does have more professional and educational credentials than the previous officeholder.

Local officials at all levels need to have adequate knowledge of the complex investment tools that are common in municipal finance today. It is necessary but not sufficient for the local treasurer to be a financial expert. County elected officials, county staff, city elected officials, city staff, school board members, and special district officials all need to have more familiarity with both "plain vanilla" securities and riskier investments. Local officials have a duty to make sure that public funds are safe and liquid. Local governments should offer opportunities to educate their elected leaders about financial markets and should regularly call in objective experts for professional advice when they are making difficult financial decisions. Improving officials' knowledge of finances will help to prevent local fiscal problems and will go a long way toward restoring the public's confidence in their local leaders' abilities to manage the taxpayer's money.

3. Municipal bankruptcies should be avoided by local governments and state governments, even if extraordinary efforts are required.
It is very rare for any municipality to declare bankruptcy, and no large urban body before had taken this drastic step. So when the fifth most populous U.S. county filed for Chapter 9 protection, it was a highly controversial event. What we have learned from the Orange County episode is that it is best for local and state governments to stay away from municipal bankruptcies. A bankruptcy offers only limited protection and can have far-ranging consequences for local governments.

Orange County actually filed two requests for bankruptcy protection in December 1994. One was for the county government, and the other was for the county pool. However, the courts eventually disallowed the latter. The purpose of the bankruptcy filing was to buy time and hold off the major creditors so that the county government could reorganize its finances. This legal move was supposed to end the collateral calls on the reverse repurchase agreements by the investment firms, which had begun in the early days of December, when the lenders lost confidence in the county pool. However, after the bankruptcy the investment firms continued to sell most of the billions of dollars in securities that they held as collateral. They claimed that these kinds of debts were exempt from the Chapter 9 filing, while the county government argued that they were not. The court has still not ruled on this issue, but it is clear that the bankruptcy filing did not accomplish one of its main goals. It did not halt the highly adverse actions against the county pool by the Wall Street investment firms.

The municipal bankruptcy also froze the county, city, school, and special district funds that were on deposit in the county pool. It was important to prevent a run on the money, but it may not have been necessary to take such a drastic action. Most of the pool funds were contributed by a relatively small number of local government investors. These major pool participants had been asked by county officials not to withdraw their funds a few weeks earlier, when word of the financial crisis first leaked out, and they had agreed not to withdraw their funds at that time. It is possible that they would have cooperated with the county officials again, if for no other reason than to prevent the panic selling that would place their investments at risk. For instance, San Diego County was also faced with a large paper loss in its county pool, but county leaders were able to prevent a rush for withdrawals without filing for bankruptcy. They informed the pool participants that they would have to take a share in the current losses if they withdrew their funds right away. On the other hand, they could wait until the financial markets cooled down and their investments regained their value. San Diego pool participants chose to wait. The Orange County bankruptcy created a great deal of ill will between the county government and local governments and created a new set of problems. For instance, a process had to be approved by the bankruptcy court to allow the local governments to access their funds from the county government in a fairly short time so that they could maintain services. Later on, a settlement plan would have to be negotiated between the county government and the cities, schools, and special districts, and approved by the bankruptcy court, in order to divide the money that was frozen in the county pool.

The label of bankruptcy also carries a stigma for Orange County. The credit markets had a negative perception of this filing. The immediate implication was that the county government may not pay its debt, and the Wall Street investment firms reacted harshly to this news. The county government will pay a penalty for the bankruptcy filing whenever it accesses the credit markets, since its bond offerings will have to include insurance and higher interest rates for the investors. Finally, the notoriety of the Orange County bankruptcy has created negative perceptions that lessen the attractiveness of the region as a business or residential location.

There has also been damage to the state of California as a result of the bankruptcy filing. The state treasurer noted, "While it is impossible to quantify the yield penalty that California issuers will pay as a result of the Orange County crisis, it could be as much as $200 million or more annually on a statewide basis" (*Cal-Tax News,* 1995, p. 2). This so-called Orange County premium would affect state and local governments. This is because the bankruptcy indicated new risks in California that the financial markets had not previously taken into account. Notably, it raised questions about the governments' abilities to access funds after Proposition 13.

There were also national repercussions of the Orange County bankruptcy. The fact that a large municipality such as Orange County signaled that it may not pay its debt raised questions about the safety of municipal bonds. Local governments are supposed to stand behind their bonds with their "full faith and credit," which includes raising taxes or whatever is necessary to pay back their debts. Orange County seemed to have taken the step toward bankruptcy fairly early in the judgment of some financial experts, that is, without exploring all of the avenues for paying its debts. This caused some concerns that a precedent was being set for municipalities to walk away from their obligations.

When all of the implications of the bankruptcy filing are considered, there seems to be only one consequence that was positive. The bankruptcy court provided a structure around which the local government investors could organize. The judge asked the local officials to form a committee of pool investors within days of the Chapter 9 filing. This included the representatives from the cities, schools, and special districts that were among the largest depositors. This committee was charged with defining the needs of the local government investors and negotiating with the county government. This court-imposed structure was essential to resolving the fiscal crisis since there had previously been little cooperation among these pool members. But surely there are ways for local officials to meet and work together other than in court.

Other municipalities in trouble should not follow the example of Orange County. If at all possible, those in fiscal distress should avoid filing bankruptcy. The traditional model of the state and local government working together to avoid bankruptcy and bond default is a much less costly approach. This could include the state government extending credit, guaranteeing the safety of local bonds, or otherwise allowing the local government to continue to have access to the credit market. Orange County had assumed that there were more similarities between corporate bankruptcy and municipal bankruptcy than is really the case. As some observers noted, "Even though it has filed for bankruptcy, it must continue to provide for the health and welfare of its residents. . . . The county needs continued access to capital markets" (Burr et al., 1995, p. 8).

4. The state of California should revise the general law governing its counties, since currently general-law counties have a structure that is lacking in local leadership.

Many have observed that a lack of political leadership was evident during the bankruptcy. This sentiment placed Orange County at an extreme disadvantage. When the fiscal crisis occurred, there was a perception within the county government, at other local government offices, and among the public and media that no one was in charge. Concerned parties had much difficulty getting information about what was going on during the fiscal emergency. It was also hard to know who among the various sources could be believed when information was given. This led to a perception of chaos and confusion within county government that led some to panic over the bankruptcy.

One of the reasons people perceived a lack of political leadership was that there was no single person in charge at the top level of county government. There were five members of the Board of Supervisors who were each elected to represent one local district. The chair of the Board of Supervisors was a position that was rotated among the five members from year to year. The chair's duties were largely honorific, such as presiding over the weekly board meetings. At the time of the bankruptcy, to add to the weakness, the current chair of the board was retiring.

There were other officials in county government, although no one position had the characteristics of county leadership. The county administrative officer was appointed by the Board of Supervisors and reported to this legislative body, but did not have any direct authority over the other county departments. The current officeholder was aware of his powerlessness and had asked the board to appoint a chief executive officer. There were also county officials who were elected, such as the county treasurer, auditor-controller, and sheriff-coroner, each of whom performed specific county functions in a fairly autonomous manner. Then there were the department heads who administered county programs such as health care and environmental planning and were appointed by the Board of Supervisors.

The county government was not a cohesive organization. The Board of Supervisors had little experience with teamwork. The five members had an informal agreement to live by the rules of the "district prerogative." They focused on satisfying their local districts' voters and their supporters. The county departments were not centrally managed, so there was little in the way of internal coordination. There was no emphasis on communication within county government, since this decentralized structure focused the attention of employees at the department level. No one had the responsibility of communicating for the county government to the outside world.

Another reason for the perception that no one was in charge is that the county government leaders were practically invisible to the public in Orange County. In the months before the bankruptcy, when asked to list the county leaders, many voters could not name one leader and few mentioned members of the Board of Supervisors. Even the race for county treasurer generated little interest, despite some heated exchanges about the risks in the county fund. The county sheriff was by far the most popular and well-known figure, which is almost certainly a carryover from the Wild West era. Only the most informed voters and self-interested businesses, such as the developers and vendors, took notice of the county supervisors and other county officials.

Some said that the lack of county leadership was a reflection on the individuals in office during the fiscal crisis. The public's perception of the county's elected officials was certainly most unflattering. The board members were proven to be ignorant about the county treasurer's investments, seemed slow in responding to the fiscal crisis, and were generally powerless to do anything to resolve the budget problems. The voters took a very dim view of the Board of Supervisors and grew more negative toward them as time went on. It is possible that the elected officials who were in power did lack leadership qualities and other skills. However, it is difficult to see how they could express any leadership qualities within this structure of local government.

The county government was able to make some modifications to its structure during the fiscal crisis. The Board of Supervisors appointed three department heads to a crisis management team that determined what areas of government needed funding in order to maintain services. The members included the county sheriff, who had by far the most experience in county government in terms of dealing with emergencies. The Board of Supervisors also appointed a chief executive officer who had previously headed a fiscally distressed company. This official became the point of contact both inside and outside of county government. These efforts did bring more leadership and coordination to a situation in which these traits were badly needed.

The Orange County bankruptcy has pointed out an important deficiency in the large counties that operate under general law. They lack strong leadership, and this can hurt their efforts to cope with an emergency, such as a financial crisis. Suburban metropolitan regions such as Orange County would be better served if they had a mayor who was elected countywide and highly visible to the people. Their governmental structure would also be improved by having a chief executive officer with authority over the budget and personnel in all county departments. For instance, there were, by comparison, few comments about the lack of political leadership during the earthquake emergencies in San Francisco and Los Angeles. The state government should consider requiring the large counties that do not currently have a county charter, such as Orange County, to create a new organizational structure that will provide them with county leadership. The state would better serve its constituents if it updated the general law governing its counties.

5. The local governments in suburban counties need to be encouraged by the state government to engage more actively in regional cooperation. The Orange County fiscal crisis exposed the reality that local governments in the area did not have many positive relations with one another. The fact that nearly all of them had funds on deposit in the Orange County Investment Pool was their common tie. Even here, though, the county agencies, cities, schools, and special districts all made the same blunder, without talking to one another, and went after high returns by taking high risks in the fund managed by Bob Citron. Before the bankruptcy the local government officials never met to discuss how much they had invested in the county pool or to compare notes on the promises Bob Citron had made to them about the safety of their principal. The first time the local government investors met as an organized group to discuss their investments was in U.S. bankruptcy court in those stressful days in December 1994. The lack of positive relationships among the local governments was later viewed by many insiders as one of the important hindrances to resolving the Orange County financial crisis.

The county and the city governments actually had a long history of poor relations. The county leaders thought of themselves as having a superior role since they were the main providers of regional services. The city leaders resented being treated in a condescending way. The cities also saw the county government as diminishing in importance as new municipalities were being carved out of the unincorporated areas.

In a recent confrontation, the county and cities were feuding over a plan to convert the El Toro Marine Air Base into a large commercial airport. Several of the cities had complained bitterly that the county government had excluded them from the planning process. This was the charged atmosphere in which the cities and county government had to reach an agreement on how to divide the funds that remained in the county pool.

Relations between city government leaders were also not very good. The cities competed with one another to attract the large employers, retail businesses, entertainment complexes, and housing developments that would provide a local tax base. They rarely found issues that put them into a cooperative relationship. Most but not all of the municipalities were members of the Orange County Division of the League of California Cities. This was a voluntary organization that brought its members together periodically for discussions, but it did not have a formal policymaking role. A recent event involved a north-versus-south conflict over NIMBY land use issues. The elected officials in the south were opposed to having a commercial airport at a closing marine base, while those in the north favored this proposal. These same cities had to reach consensus on a pool settlement with the county leaders.

There were also the regional transportation agencies, local school districts, local water districts, the county sanitation district, and other local special districts in Orange County. Most were focused on highly specific tasks, and some were responsible for small geographic areas. There was little reason for these local special districts to have much to do with one another. They also functioned independently of the county government and the city governments. The local special districts were forced into a close relationship with city and county governments, and each other, only when they were required to make joint decisions about the settlement plan for the county pool.

The Orange County fiscal crisis is one type of regional emergency in which the county government, cities, schools, and special districts needed to cooperate. They were limited by their lack of experience in working together. As a result, county business leaders had to be called in to negotiate the pool settlement and the financial recovery plan. One can imagine more life-threatening situations, such as floods or earthquakes, that would require even more urgent regional cooperation. This is why local governments in suburban regions need incentives from the state to cooperate more. It is typical for local governments to resist any efforts that are associated with regional governance, such as land use policy coordination or local service consolidation. There is evidence, however, that local officials will look more favorably toward regional efforts when the state government is involved (Kanarek and Baldassare, 1996). The state should find ways to provide fiscal incentives to increase the amount of regional cooperation.

6. *County governments need more flexibility in spending the state government funds they receive, especially during a local fiscal emergency.*
Orange County learned the hard way. It had few options for cutting spending after the collapse of the county investment pool. The county government had a total budget of $3.73 billion in 1994–1995. However, most of the county's revenues were from state and federal agencies and were assigned for specified programs. The largest category of revenues was $1.64 billion for the general fund; however, 72 percent of these funds were from intergovernmental revenues and could be used only for certain purposes. Thus, the county government struggled to erase a $170 million deficit in 1994–1995 even though this was less than 5 percent of the total budget. This is because the deficit accounted for a third of all of the unrestricted revenues. Still, the unrestricted revenues went to pay for programs and services of an essential nature.

Since Proposition 13 passed, the trend in state and local government finance is for much of the county government budget to be on "automatic pilot." There are mandated programs for which the state government provides all of the funds. There are also mandated programs for which the state provides a proportion of the funds and requires the county government to provide the rest. At the end of this budget process, there is little left in the way of discretionary revenues or expenditures for other kinds of county government programs. Instead, the county government has to spend some of its unrestricted funds to pay for state-mandated programs.

The fact that local government funds were needed to pay for state-mandated programs made it very difficult for Orange County to respond to the fiscal emergency. The county leaders could find very few places to cut expenses when they faced a budget deficit and revenue shortfall the next year. This is in stark contrast to the perceptions of the distrustful local voters, who believe that by cutting government waste their leaders can resolve the fiscal problems. State Assemblyperson Marilyn Brewer from Orange County made this observation during the bankruptcy: "The federal government mandates without providing funds, the state government mandates without funds and this places burdens beyond the capability of counties. We're in an era where government needs to reexamine how it does business" (*California Journal Weekly*, 1994, p. 11).

The county government clearly has a responsibility to provide services that are needed by its residents and to spend the federal and state funds it receives for their intended purposes. However, there should be some conditions when county leaders can seek approval from federal and state agencies to make modest and temporary cuts in the level of local funding that they are required to provide for services. A fiscal emergency such as the Orange County bankruptcy would be one such circumstance. Orange County Supervisor Marian Bergeson gave one such example when she noted, "I don't think we should have a bailout, but counties need the flexibility to solve problems. By freeing up maintenance of effort requirement, the state could give some freedom in those areas that help the county" (*California Journal Weekly*, 1994, p. 11).

Unfortunately, most of the state leaders during the bankruptcy did not seem to be highly focused on how the state government could ease the fiscal requirements that are placed on county governments. Political rivalries were interfering with the ability of state legislators to rationally address the fundamental issue of how much a county government is able to cope with a fiscal emergency. Assembly Speaker Willie Brown said, "I'm going to treat Orange County with the same degree of consideration that Orange County legislators have treated the rest of the state in its times of crisis," and State Assemblyperson Marguerite Archie-Hudson added, "We are having a little bit of fun with Orange County because they have always beaten up on the rest of us" (*California Journal Weekly*, 1995, p. 9). These state officials seemed to be referring to their political battles and partisan disputes with state legislators from Orange County in the state legislature. They had lost sight of the local officials who were struggling with a problem they partly caused and the fact that local residents were facing the prospects of having their county services either reduced or eliminated. In order for county governments to help themselves out of fiscal crises, state officials will need to provide local governments with more flexibility in spending state funds than was available to Orange County.

7. *The state government should closely monitor the fiscal conditions of its local governments, rather than waiting for serious problems to surface.*
The state officials were largely in the dark about the fiscal conditions of county governments. They had no knowledge of the risky strategies

that led to the big losses in the Orange County Investment Pool until the days before the bankruptcy filing. The state officials were unaware of the fact that Monterey, Placer, San Bernardino, San Diego, Solano, and Sonoma counties were also heavily involved in leveraging and derivatives until Moody's Investors Service issued a report in December 1994. They also had no advance warning of the $1.2 billion budget deficit confronting Los Angeles County in the same year as a result of the high costs of providing health care to the welfare and immigrant population. Finally, the state government did not realize that there were eight small counties near fiscal collapse until the counties approached the state legislature for a $15 million bailout in the fall of 1994.

The state controller currently collects budget data from county governments and presents them in an annual reported entitled "Financial Transactions Concerning Counties of California." These include detailed information on types of revenue sources, such as funds from state agencies, federal agencies, property taxes, sales tax, user fees, and interest income. Also reported are the categories of expenditures, such as public assistance, public protection, general government, health, and education. The information is collected by the state, but it is not analyzed in a systematic fashion to determine which of the county governments may have abnormal sources of revenues or patterns of expenditures or may be showing signs of fiscal distress. For instance, a review of the financial data for the 1990s would have indicated that Orange County had a large amount of interest income and that that source represented a much higher percentage of revenues than for other counties in the state. This information alone should have been sufficient to uncover the problems that Orange County was facing. There should have been warning signs and an opportunity to recommend some adjustments. However, no one at the state level was systematically monitoring the fiscal conditions of counties.

Several state authorities certainly mounted a major effort to evaluate the financial crisis in Orange County after the bankruptcy. The governor sent the California state auditor to audit the Orange County Investment Pool. The state treasurer had the Task Force on Local and State Investment Practices hold hearings on the Orange County financial crisis and make recommendations to the governor. The California Debt Advisory Commission heard expert testimony about the impacts of the bankruptcy and provided a background paper on bond offerings and credit ratings. The Senate Special Committee on Local Government Investments called witnesses to their investigation of the Orange County financial crisis, as did the Assembly Select Committee on the Insolvency of Orange County. Unfortunately, this state involvement took place after the problem was too far advanced to be easily solved. When the problem came to the state's attention, it was already too late to avert the financial crisis that would have implications for Orange County, other local governments, and the state government.

The state government is vitally concerned with the fiscal trends in local governments for several reasons. State officials do not want residents to suffer because their localities are having a fiscal crisis. Also, the state government often has to consider a bailout or some other form of assistance if a local fiscal situation has deteriorated. It would thus make sense for the state to have an early-warning system that would track the fiscal health of counties, cities, and school districts. Gold (1990, p. 214) recommends that the following components be monitored: tax revenue, tax rates, expenditures, beginning and ending cash balances, federal aid, state aid, user charges, tax bases, indebtedness, fiscal capacity, fiscal effort, needs, and a measure of fiscal stress. The purpose of the monitoring is to "give state officials the tools they need to keep tabs on local developments and to improve the targeting of local assistance" (Gold, 1990, p. 216).

State monitoring would give state leaders an opportunity to discuss fiscal problems and solutions with local officials before they reach the crisis stage. It would also provide the information that state officials require to distinguish real needs for state assistance from the less valid complaints, and compare the relative needs of local governments in financial stress.[1] State monitoring of local government finance certainly would have improved the chances of avoiding the Orange County bankruptcy. It would also have provided a much-needed and timely source of objective data on whether or not the state actually needed to respond to this local crisis.

8. The Brown Act's requirements for public meetings by local legislators should be suspended during fiscal emergencies, as they are for other types of emergencies.

The Brown Act was cited by many county leaders as a severe hindrance to their need for frequent and open communications during the Orange County fiscal emergency. This state-imposed law may have added to the coordination problems that were already present to a

---

1. Gold (1990, p. 216) also reports that some states, such as New York and Georgia, already have information systems for monitoring local government finance.

large degree because of the political fragmentation of county government. Perhaps there were even decisions made in the crisis mode, such as declaring bankruptcy, without proper discussion because of the state laws that restrict local legislators from having private conversations in a group.

The Brown Act governs the rights of the public to attend and participate in meetings held by their county supervisors. This state legislation was passed in 1953. A meeting is defined as a majority of the board members getting together and discussing any matter that is related to their local jurisdiction. For most California counties, this means that a conversation by three or more board members would be classified as a meeting. A regular meeting requires seventy-two-hour public notice of an agenda, and special meetings require twenty-four-hour notice. Emergency meetings are allowed with only one-hour notice, but these are limited to emergencies involving work stoppages or crippling disasters. Closed meetings are permitted in rare circumstances, such as for labor negotiations or litigation. There are criminal penalties for county supervisors who are found guilty of attending meetings in violation of the Brown Act.

The rules against private meetings prevented the Orange County Board of Supervisors from meeting as a group during some of the worst times of the fiscal crisis. They were called to their offices on Sunday morning, December 4. Once they arrived, they were separately briefed by county staff, and each one was told that the Wall Street investment firms would be selling off the collateral on the county's loans in the next few days. The county officials had to make some important decisions at this time. The Board of Supervisors agreed to ask for the resignation of Bob Citron and would have their staff make one last effort to sell the risky securities in the county pool. These efforts did not restore calm to the financial markets, and two days later the county government filed for bankruptcy.

A number of occasions during the fiscal emergency called for more candid conversations. Although they were allowed to meet in the hours leading up to the bankruptcy filing to discuss legal matters, a more expansive suspension of the Brown Act would have allowed them to hold more group meetings on their own. They could have had an opportunity to brainstorm and honestly discuss their fiscal problems and evaluate their options without staff present. The county's elected officials may have also been more likely in a group setting, rather than one on one, to ask probing questions and engage in a lengthy dialogue with their staff about the fiscal conditions and suggested solutions. The possibilities for miscommunications are also heightened through separate communications by staff members with each of the supervisors. The county staff may also have too much power in these situations, since they are allowed to meet and agree on a course of action while the board cannot have such discussions.

Another point worth mentioning is that the public meetings of the Board of Supervisors were not at all conducive to good decision making during the financial crisis. The public was angry and used these public sessions as an opportunity to vent their frustrations against all of their elected officials. The meetings often had a circuslike atmosphere, and some members of the public were personal in their verbal attacks on the board members. These county officials were not used to such a display of emotion and sometimes took these public criticisms personally. The public meetings were not a good setting for county elected officials to say what was on their minds, make hard decisions, and maintain a rational perspective on the fiscal emergency.

The state legislature has made a number of reforms of local government investing practice based on the experience of the Orange County bankruptcy. They have also made changes so that the county officials are more fiscally accountable. It is also important that they enact some changes to the Brown Act. A fiscal disaster should be treated in the same way as a crippling act of nature. Emergency meetings with one-hour notice should thus be allowed during a fiscal crisis, and closed meetings should be permitted when a local legislative body needs to make fast decisions about complex fiscal issues.

9. There are equity issues that need to be considered in fiscal emergencies. Since the poor rely heavily on county services, their voices need to be heard in decisions about budget cuts.

Despite the region's image as a wealthy suburban enclave, there were over 200,000 individuals living below the poverty line in Orange County in 1990 according to the census. Many of the poor are recent immigrants from Mexico and Asia with limited English skills. They have little political power. They are not politically organized. They do not vote in large numbers compared with the middle-class population. As a result, the poor and recent immigrants did not have a voice in the decisions that were made during the bankruptcy that hurt them. Nor did anyone in government represent their interests. This raises equity issues about the response to the local fiscal emergency.

Those who live below the poverty line are the most dependent on the county government for their well-being and survival. County agencies provide them with a range of health, welfare, and social services. If these services are reduced or eliminated, no other sources are available to them. Many cannot afford to pay for private service providers and lack insurance coverage. This argues for protecting the county services for the poor from any cuts during a fiscal emergency. However, the budget decisions that were made by county leaders seemed to have the greatest consequences for those residents who were most in need of county services.

One of the reasons that the poor were treated unequally is because of the dominant political perspective in Orange County that cuts across party lines. Most of the middle-class voters have negative perceptions of people who are highly dependent on government assistance. There is a strong belief that welfare bureaucracies do more harm than good. In the fall of 1994 a statewide initiative to prohibit government services for illegal immigrants raised the public's perception that there were undeserving people receiving public assistance. This ballot measure won by a wide margin in Orange County. There were almost no political risks associated with the county leaders' decision to take funds away from the services for the poor. The middle-class voters were in favor of this move, while the poor and immigrants would not be heard on the issue. On the other hand, there would be a great outcry from the middle class if their county services were cut.

The poor were disproportionately affected by the budget cuts that were made in response to the $170 million budget deficit. The budget for Community and Social Services was reduced by 27 percent, from $74 million to $54 million. The budget for Health Services was reduced by 35 percent, from $40 million to $26 million. Of the 1,600 job losses in county government, 990 were in Community and Social Services and 139 were in Health Services. The Social Service Agency closed four neighborhood offices, which made it more difficult for the poor to access services (*Orange County Register*, 1996b). A program for the homeless was eliminated, a prenatal clinic was closed, fifteen clinics for children were shut down, and a child abuse prevention program was cut by 50 percent (*New York Times*, 1995e). The recovery plan that took funds from the regional transportation agency also hurt the poor. The head of the Orange County Transportation Agency has said that the county tax diversion would result in cuts in bus service. The poor are the most dependent on public transit, since they are less likely to own an automobile and need to ride public buses to work and other destinations.

It is clear that equity issues were not at the forefront when the county leaders were trying to resolve the financial crisis. Although some state and local elected officials were concerned about the impacts on the poor, the county budget cuts that were implemented fell largely in areas that would be felt most by those in poverty. By contrast, few residents from the middle class were affected by the financial crisis, and most did not even notice any service cuts in areas that affect them. The poor were silent and without representation during the bankruptcy. The county officials heeded the preferences of the middle class throughout the crisis, including their overwhelming rejection of a tax increase. The disadvantaged have much to lose when county services are cut. In the future, the voices of the poor need to be included in the decision making when there are local fiscal emergencies.

10. Local officials need to be more wary about citizens' pressures to implement local fiscal policies that are popular in the short run but financially disastrous over time.
The distrustful voters of Orange County had placed impossible demands on their elected officials. Many didn't want to see their local taxes raised under any circumstances. If the county's elected leaders even mentioned the "T" word, they would be writing their political obituaries. Yet these same local voters were also unwilling to approve cuts in county services for middle-class residents. In fact, most would say that they expect the quality and availability of their services to be improved. The only form of spending they were willing to cut was welfare and county programs for the poor. However, most of the county programs for the poor were required through state and federal mandates, so their budgets could not be reduced.

The voters in California have displayed some unrealistic and contradictory policy preferences. Proposition 13 and the tax revolt that followed have been described by Sears and Citrin (1982) as the voters' desire to have "something for nothing." Many of the New Fiscal Populist leaders in the 1980s and 1990s have chosen to try to meet their voters' demands anyway, for the sake of their political survival. This is because the New Fiscal Populists have been elected by going directly to the voters, rather than the parties or special interests, and saying they will meet their wishes. In other words, elected officials cannot afford to go against their voters. These citizens' pressures contributed to the risky policies that led to the bankruptcy.

In many prior circumstances, voter distrust had been described as the catalyst that resulted in local government reforms. Middle-class voters who were fiscal conservatives and social liberals elected New Fiscal Populist leaders in the older central cities. They found ways to break the bad habit of too much spending. These elected officials brought rational decision making back to the budget process by avoiding escalating debts when their tax revenues had fallen off. They would find novel ways to increase the productivity of municipal employees. They would cut government costs by contracting out for local public services. These leaders would also find ways to save money by improving technology in their city governments. The fiscally conservative voters and their New Fiscal Populist leaders were seen as a breath of fresh air in the depressing world of declining central cities and urban fiscal strain.

The quest for higher returns through the Orange County Investment Pool showed that following the wishes of distrustful voters does have a dark side. Local elected officials met their citizens' policy preferences and maintained local services without raising taxes. They raised the revenues to meet these purposes by depositing public funds in a risky pool that promised to generate more cash by earning higher interest rates. When the state cut local revenues during the recession, these local leaders placed even more money in the county pool and even borrowed money to deposit in the pool with the hope of earning more interest income to make up for lost funding. Local elected officials placed pressures on the county treasurer to keep up the high rate of return. The treasurer responded by increasing the amount of leveraging and buying more risky securities. The county leaders preferred to take these risks rather than face the voters' wrath by cutting spending and services that affected middle-class residents.

The policy preferences of distrustful voters are based on the assumption that there is considerable waste in government bureaucracy. Therefore, they think that municipalities should be able to cut taxes without doing harm to their local services. The New Fiscal Populist leaders have fueled these perceptions in their campaign promises. The result is a search for hidden revenue sources, such as interest income from the county pool, that are not easily recognized by the public. Most voters are ignorant about the fiscal conditions faced by local governments and the services they must provide. This was the case in Orange County. Voters are not in a position to judge the amount of waste in government bureaucracy and whether a tax cut is possible.

Fiscal conservatism, driven by middle-class voter distrust, is not the only type of citizen pressure that can have negative fiscal consequences for local governments. "New Deal" Democrats can ask for high debts that can and have bankrupted municipalities. "New Deal" Republicans can demand budget cuts that reduce local services to dangerously low levels. Local officials need to do a better job of informing their voters about how a local government pays its bills and for what necessary services. They also have to show more courage in opposing the voters' wishes when they know they will threaten the public good. State government should also note that there are no checks and balances against citizen initiatives that can end up having disastrous impacts on county services. Perhaps legislative review and gubernatorial approval is needed for voter-approved initiatives on taxes and spending.

REINVENTING STATE AND LOCAL GOVERNMENTS

In retrospect, a county government in California was the most likely place for a municipal bankruptcy to occur. County governments are charged with the task of providing all of the local services for unincorporated areas and some services such as public health care, jails, courts, and welfare for the entire county. Many of the fiscal problems California counties face today are tied to Proposition 13 and the adjustments that the state government has made to cope with property tax limitations. The problem began when property taxes, the major source of county revenue, were drastically reduced nearly two decades ago. The state government then agreed to provide more funding for the county government but placed conditions on how most of that money could be spent. As one county supervisor noted on the tenth anniversary of Proposition 13, "Now, counties find themselves in control of budgets that are 90 percent driven by state requirements" (Hahn, 1988, p. 38).

Too often, state officials have not provided all of the funds that are needed for the services the state is requiring from county governments. This has forced county leaders to use what little discretionary funding they have on hand to cover their state-mandated programs. However, middle-class residents continue to expect their county governments to be responsive to their every need and provide them with more and better services. They don't trust their local leaders enough to raise taxes. As one county supervisor observed, "The constituents in our county still want us to be able to do everything that we could do before Proposition 13. They want us to provide new and innovative programs. They want us to have our county offices open all day every day" (Hahn,

1988, p. 39). County leaders have been placed in the unenviable position by middle-class voters and state officials of having to provide more
services with less money.

The events in the 1990s led to even more difficulties for county governments. Large counties such as Orange, San Diego, and Los Angeles
experienced rapid population growth through foreign immigration.
This led to an increase in service demands. State funding to counties
was reduced as a result of a recession that resulted in a large state budget deficit. It is no wonder, then, that all three of the major counties
faced fiscal problems by 1994. There was little flexibility in terms of
raising taxes and fees at the county level, because of Proposition 13 and
other restrictions. However, as one observer noted, "County folks are
very creative in finding ways to fund the services their constituents are
asking them to provide" (Hahn, 1988, p. 15).

When Orange County faced a financial squeeze, it turned to investing its surplus funds in risky investments as a way of generating a sizable amount of interest income for the purpose of discretionary
spending. Once this revenue-generating approach had been carried to
an extreme, the investment fund faced massive losses and the county
government had to declare bankruptcy. As the county government tried
to resolve its bankruptcy, it once again recognized how little say it had
in the revenues and expenditures that fall in the county budget after
Proposition 13. It was difficult to balance the general fund budget and
impossible to find the funds that were needed to pay its debt. The
county leaders had to turn to the state legislature, which then gave the
county government permission to divert some county tax funds that
could be allocated to new bonds to pay off the existing debt. This recovery plan means that Orange County can expect a tight budget with
little flexibility for many years.

"Counties are in a world full of hurt. . . . The legislature must take
some action and make some changes," observed Alvin Sokolow at
the tenth anniversary of Proposition 13 (Hahn, 1988, p. 5). The
Orange County bankruptcy should have served as a wake-up call;
however, there have been no changes in state and local government
relations as the twentieth anniversary approaches. There have been a
number of proposals in the 1990s for revising the state constitution.
A major reason for reform is to bring logic and efficiency to state
and county government relations. Such an effort would require the
approval of the governor, the state legislature, and the voters (Cain
and Noll, 1995).

The twenty-three-member California Constitution Revision Commission began its work in 1994 and provided its recommendations two years later. At this point, they have not been acted upon by the governor or the state legislature. A major goal is to reduce the confusion over the services shared by state and local governments. The commission would require the governor to submit a plan that explicitly assigns responsibilities and finance sources for state and local services. It would also require a charter for each county and a plan for delivering government services within the area. There would be a requirement that state programs be funded with state revenues. An incentive for having a charter is that the state government would be prohibited from taking back the property tax revenues allocated to county governments. Local governments would also be given greater control over generating revenues by being allowed to pass tax and bond measures with a simple majority vote (California Constitution Revision Commission, 1996, pp. 9–10).

Other ideas are being offered for "reinventing" state and local government relations. One proposal requires the state to set minimum service standards for core public services; however, the state would have to pay for this level of service with state funds only (Cain and Noll, 1995). A proposal by the California Business Roundtable (1995) would give all programs that deliver services to the public to local governments, and all programs that are of statewide concern, such as the judicial system, to state governments. The business group also recommends allowing local governments to refuse to carry out unfunded mandates. It also seeks a state plan to consolidate local special districts in order to create a more efficient delivery system. The legislative analyst (1993b, p. 11) has concluded that "California's existing 'system' of state and local government clearly does not work." This office calls for changes in state and local government responsibilities, with the state given only certain statewide functions and local governments given authority over local programs. Local governments would receive a larger share of property tax revenues to pay for these services.

One of the factors that will slow down the efforts to restructure county and state government relations is the state budget process. The state government faces revenue limits and expenditure limitations. State legislators have also seen their flexibility shrink in terms of state spending through constitutional mandates such as minimum funding for K-12 education through Proposition 98, state mandates such as funding for youth corrections, and federal legislative mandates such as

Medicaid (Ellwood and Sprague, 1995). The state leaders will be reluctant to require that state mandates be fully funded by the state because they now have so little discretion over state government spending.

State and local government relations in California will be further complicated by two recent state policy changes. The state voters passed Proposition 218 in November 1996. This citizen initiative will place restrictions on raising local taxes and fees that were not covered in Proposition 13. The federal government passed welfare reform, which places the responsibility of caring for the poor more firmly in the hands of state governments. One possible outcome is that the state government will pass on the responsibilities to local governments without providing adequate funds.

In the future, state governments will have to take more of a leadership role in developing a comprehensive system that determines who delivers what local public services and how they will be funded. State leaders have the capability of easing the fiscal burdens now facing many local governments (see Campbell and Bahl, 1976; Callahan and Bosek, 1976). County governments will need to change, since the general laws were designed to govern rural counties. States can also provide incentives for counties to create charter governments that may better fit their urban character.

The Orange County bankruptcy may have been averted if the state government had taken a more active role in state and local government relations. For instance, a state requirement for a county charter would have helped to move Orange County toward a county government structure that is less fragmented and has more oversight and fiscal accountability. A lower threshold for passing local bonds and tax increases than the current two-thirds majority would have eased the fiscal pressures on local officials. If county leaders had been given more control over state-mandated spending, there would have been less temptation to increase the discretionary funds through risky investments. This is an era when all governments are challenged to meet growing needs with limited resources. State and local fiscal reform can provide greater certainty about who will pay for services and how they will be delivered to the public in the most efficient and effective manner.

Right now, Orange County's future is in hock because of its past mistakes. What happened there, for all of the reasons presented in this book, could happen elsewhere. In some sense, what occurred in Orange County is really a failure of governance and not only government. By this I mean that the responsibility for preventing what occurred in Orange County lies not just with the elected and appointed officials but also with the voters. They showed both little interest in who was being elected and a great distrust of government, as shown by the large numbers who did not vote in local elections and the overwhelming support for tax limits and term limits by those who did go to the polls. They put their elected officials in an impossible situation by constraining their ability to raise revenues and at the same time demanding the same or better services. When the county pool collapsed and the interest income that had provided a steady stream of revenues vanished, the voters turned their backs on the problem and refused to honor the debts that were incurred to give them the services they had taken for granted. In some sense, the voters' actions can be seen as a breach of contract between the governing and governed. Voters were not, of course, the only parties who failed to honor their responsibilities, considering, for instance, the actions of Bob Citron, the investment firms, county government officials, local government officials, state officials, and the press. However, the voters' role in the Orange County bankruptcy offers the greatest lesson of all. It sounds a warning that there is a disturbing trend toward a lack of civic participation that can have profound implications for the future of U.S. communities.

Time Lines

One of the research tasks involved in writing this book was establishing the dates for the major occurrences during the Orange County financial crisis. These include the events leading up to the bankruptcy, the response to the fiscal emergency, the road to bankruptcy recovery, and local government reforms after the bankruptcy.

These dates were determined largely by reviewing the daily newspaper stories and consulting the chronological tables that were published in the local newspapers. The newspaper sources that were used for the tables in this appendix include the *Los Angeles Times* Orange County edition (1995a, 1996a, 1996c, 1997a, 1997d) and the *Orange County Register* (1995b, 1996b). Internal documents provided by the county government (County of Orange, 1996a, 1996b), the local government investors in the county pool (Orange County Investment Pool, 1995a, 1995b, 1995c, 1995d), and the Orange County Division of the League of California Cities (Huston, 1995) also contained information on the timing of key events during the financial crisis.

The dates for important events during the Orange County bankruptcy are discussed in the text. To provide a more detailed picture, I have summarized the time lines in chronological order in the tables in this appendix.

TABLE A-I   EVENTS OF 1994 LEADING
UP TO THE BANKRUPTCY

February 4	Federal Reserve Board raises interest rates for the first of six times in 1994
April 13	City of Tustin withdraws all funds from the investment pool
May 31	John Moorlach warns Board of Supervisors about investment pool
June 7	Bob Citron defeats John Moorlach and is reelected treasurer
June 14	Supervisors vote for $600 million in bonds to invest in pool
October 24	CAO informed of problems with pool by treasurer's office
October 31	Treasurer assures largest investors of adequate cash in the pool
November 3	Consultant retained by county government to review pool
November 15	Irvine Ranch Water District requests withdrawal of millions from pool
November 16	Consultant report indicates $1.5 billion loss in pool
November 29	Treasurer urges ten largest pool investors not to withdraw funds
November 30	Investment firms asked to extend loans and to seek no collateral
December 2	Orange County publicly announces $1.5 billion paper loss
December 3	Attempt to obtain financial help from investment firms fails; county officials decide to liquidate investment pool
December 4	Supervisors briefed by CAO on worsening financial crisis; CAO asks for and receives Treasurer Bob Citron's resignation
December 6	CS First Boston seizes over $2 billion in county collateral for loans due; Orange County files for Chapter 9 bankruptcy

TABLE A-2 MEASURES TOWARD DAMAGE CONTROL AND LIMITING LOSSES AFTER THE BANKRUPTCY

December 7, 1994	Orange County credit rating falls to "junk" status after bankruptcy filing
December 8	County defaults on $110 million pension bond
	Wall Street investment firms sell off securities held as collateral
	Tom Hayes named by supervisors to manage investment pool
December 12	County management team begins to meet with department heads
December 13	Tom Hayes decides on strategy of a speedy sale of all risky holdings; Salomon Brothers to sell the pool's assets
December 14	U.S. trustee appoints two creditor committees
	Pool Participants Committee begins meeting daily
December 19	U.S. bankruptcy judge authorizes emergency release of $152.6 million from investment pool funds for local government agencies to meet payrolls; $115 million goes to school district payrolls
December 22	U.S. bankruptcy judge approves agreement between the county and the Pool Participants Committee to allow the release of up to $1 billion from investment pool on a hardship basis if approved by Pool Participants Committee
December 26	$60.5 million in hardship approvals granted by Pool Participants Committee
December 30	Pool Participants Committee begins to meet on regular basis to review, discuss, and approve hardship distributions
January 2, 1995	Supervisors Jim Silva and Marian Bergeson join the board
January 12	County files a $2 billion lawsuit against Merrill Lynch
January 20	All risky securities in the county pool are sold; loss is $1.64 billion

TABLE A-3   INVESTMENT POOL SETTLEMENT,
BUDGET CUTS, AND HOUSE CLEANING

January 20, 1995	Orange County Business Council names task force to assist in negotiating investment pool settlement
January 23	Supervisors reassign CAO Ernie Schneider
February 7	Orange County Business Council proposes pool settlement plan
February 10	Supervisors appoint Chief Executive Officer William Popejoy
February 17	Governor calls legislature into special session on Orange County
February 25	CEO fires former CAO and assistant treasurer, asks for resignation of county counsel and elected auditor-controller
March 7	CEO proposes 1,040 layoffs and 563 job eliminations in county
March 15	CEO proposes half-cent sales tax for bankruptcy recovery
March 17	Orange County Business Council supports tax increase
March 21	John Moorlach chosen by supervisors as acting treasurer
March 26	County and pool participants reach agreement
March 29	Supervisors approve sales tax measure for June 27 election
April 27	Former treasurer Bob Citron pleads guilty to six felony charges
May 2	Judge approves agreement reached by county and pool members
May 15	Governor signs legislation to allow debt refinance for pool IOUs
May 16	Former assistant treasurer is indicted by grand jury
May 23	Cities, schools, and others withdraw nearly $2.3 billion from pool

TABLE A-4   THE ROAD TO BANKRUPTCY RECOVERY

June 2, 1995	County says it will roll over $800 million in short-term notes and pay extra interest; investors describe this offer as a default on bonds
June 13	County sells $279 million in recovery notes for investment pool IOUs
June 27	Voters reject Measure R sales tax increase
June 29	Board of Supervisors tells CEO Popejoy that they will set policy
July 7	Investors agree to roll over $800 million in short-term notes for one year
July 13	CEO William Popejoy announces resignation as of July 31
July 14	Supervisors appoint Jan Mittermeier as interim CEO
August 2	Governor Wilson vetoes bus tax diversion plan to cover bankruptcy debts
August 7	Supervisor Vasquez, chair of board, announces September 22 resignation
August 21	Supervisors approve county consensus plan to divert tax funds from other county agencies to general fund in order to pay bondholders and vendors; local governments agree to wait for lawsuit proceeds to pay IOUs
October 9	Governor signs legislation allowing the diversion of tax funds
December 20	County files $3 billion lawsuit against auditor KPMG Peat Marwick
December 21	Bankruptcy escape plan is filed in bankruptcy court
June 5, 1996	County sells $880 million in bonds
June 11	County files lawsuits against other investment banking firms
June 12	County pays investors $800 million in overdue notes; Orange County officially ends the bankruptcy

TABLE A-5   LEGAL ACTIONS
AGAINST COUNTY OFFICIALS

April 27, 1995	Robert Citron, former Orange County treasurer Pleaded guilty to six felonies, including skimming interest earnings from schools, cities, and agencies to put into a county account; sentenced to one year in jail and $100,000 fine; served eight months time in a work release program in the county jail during the day
May 16	Matthew Raabe, former Orange County assistant treasurer
	Grand jury criminal indictment on same charges as Citron, including skimming interest earnings
December 13	Ron Rubino, former Orange County budget director
	Grand jury criminal indictment in the interest diversion scheme
	Roger Stanton and William Steiner, Orange County supervisors
	Orange County grand jury files civil accusations to remove them from office for "official misconduct"
	Steven Lewis, Orange County auditor-controller
	Orange County grand jury files civil accusations to remove him from office for "official misconduct"
September 13, 1996	Hung jury in Ron Rubino trial; Rubino enters guilty plea to a misdemeanor charge of falsifying public records; sentenced to two years of probation and 100 hours of community service
November 26	State appeals court dismisses all charges against supervisors Roger Stanton and William Steiner
May 2, 1997	Matthew Raabe found guilty on five felony counts; three-year prison sentence currently under appeal
December 6	Attorney general's office recommends dropping the pending case against Steven Lewis

TABLE A-6   REFORMING LOCAL GOVERNMENT

October 12, 1995	Governor signs legislation on county treasurer reforms
October 26	Council of governments proposal reviewed by Orange County Division of League of California Cities
November 28	Supervisors vote to place charter proposal on March ballot
December 12	Bankruptcy recovery plan filed in court
January 1, 1996	County treasurer reforms become state law
March 26	Charter proposal for county government reform defeated
April 9	Supervisors ask CEO for county government restructuring plan
June 3	Council of governments formed
June 12	Orange County officially ends the bankruptcy
June 20	CEO's plan for county government restructuring approved
November 5	Term limits measure for supervisors passes; term limits established in seven cities
November 19	CEO's plans for budget cuts and reorganization approved
May 16, 1997	CEO announces elimination of 220 county positions

Orange County Annual Surveys

The Orange County Annual Survey has been conducted at the University of California at Irvine each year since 1982. Its purpose is to measure political, social, and economic trends in the county. The Orange County Annual Survey was begun by Mark Baldassare and has been codirected since 1986 by Mark Baldassare and Cheryl Katz.

This is a random-digit-dial telephone survey that always includes interviews with 1,000 Orange County adult residents. The survey is generally conducted in late August and early September. The methodology has been the same for all fifteen surveys.

Telephone interviewing is conducted on weekend days and weekday nights, using a computer-generated random sample of telephone numbers. Up to four callbacks are made for each random telephone number. Within a household, adult respondents are randomly chosen for interviewing. Each year the interview includes about 100 questions and takes an average of twenty to twenty-five minutes to complete. Some of the survey questions are repeated each year, for the analysis of time trends; other questions are asked less frequently. Most of the questions are closed-ended. The topics have included attitudes toward local government, local policy preferences, political attitudes, economic attitudes, residential satisfaction, housing, and demographics.

The telephone interviewing is in English and Spanish, as needed. The field work has been conducted by professional interviewing firms. The completion rate for the survey is generally around 65 to 70 percent. Once the surveys are completed, the sample characteristics are compared with the U.S. census and state population figures by city and subregion within Orange County. The survey data are statistically weighted as needed by population size, age, gender, or other characteristics to correspond to the actual regional distribution and demographic features of Orange County residents.

The sampling error for the total sample of 1,000 in the Orange County Annual Survey is ±3 percent at the 95 percent confidence level. This means that 95 times out of 100, the results will be within three percentage points of what they would be if all adults in Orange County were interviewed. The sampling error for any subgroup is larger.

The final reports for the 1982 to 1996 Orange County Annual Surveys, including all of the questions, are archived at the University of California at Irvine main library.

In this book we include the results of Orange County Annual Surveys that were conducted before, during, and after the Orange County bankruptcy. The survey results are discussed in the text. In order to provide the specific questions and more detailed results, I have summarized the Orange County Annual Survey findings in the tables in this appendix.

TABLE B-1   ORANGE COUNTY'S TRENDS IN
MEDIAN HOUSEHOLD INCOME, 1982–1994

1994	$47,000
1993	47,000
1992	45,000
1991	49,000
1990	49,000
1989	45,000
1988	44,000
1987	42,000
1986	41,000
1985	39,000
1984	36,000
1983	32,000
1982	29,000
Percent change, 1990–1994	– 4
Percent change, 1982–1990	69

SOURCE: Baldassare and Katz (1994).

TABLE B-2   PERCEIVED SOCIAL AND ECONOMIC
STATUS IN ORANGE COUNTY

Orange County Trends over Time

Social Class	1992	1986
Upper or upper middle class	27%	34%
Middle class	55	54
Lower or lower middle class	18	12

National Comparisons, 1996

Household Income	Orange County	U.S.
Not enough	17%	19%
Just enough	51	57
More than enough	32	24

SOURCE: Baldassare and Katz (1986, 1996).

TABLE B-3   ORANGE COUNTY'S POLITICAL
PROFILE BY PARTY, 1994

"Would you consider yourself to be politically . . ."

	All Adults	Democrats	Republicans
Very liberal	7%	14%	2%
Somewhat liberal	19	33	10
Middle-of-the-road	27	32	21
Somewhat conservative	31	16	42
Very conservative	16	5	25

SOURCE: Baldassare and Katz (1994).

TABLE B-4   ATTITUDES TOWARD LOCAL GOVERNMENT
BEFORE THE BANKRUPTCY

	Voters	Democrats	Republicans

"How would you rate the performance of your city government in solving problems in your community?"

	Voters	Democrats	Republicans
Excellent/good	39%	39%	41%
Fair	37	37	36
Poor	13	15	12
Don't know/other	11	9	11

"Do you think the current system of county government and city governments sharing responsibilities for solving problems is effective, or not?"

	Voters	Democrats	Republicans
Yes	56%	54%	58%
No	39	32	27
Don't know	5	14	15

"Compared to the way it is now, would you prefer to see the county government have more responsibility or the city government have more responsibility in your community?"

	Voters	Democrats	Republicans
County	28%	29%	25%
City	58	56	62
No change	6	9	6
Other/don't know	8	6	7

"Would you favor or oppose the merger of county government and city governments into one large countywide government?

	Voters	Democrats	Republicans
Favor	29%	31%	23%
Oppose	63	60	69
Don't know	8	9	8

SOURCES: Baldassare (1985); Baldassare and Katz (1991).

TABLE B-5   THE DECLINE IN LOCAL SERVICE
RATINGS IN ORANGE COUNTY, 1982–1991

"I'd like to ask you how you would rate some of the main public services you are supposed to receive—excellent, good, fair, or poor?"

	Percent Excellent or Good Ratings	
	1991	1982
Parks and recreation	71	82
Police protection	59	76
Streets and roads	58	72
Public schools	28	45

SOURCE: Baldassare (1982); Baldassare and Katz (1991).

TABLE B-6 OPINIONS ABOUT THE LOCAL
GOVERNMENT STRUCTURE, AUGUST 1995

	1995	1985

"Do you think the current system of county government and city governments sharing responsibilities for solving problems is effective, or not?"

Yes	41%	56%
No	51	39
Don't know	8	5

"Compared to the way it is now, would you prefer to see the county government have more responsibility or the city government have more responsibility in your community?"

County	22%	28%
City	66	58
Other, don't know	12	14

"Would you favor or oppose the merger of county government and city governments into one large countywide government?"

Favor	26%	29%
Oppose	68	63
Don't know	6	8

SOURCE: Baldassare and Katz (1995).

TABLE B-7   OVERALL RATINGS OF ORANGE COUNTY,
SEPTEMBER 1996

	1996	1995	1994
"How would you rate the economy in Orange County today?"			
Excellent/good	44%	19%	28%
Fair	45	50	54
Poor	10	30	7
Don't know	1	1	1
"Thinking about the quality of life in Orange County, how do you think things are going?"			
Going well	82%	68%	71%
Going badly	18	32	29
"In general, do you think that buying a home in Orange County today is an excellent, good, only fair, or a poor investment?" (homeowners)			
Excellent/good	60%	50%	57%
Fair	30	31	28
Poor	8	18	14
Don't know	2	1	1

SOURCE: Baldassare and Katz (1996).

TABLE B-8   RATINGS OF LOCAL SERVICES, SEPTEMBER 1996

"I'd like to ask you about some of the local public services you are supposed to receive—excellent, good, fair, or poor?"

	Excellent/Good		Fair	Poor	Don't Know
	1996	1991			
Police protection	75%	59%	19%	4%	2%
Parks and recreation	74	71	19	4	3
Public libraries	66	NA	19	6	9
Streets and roads	60	58	30	9	1
Public schools	42	28	30	14	14

SOURCE: Baldassare and Katz (1996).

TABLE B-9   CONFIDENCE IN LOCAL GOVERNMENT, SEPTEMBER 1996

"How would you rate the performance of your county government (and city government) in solving problems in your community?"

	County Government	City Government
Excellent/good	23%	42%
Fair	53	43
Poor	20	9
Don't know/NA	4	6

"When your county government leaders decide what policies to adopt, how much attention do you think they pay to what the people think?"

	September 1996	June 1995
A lot of attention	7%	5%
Some attention	52	40
Very little/no attention	38	53
Don't know	3	2

"In general, do you think that the people who run county government waste a lot of the money we pay in taxes, waste very little of the money we pay in taxes, or waste none of the money we pay in taxes?"

	September 1996	June 1995
Waste a lot of money	39%	51%
Waste some money	45	40
Waste very little or none	11	6
Don't know	5	3

SOURCE: Baldassare and Katz (1996); Times Orange County Poll (1995d).

The Times Orange County Polls

The Times Orange County Poll is commissioned by the *Los Angeles Times* Orange County edition. It has been conducted since 1988. Its purpose is to monitor politics and elections, business and economic issues, and lifestyle trends in Orange County. The surveys are designed and conducted by Mark Baldassare and Cheryl Katz as consultants to the editorial staff of the *Los Angeles Times* Orange County edition.

These are random-digit-dial telephone surveys that typically include interviews with 600 Orange County adult residents. Telephone interviewing is conducted on weekend days and weekday nights, using a computer-generated random sample of telephone numbers. Within a household, adult respondents are randomly chosen for interview. For election surveys, an additional screening question asks to speak to an adult respondent in the household who is registered to vote.

The Times Orange County Poll is generally conducted four times a year. A survey usually contains about forty questions and takes from ten to twelve minutes to complete. Most of the questions are closed-ended. The topics vary depending on the news issues in Orange County. The issues have included attitudes toward local government, local policy preferences, election preferences, and political attitudes.

The telephone interviewing is in English and Spanish, as needed. The field work has been conducted by professional interviewing firms. The survey samples are compared to the U.S. census and state figures by city for Orange County. When necessary, the data are statistically weighted to represent the actual regional distribution and demographic characteristics of Orange County residents. The survey samples thus have population distributions and demographic characteristics that are comparable to the U.S. census and other survey data, including the Orange County Annual Surveys.

The sampling error for the total sample of 600 in the Times Orange County Polls is ±4 percent at the 95 percent confidence level. This means that 95 times out of 100, the results will be within four percentage points of what they would be if all adults in Orange County were interviewed. The sampling error for any subgroup would be larger. The results of the Times Orange County Poll are published in news articles in the *Los Angeles Times* Orange County edition. In this book, we report the results of several surveys that were designed to measure the public's reactions to the Orange County financial crisis in 1994, 1995, and 1996. In addition, we refer to earlier Times Orange County Polls on political preferences and attitudes toward local government. The tables in this appendix give the full question wording and response categories.

TABLE C-1   ORANGE COUNTY'S FISCAL CONSERVATISM
AND SOCIAL LIBERALISM

	Voters	Democrats	Republicans
"When something is run by the government, it is usually inefficient and wasteful."			
Agree	76%	61%	83%
Disagree	22	35	16
Don't know	2	4	1
"Poor people have become too dependent on government assistance programs."			
Agree	83%	75%	87%
Disagree	14	23	9
Don't know	3	2	4
"The federal government controls too much of our daily lives."			
Agree	67%	55%	74%
Disagree	31	44	24
Don't know	2	1	2
"There needs to be stricter laws and regulations to protect the environment."			
Agree	73%	84%	66%
Disagree	25	14	31
Don't know	2	2	3
"Do you favor or oppose a law that would prohibit abortion in most cases?"			
Favor	29%	26%	33%
Oppose	66	72	61
Don't know	5	2	4

SOURCE: Times Orange County Poll (1992, 1994b).

TABLE C-2 PUBLIC PERCEPTIONS OF ORANGE COUNTY LEADERSHIP, MAY 1994

"When it comes to Orange County's leaders, what names come to mind?"
(open-ended, up to three)

Number of Mentions

No one named	56%
One named	22
Two named	11
Three named	11

Specific Names Mentioned

Tom Riley, supervisor	11%
Gaddi Vasquez, supervisor	11
Brad Gates, sheriff	10
Harriet Wieder, supervisor	8

SOURCE: Times Orange County Poll (1994a).

TABLE C-3 POPULARITY AND NAME IDENTIFICATION OF SUPERVISORS, MAY 1994

"Do you have a favorable or an unfavorable opinion of the following people in Orange County politics, or don't you know enough about them to have an opinion?"

	Favorable	Unfavorable	Don't Know
Tom Riley	26%	16%	58%
Gaddi Vasquez	24	11	65
Harriet Wieder	24	18	58
Roger Stanton	17	9	74
William Steiner	16	6	78

SOURCE: Times Orange County Poll (1994a).

TABLE C-4   JOB PERFORMANCE RATINGS OF THE SUPERVISORS, MAY 1994

	Voters	Democrats	Republicans
"How would you rate the Orange County Board of Supervisors in terms of providing overall leadership?"			
Excellent/good	28%	29%	28%
Fair	50	50	51
Poor	15	17	13
Don't know	7	4	8
"How would you rate the Orange County Board of Supervisors in terms of representing the views of local residents?"			
Excellent/good	25%	27%	27%
Fair	42	41	42
Poor	27	27	24
Don't know	6	5	7

SOURCE: Times Orange County Poll (1994a).

TABLE C-5   JOB PERFORMANCE RATINGS OF THE COUNTY TREASURER, SHERIFF, AND DISTRICT ATTORNEY, MAY 1994

	Voters	Democrats	Republicans
"How would you rate the job performance of Orange County Sheriff Brad Gates?"			
Excellent/good	51%	46%	58%
Fair	31	34	28
Poor	10	12	7
Don't know	8	8	7
"How would you rate the job performance of Orange County District Attorney Mike Capizzi?"			
Excellent/good	34%	37%	32%
Fair	23	23	24
Poor	7	6	6
Don't know	36	34	38
"If the election for Orange County Treasurer/Tax Collector were held today, would you vote for . . ."			
Bob Citron	41%	39%	43%
John Moorlach	22	19	23
Other	1	1	1
Don't know	36	41	33

SOURCE: Times Orange County Poll (1994a).

TABLE C-6   PUBLIC REACTIONS OF FEAR AND ANGER,
DECEMBER 1994

"How do you feel about the actions of local officials that led to the Orange County financial crisis?"

Very angry	39%
Somewhat angry	36
Not too angry	10
Not at all angry	11
Don't know	4

"In general, how worried are you about these events in Orange County?"

Very worried	28%
Somewhat worried	40
Not too worried	18
Not at all worried	13
Don't know	1

"How much confidence do you have in the ability of the Orange County Board of Supervisors to solve the county's financial crisis?"

Great deal	10%
Some	41
Very little	31
None	16
Don't know	2

SOURCE: Times Orange County Poll (1994c).

TABLE C-7   PERCEIVED IMPACTS OF THE
BANKRUPTCY, DECEMBER 1994

*"Do you think that . . . will have to be reduced a lot, somewhat, very little,
or not at all as a result of the investment fund losses?"*

	County Services	City Services	School Programs
A lot	30%	17%	22%
Somewhat	41	46	37
Very little	12	18	17
Not at all	9	13	17
Don't know	8	6	7

*"How worried are you that you or a family member will be hurt financially
as a result of the crisis involving the county's investment fund?"*

Very worried	16%
Somewhat worried	27
Not too worried	23
Not at all worried	33
Don't know	1

*"Do you or a member of your family currently receive a salary, contract or
other payments from the county, a city, school district, or other agency that is
affected by Orange County's financial crisis?"*

Yes	17%
No	83

SOURCE: Times Orange County Poll (1994c).

TABLE C-8   EARLY REACTIONS TO POSSIBLE SOLUTIONS, DECEMBER 1994

	All Voters	Democrats	Republicans

"Do you favor or oppose asking the state for money to help Orange County out of its financial problems?"

	All Voters	Democrats	Republicans
Favor	52%	52%	47%
Oppose	41	41	45
Don't know	8	7	8

"Do you favor or oppose raising local taxes to help restore the Orange County investment funds that were lost?"

	All Voters	Democrats	Republicans
Favor	17%	18%	17%
Oppose	80	79	80
Don't know	3	3	3

SOURCE: Times Orange County Poll (1994c).

TABLE C-9   POLITICAL FALLOUT, JANUARY 1995

"Who do you think is most to blame for the Orange County financial crisis?"

Supervisors	22%
Citron	16
Merrill Lynch, brokers	2
County administrator	1
Local government investors	0
All of the above	52
Other answers	7

"Some people have asked for the recall of the three members of the Orange County Board of Supervisors who were in office when the Orange County financial crisis began. Do you favor or oppose the recall of . . ."

	Gaddi Vasquez	Roger Stanton	Bill Steiner
Favor	48%	48%	46%
Oppose	28	27	29
Don't know	24	25	25

"Do you favor or oppose removing from office County Administrator Ernie Schneider, who was also in office when the Orange County financial crisis began?"

Favor	53%
Oppose	25
Don't know	22

SOURCE: Times Orange County Poll (1995b).

TABLE C-10   PREFERRED SOLUTIONS, JANUARY 1995

	All Voters	Democrats	Republicans

"The county government has a budget shortfall of about 170 million dollars over the next six months as a result of the failed investment pool. Which of the following do you think is the best solution to this loss?"

	All Voters	Democrats	Republicans
Cut spending	31%	27%	34%
Raise user fees	15	14	16
Raise taxes	4	8	3
More than one of the above	40	46	36
Other answer	10	5	11

"Would you favor or oppose increasing county fees?"

	All Voters	Democrats	Republicans
Favor	60%	59%	61%
Oppose	38	40	38
Don't know	2	1	1

"Do you approve or disapprove of selling John Wayne Airport?"

	All Voters	Democrats	Republicans
Approve	50%	47%	50%
Disapprove	36	41	36
Don't know	14	12	14

"Would you favor or oppose raising taxes so that investors who bought Orange County bonds can be paid back in full?"

	All Voters	Democrats	Republicans
Favor	18%	22%	15%
Oppose	78	76	81
Don't know	4	2	4

SOURCE: Times Orange County Poll (1995b).

TABLE C-11 PERCEPTIONS OF THE ROOT CAUSES,
JANUARY 1995

	All Voters	Democrats	Republicans

"Some people say Orange County's financial crisis was caused at least in part by Proposition 13, which made it so hard to raise taxes that schools and local governments were forced to make risky investments to get enough money to pay for their operations. Do you agree or disagree with this view?"

Agree	19%	27%	12%
Disagree	77	69	85
Don't know	4	4	3

"Others say the financial crisis came about in part because county government was overstaffed and wasted taxpayers' money for years. Do you agree or disagree with this view?"

Agree	67%	64%	70%
Disagree	27	32	25
Don't know	6	4	5

SOURCE: Times Orange County Poll (1995b).

TABLE C-12 PUBLIC REACTIONS TO THE
MEASURE R SALES TAX, APRIL 1995

"If the election were held today, would you vote yes or no on Measure R, the Bankruptcy Recovery Tax?"

	Yes	No	Don't Know
All voters	36%	57%	7%
Democrats	45	49	6
Republicans	31	62	7
18 to 34	35	51	14
35 to 54	38	59	3
55 and older	34	59	7
Supervisors given excellent/good rating	56	35	9
Supervisors given fair rating	38	56	6
Supervisors given poor rating	28	65	7

SOURCE: Times Orange County Poll (1995c).

TABLE C-13   VOTERS' REASONS FOR SUPPORTING OR
OPPOSING THE MEASURE R SALES TAX, APRIL 1995

"Why would you vote no on Measure R?"

Unfair to pay for others' mistakes	45%
No new taxes	26
Other ways to raise money	14
Supervisors must quit first	6
Other answers	9

"Why would you vote yes on Measure R?"

Only way to raise enough money	57%
Maintain county services	8
Protect schools, law enforcement	7
Avoid hurting the economy	7
No more budget cuts, layoffs	5
Avoid bond defaults	4
Other answers	12

SOURCE: Times Orange County Poll (1995c).

TABLE C-14   RATINGS OF COUNTY OFFICIALS, APRIL 1995

	April	December

"How would you rate the job performance of the Orange County Board of Supervisors in handling the county's financial crisis?"

	April	December
Excellent/good	13%	21%
Fair	33	35
Poor	48	34
Don't know	6	10

"How would you rate the job performance of county Chief Executive Officer William Popejoy in handling the county's financial crisis?"

	April	December
Excellent/good	30%	NA
Fair	35	
Poor	15	
Don't know	5	

SOURCE: Times Orange County Poll (1995c).

TABLE C-15   PERCEIVED IMPACTS OF THE
BANKRUPTCY, APRIL 1995

	April	January

"Have you heard or read about any cuts in local services that will directly affect you and your household this year?"

	April	January
Yes	32%	22%
No	68	78

"Do you think the investment fund losses will hurt the quality of life in Orange County . . ."

	April	January
A lot	28%	17%
Somewhat	48	57
Not much	12	18
Not at all	8	7
Don't know	4	1

"Do you think the investment fund losses will hurt the quality of education in your school district . . ."

	April	January
A lot	34%	22%
Somewhat	42	40
Not much	11	21
Not at all	8	12
Don't know	5	5

SOURCE: Times Orange County Poll (1995c).

TABLE C-16   PUBLIC REACTIONS TO
A THREATENED STATE TAKEOVER, APRIL 1995

"Do you favor or oppose having a state panel take over and run Orange County government?"

	All Voters	Democrats	Republicans
Favor	28%	33%	26%
Oppose	52	48	54
Don't know	20	19	20

SOURCE: Times Orange County Poll (1995c).

TABLE C-17   VOTER DISTRUST BEFORE THE
MEASURE R SALES TAX VOTE, JUNE 1995

"In general, do you think the people who run county government waste a lot, some, very little, or none of the money we pay in taxes?"

	All Voters	Democrats	Republicans
Waste a lot	51%	47%	53%
Waste some	40	42	40
Waste very little or none	6	7	6
Don't know	3	4	2

"When your county government leaders decide what policies to adopt, how much attention do you think they pay to what the people think?"

	All Voters	Democrats	Republicans
A lot of attention	5%	6%	5%
Some attention	40	38	44
Very little/no attention	53	54	49
Don't know	2	2	2

Effects of Distrust

	Yes on Measure R	No on Measure R	Don't Know
Voters who say county government wastes a lot of tax money	31%	56%	13%
Voters who say county government pays little or no attention to people	33	53	14

SOURCE: Times Orange County Poll (1995d).

TABLE C-18   PERCEIVED IMPACTS OF THE
BANKRUPTCY, JUNE 1995

	June	April

"As for the impacts of the Orange County investment fund losses, have you heard or read about any cuts in local services or public school programs that will directly affect you and your household this year?"

	June	April
Yes	31%	32%
No	69	68

"Do you think the investment fund losses will hurt the quality of life in Orange County . . ."

	June	April
A lot	22%	28%
Somewhat	56	48
Not much	12	12
Not at all	6	8
Don't know	4	4

"Do you think the investment fund losses will hurt the quality of education in your school district . . ."

	June	April
A lot	28%	34%
Somewhat	44	42
Not much	12	11
Not at all	10	8
Don't know	6	5

SOURCE: Times Orange County Poll (1995d).

TABLE C-19   VOTER INTEREST IN THE MEASURE R
SALES TAX ELECTION, JUNE 1995

"How interested are you in the June 27 Measure R special election—very interested, somewhat interested, not too interested, or not at all interested?"

	Percent Very Interested
All voters	54
Vote yes on R	49
Vote no on R	60
Republicans	56
Democrats	53
18 to 34	32
35 to 54	60
55 and older	66
Homeowner	59
Renter	43
Under $50,000 household income	48
$50,000 or more household income	57
Child in public schools	58
No child in public schools	53

"Thinking about the . . . election, will you definitely vote, probably vote, probably not vote, or definitely not vote?"

	Percent Definitely Voting
October 1992 Presidential	94
October 1990 Governor/Measure M sales tax	86
October 1994 Governor	83
June 1995 Measure R sales tax, special	69
October 1989 Measure M sales tax, special	66

SOURCE: Times Orange County Poll (1995d).

TABLE C-20   JOB RATINGS FOR COUNTY
OFFICIALS, JUNE 1995

"How would you rate the job performance of the Orange County Board of Supervisors in handling the county's financial crisis?"

	June	April
Excellent/good	12%	13%
Fair	33	33
Poor	49	48
Don't know	6	6

"How would you rate the job performance of county Chief Executive Officer William Popejoy in handling the county's financial crisis?"

	June	April
Excellent/good	35%	30%
Fair	33	35
Poor	16	15
Don't know	16	20

How would you rate the job performance of Orange County Sheriff Brad Gates?"

	June	May 1994
Excellent/good	51%	51%
Fair	28	31
Poor	8	10
Don't know	13	8

SOURCE: Times Orange County Poll (1995d).

TABLE C-21   VOTER ATTITUDES TOWARD
COUNTY REFORM, MARCH 1996

	All Voters	Democrats	Republicans

"Do you favor or oppose setting term limits to members of the Orange County Board of Supervisors to no more than two consecutive four-year terms in office?"

	All Voters	Democrats	Republicans
Favor	79%	79%	80%
Oppose	13	13	13
Don't know	8	8	7

"Do you favor or oppose authorizing Orange County government to contract out with private companies to provide county services?"

	All Voters	Democrats	Republicans
Favor	65%	53%	71%
Oppose	25	34	21
Don't know	10	13	7

"Do you favor or oppose having a county executive officer appointed by the Board of Supervisors to manage all day-to-day operations and supervise department heads?"

	All Voters	Democrats	Republicans
Favor	54%	54%	56%
Oppose	30	32	27
Don't know	16	14	17

"Do you favor or oppose changing the Orange County treasurer, clerk, and auditor from elected positions to appointed positions in Orange County government?"

	All Voters	Democrats	Republicans
Favor	34%	33%	37%
Oppose	51	50	48
Don't know	15	17	15

SOURCE: Times Orange County Poll (1996a).

TABLE C-22   VOTER ATTITUDES TOWARD COUNTY SUPERVISORS, MARCH 1996

"How would you rate the performance of the Orange County Board of Supervisors in handling the county's financial crisis?"

	March 1996	April 1995
Excellent/good	17%	13%
Fair	35	33
Poor	43	48
Don't know	5	6

"Do you think the Orange County supervisors who were in office when the bankruptcy occurred should finish their terms in office, or should they resign before their terms are over?"

	All Voters	Democrats	Republicans
Finish terms	28%	25%	29%
Resign	64	65	63
Don't know	8	10	8

"Do you think county government funds should or should not be used to pay for the legal defense of current county supervisors against charges that they failed to properly oversee the Orange County fund losses?"

	All Voters	Democrats	Republicans
Should	17%	16%	18%
Should not	77	79	75
Don't know	6	5	7

SOURCE: Times Orange County Poll (1996a).

TABLE C-23   SUPERVISORS' JOB RATINGS AFTER
THE BANKRUPTCY, OCTOBER 1996

	October 1996	May 1994
"How would you rate the Orange County Board of Supervisors in terms of providing overall leadership?"		
Excellent/good	11%	28%
Fair	38	50
Poor	39	15
Don't know	12	7
"How would you rate the Orange County Board of Supervisors in terms of representing the views of local residents?"		
Excellent/good	12%	25%
Fair	38	42
Poor	33	27
Don't know	17	6
"How would you rate the Orange County Board of Supervisors in terms of managing the County Budget?"		
Excellent/good	11%	19%
Fair	25	40
Poor	54	29
Don't know	10	12

SOURCE: Times Orange County Poll (1996b).

In-Depth Interviews

In-depth interviews were conducted with some of the individuals who participated in the events surrounding the Orange County financial crisis. These included county officials, city officials, school officials, water district officials,
business leaders, consultants, and attorneys. Most of the interviews were conducted in person and in Orange County. The exceptions were one interview
conducted in a Los Angeles attorney's office and a telephone interview with
an attorney in San Diego. The interviews generally lasted between thirty and
forty-five minutes. They were all completed between June and August 1996.
All of the initial contacts and interviews were conducted by Mark Baldassare.

The purpose of the in-depth interviews was to gather background information about the events, from a variety of perspectives, by those who were
highly involved in the crisis and its resolution. This was not designed to be a
representative or comprehensive study of the participants. For instance, three
of the key participants in the county's financial crisis were asked to be interviewed but did not make themselves available for one reason or another.
These include Bob Citron, the former county treasurer; Gaddi Vasquez, a former member of the Board of Supervisors; and Terry Andrus, the former
county counsel. These were designed to be open-ended, qualitative interviews
to assist in better understanding what had occurred during the financial crisis,
rather than to gather specific facts.

All of those interviewed were asked to comment on five questions:

1. What were your thoughts—back in 1994—when you first learned
about the losses in the investment pool and that the county government was
going to declare bankruptcy?
2. What do you think were the main causes of the financial crisis?
3. How would you describe the initial response to the financial crisis?
4. What are your thoughts about how the financial crisis was resolved?

5. What are the lessons to be learned for public policy in California and elsewhere in the nation?

Interviewees were also invited to make any other comments about the financial crisis and bankruptcy.

Twenty-three participants were interviewed. This number does not include aides or colleagues who were present during the interview. The participants are named below along with their affiliations during the financial crisis. They are listed in the order in which the interviews took place.

William Popejoy, Chief Executive Officer, County of Orange
Paul Brady, City Manager, City of Irvine
Gary Hunt, task force member, Orange County Business Council
Todd Nicholson, President, Orange County Business Council
Hank Adler, board member, Irvine Unified School District
Janet Huston, Executive Director, Orange County Division, League of California Cities
Peer Swan, board member, Irvine Ranch Water District
Michael Ruane, Executive Director, Environmental Management Agency
Stan Oftelie, Chief Executive Officer, Orange County Transportation Authority
Tom Sutton, task force member, Orange County Business Council
Ernie Schneider, Chief Administrative Officer, County of Orange
Donald Saltarelli, Board of Supervisors, County of Orange
Gary Hausdorfer, consultant and former mayor, City of San Juan Capistrano
Dan Young, consultant and former mayor, City of Santa Ana
William Steiner, Board of Supervisors, County of Orange
Roger Stanton, Board of Supervisors, County of Orange
Brad Gates, Sheriff/Coroner, County of Orange
Marian Bergeson, Board of Supervisors, County of Orange
Jan Mittermeier, Chief Executive Officer, County of Orange
Bruce Bennett, attorney representing the County of Orange
Patrick Shea, attorney representing the county investment pool participants
John Moorlach, Treasurer/Tax Collector, County of Orange
George Argyros, task force member, Orange County Business Council

References

Adams, James Ring. 1984. *Secrets of the Tax Revolt*. New York: Harcourt Brace Jovanovich.

Arthur Andersen. 1995. "County of Orange, California: Presentation to the Board of Supervisors." January 4. Santa Ana, CA: Arthur Andersen and Company.

Assembly Select Committee on the Insolvency of Orange County. 1995. *Hearing on the Subject Matter of Insolvency Legislation*. May 9. Sacramento: State of California.

Baldassare, Mark. 1982. *Orange County Annual Survey: 1982 Final Report*. Irvine: University of California.

———. 1984. *Orange County Annual Survey: 1984 Final Report*. Irvine: University of California.

———. 1985. *Orange County Annual Survey: 1985 Final Report*. Irvine: University of California.

———. 1986. *Trouble in Paradise: The Suburban Transformation in America*. New York: Columbia University Press.

———. 1989. "Citizen Preferences for Spending and Taxes in a Suburban Context." *Research in Urban Policy* 3:3–14.

———. 1992. "Suburban Communities." *Annual Review of Sociology* 18:475–494.

———. 1994. *Los Angeles Riots: Lessons for the Urban Future*. Boulder, CO: Westview Press.

———. 1996. "New Immigrant Communities in a Suburban Region." *Research in Community Sociology* 6:105–122.

Baldassare, Mark, Joshua Hassol, William Hoffman, and Abby Kanarek. 1996. "Possible Planning Roles for Regional Government: A Survey of City Planning Directors in California." *Journal of the American Planning Association* 62:17–29.

Baldassare, Mark, and Cheryl Katz. 1986. *Orange County Annual Survey: 1986 Final Report.* Irvine: University of California.

———. 1991. *Orange County Annual Survey: 1991 Final Report.* Irvine: University of California.

———. 1992. *Orange County Annual Survey: 1992 Final Report.* Irvine: University of California.

———. 1993. *Orange County Annual Survey: 1993 Final Report.* Irvine: University of California.

———. 1994. *Orange County Annual Survey: 1994 Final Report.* Irvine: University of California.

———. 1995. *Orange County Annual Survey: 1995 Final Report.* Irvine: University of California.

———. 1996. *Orange County Annual Survey: 1996 Final Report.* Irvine: University of California.

Baldassare, Mark, and Georjeanna Wilson. 1995. "More Trouble in Paradise: Urbanization and the Decline in Suburban Quality-of-Life Ratings." *Urban Affairs Quarterly* 30:690–708.

Benjamin, Gerald, and Charles Brecher. 1988. *The Two New York's: State-City Relations in the Changing Federal System.* New York: Russell Foundation.

Bergeson, Marian. 1995. "Orange County 2001." July 3. Santa Ana, CA: County of Orange.

Bollens, Scott. 1986. "A Political-Ecological Analysis of Income Inequality in the Metropolitan Area." *Urban Affairs Quarterly* 22:221–241.

Bollens, Scott. 1997. "Fragments of Regionalism: The Limits of Southern California Governance." *Journal of Urban Affairs* 19 (forthcoming).

Brody, Michael. 1986. NASA's Challenge: Ending Isolation at the Top." *Fortune,* May 12, pp. 26–32.

Burnell, B., and J. Burnell. 1989. "Community Interaction and Suburban Zoning Practices." *Urban Affairs Quarterly* 24:470–482.

Burr, James, Mary Francoeur, Brad Gewehr, Patricia McGuigan, and Katherine McManus. 1995. "Bankruptcy Aftershocks: Will Public Finance Foundations Be Shaken?" *Moody's Municipal Issues,* pp. 3–11.

Cain, Bruce, and Roger Noll. 1995. *Constitutional Reform in California.* California Policy Seminar Brief, vol. 17, no. 14. Berkeley: California Policy Seminar.

Cal-Tax News. 1993. Trailer Bills Spell out Details of Budget Compromises. July 1, 34 (13):3.

———. 1995. "Orange County Bankruptcy Hikes Government Debt Interest." March 1, 36 (5):2.

Calavita, Kitty, and Henry N. Pontell. 1992. "The Savings and Loan Crisis." In M. David Ermann and Richard J. Lundman (eds.), *Corporate and Governmental Deviance: Problems of Organizational Behavior in Contemporary Society.* New York: Oxford University Press, pp. 233–258.

California Association of County Treasurers and Tax Collectors. 1996. "Memo on Elected Treasurers from Phil Franey." November 25. Sacramento: California Association of County Treasurers and Tax Collectors.

California Attorney General's Office. 1994. "The Brown Act: Open Meetings for Local Legislative Bodies." Sacramento: State of California.

California Business Roundtable. 1995. "Revenue and Taxation Task Force: Agenda for Governance and Fiscal Reform." San Francisco: California Business Roundtable.

California Constitution Revision Commission. 1996. "Final Report and Recommendations to the Governor and the Legislature." Sacramento: State of California.

California Debt Advisory Commission. 1995. "Credit Implications of the Orange County Crisis." February 22. Sacramento: State of California.

California Department of Finance. 1991. *California's Growing Taxpayer Squeeze.* Sacramento: State of California.

———. 1995. *One Million in Five Years: California Demographics, Fall.* Sacramento: State of California.

———. 1996a. *Historical Census Populations of California State and Counties, 1900–1990.* Sacramento: State of California.

———. 1996b. *State and County Race/Ethnic Estimates, 1994.* Sacramento: State of California.

———. 1996c. *Population by Race and Ethnicity: 1970, 1980, 1990.* Sacramento: State of California.

———. 1997. *California Demographics, Winter 1997.* Sacramento: State of California.

California Journal Weekly. 1994. "Orange County Crisis Continues: Financial Catastrophe Could Be Catalyst for New Investment Laws." December 19, pp. 3, 11.

———. 1995. "Orange County: Political Agendas Begin to Piggyback on Attempts to Deal with the Bankruptcy." February 27, pp. 3, 9, 10.

California State Association of Counties. 1996. "Memo on County Information from Katherine Knighten." December 9. Sacramento: California State Association of Counties.

California State Auditor. 1995. "California State Auditor's Report: Orange County." March 1995. Sacramento: State of California.

California State Library Foundation Bulletin. 1988. "Special Issue—Proposition 13." July, no. 24, pp. 1–31.

Callahan, John, and Ruth Bosek. 1976. "State Assumptions of Urban Responsibilities: Exception to the Rule or Wave of the Future?" In Alan Campbell and Roy Bahl (eds.), *State and Local Government: The Politics of Reform.* New York: Free Press, pp. 79–91.

Campbell, Alan, and Roy Bahl. 1976. "The Implications of Local Government Reform: Efficiency, Equity, Cost and Administrative Dimensions." In Alan Campbell and Roy Bahl (eds.), *State and Local Government: The Politics of Reform.* New York: Free Press, pp. 185–203.

Campbell, Alan, and Judith Dollenmeyer. 1976. "Governance in a Metropolitan Society." In Amos Hawley and Vincent Rock (eds.), *Metropolitan America in Contemporary Perspective.* New York: John Wiley & Sons, pp. 355–396.

Carroll, Stephen, Kevin McCarthy, and Mitchell Wade. 1994. "California's Looming Budget Crisis." *RAND Research Review* 18 (2):1–4, 15.

Center for Demographic Research. 1996. "Orange County Cities." June 17.
Fullerton: California State University.

Chapman, Jeffrey. 1996. "The Challenge of Entrepreneurship: An Orange
County Case Study." *Municipal Finance Journal* 17:16–32.

Citrin, Jack. 1979. "Do People Want Something for Nothing?" *National Tax
Journal* 32:113–130.

Clark, Terry. 1976. "How Many More New York's?" *New York Affairs* 3 (4):
1–10.

———. 1978. "Issues in Financial Management of Local Governments. Final
Report." September. Washington, DC: U.S. Conference of Mayors.

———, ed. 1994a. *Urban Innovation.* Thousand Oaks, CA: Sage.

———. 1994b. "Municipal Fiscal Strain: Indicators and Causes."
Government Finance Review, June, pp. 27–29.

———. 1994c. "Program for a New Public Choice." In James Chan (ed.),
Research in Governmental and Nonprofit Accounting. Greenwich, CT: JAI
Press, pp. 3–28.

Clark, Terry, Daniel Crane, Ann Kelley, Joanne Malinowski, Melissa Pappas,
and Gregory Wass. 1992. "Taxes in Chicago and Its Suburbs: A
Comparison of Tax Burdens in the City of Chicago and Ten Suburbs."
Research in Urban Policy 4:3–29.

Clark, Terry, and Lorna Ferguson. 1981. "Political Leadership and Urban
Fiscal Policy." In Terry Clark (ed.), *Urban Policy Analysis: Directions for
Future Research.* Beverly Hills: Sage, pp. 81–102.

———. 1983. *City Money.* New York: Columbia University Press.

Clark, Terry, and Ronald Inglehart. 1997. "The New Political Culture." In
Terry Clark (ed.), *The New Political Culture.* Boulder, CO: Westview
Press, forthcoming.

Committee of the Whole. 1995. "Second Extraordinary Session of the
California State Assembly: Orange County Insolvency." March 8.
Sacramento: State of California.

County of Orange. 1993. *1993 Census Report, Volume 4.* Santa Ana, CA:
County of Orange.

———. 1994. *FY 1993–94 Annual Budget.* Santa Ana, CA: County of
Orange.

———. 1995a. "Financial Condition and Pool Settlement Presentation."
March 15. Santa Ana, CA: County of Orange.

———. 1995b. "Financial and Legal Update: Presentation from the Office of
the CEO." July 18. Santa Ana, CA: County of Orange.

———. 1996a. "Restructuring Plan for the County of Orange." June 20.
Santa Ana, CA: County of Orange.

———. 1996b. "First Report on the Restructuring Plan for the County of
Orange." November 19. Santa Ana, CA: County of Orange.

Courant, Paul, Edward Gramlich, and Daniel Rubinfeld. 1979. "Tax
Limitations and the Demand for Public Services in Michigan." *National
Tax Journal* 32:147–157.

———. 1980. "Why Voters Support Tax Limitation Amendments: The
Michigan Case." *National Tax Journal* 33:1–20.

Danielson, Michael. 1976. *The Politics of Exclusion*. New York: Columbia University Press.

DiMento, Joseph, and LeRoy Graymer. 1991. *Confronting Regional Challenges*. Cambridge, MA: Lincoln Institute.

Dolan, D. 1990. "Local Government Fragmentation: Does It Drive up the Cost of Government?" *Urban Affairs Quarterly* 26:28–45.

Dowall, David. 1984. *The Suburban Squeeze*. Berkeley: University of California Press.

E & Y Kenneth Leventhal. 1996. *Residential Data Trends, September 1996*. Newport Beach, CA: E & Y Kenneth Leventhal Real Estate Group.

Ellwood, John, and Mary Sprague. 1995. "Options for Reforming the California State Budget Process." In Bruce Cain and Roger Noll (eds.), *Constitutional Reform in California*. Berkeley: Institute of Governmental Studies Press.

Employment Development Department. 1996. *California Annual Average Labor Force and Industrial Employment*. Sacramento: State of California.

Farley, Reynolds, and William H. Frey. 1994. "Changes in the Segregation of Whites from Blacks During the 1980s: Small Steps Toward a More Integrated Society." *American Sociological Review* 59:23–45.

Fay, Stephen. 1996. *The Collapse of Barings*. London: Richard Cohen Books.

Federal Reserve Bank. 1996. "Federal Funds Rate History." Personal memo from Joseph Mattey, December 9. San Francisco: Federal Reserve Bank.

Fischer, Claude S. 1984. *The Urban Experience*. New York: Harcourt Brace Jovanovich.

Flickinger, Barbara, and Katherine McManus. 1996. "Bankruptcy Aftershocks." January. *Public Management*, pp. 16–23.

Frey, William. 1993. "People in Places: Demographic Trends in Urban America." In *Rediscovering Urban America: Perspectives on the 1980s*. Washington, DC: U.S. Department of Housing and Urban Development, pp. 3-1-3-106.

———. 1994. "Minority Suburbanization and Continued White Flight in U.S. Metropolitan Areas: Assessing Findings from the 1990 Census." *Research in Community Sociology* 4:15–42.

Fuchs, Ester R. 1992. *Mayors and Money: Fiscal Policy in New York and Chicago*. Chicago: University of Chicago Press.

Gold, Steven. 1990. "State Government Monitoring of Local Trends." In Terry Clark (ed.), *Monitoring Local Governments: How Personal Computers Can Help Systematize Municipal Fiscal Stress*. Dubuque, IA: Kendall/Hunt, pp. 213–217.

Government Finance Review. 1996. "SEC Actions in Orange County Investigation." April, pp. 13–15.

Government Practices Oversight Committee. 1996. "A Review of Governance in Orange County, California." August 1996. Santa Ana, CA: County of Orange.

Green, Leroy. 1979. "Staff Report on Conference Report on AB 8, July 18." Sacramento: State of California.

Hahn, Paul. 1988. "Proposition 13, Ten Years Later: Finances, Local Control and the Common Good." Berkeley: California Policy Seminar.

Harvey, Richard B. 1993. *The Dynamics of California Government and Politics*. Dubuque, IA: Kendall/Hunt.

Hector, Gary. 1995. "Securities Class-Action Lawyers Blame Merrill Lynch for Orange County's Bankruptcy." *California Lawyer*, August, pp. 36–39, 90, 91.

Hoffman, Wayne Lee, and Terry Clark. 1979. "Citizen Preferences and Urban Policy Types." In John P. Blair and David Nachmias (eds.), *Fiscal Retrenchment and Urban Policy*. Urban Affairs Annual Reviews, vol. 17. Beverly Hills: Sage, pp. 85–106.

Huston, Janet. 1995. "Council of Governments Background Materials." November 22. Santa Ana, CA: Orange County Division, League of California Cities.

Jackson, Kenneth. 1985. *Crabgrass Frontier: The Suburbanization of the United States*. New York: Oxford University Press.

Jeffe, Sherry Bebitch. 1995. "It Isn't Easy Being Orange." *California Journal* 26 (5):21.

Johnson, Craig, and John Mikesell. 1996. "The Orange County Debacle: Where Irresponsible Cash and Debt Management Practices Collide." *Municipal Finance Journal* 17: 1-15.

Johnson, Hans. 1996. *Undocumented Immigration to California: 1980–1993*. San Francisco: Public Policy Institute of California.

Johnston, Michael. 1996. "Understanding Organizations in Crisis: Local Governments and the Orange County Bankruptcy." *Municipal Finance Journal* 17:33–50.

Jorion, Philippe. 1995. *Big Bets Gone Bad*. New York: Harcourt Brace Jovanovich.

Jump, Bernard. 1996. "Six Easy Lessons: Learning from Orange County." *Municipal Finance Journal* 17:81–94.

Kanarek, Abby, and Mark Baldassare. 1996. "Preferences for State and Regional Planning Efforts among California Mayors and City Planning Directors." *Journal of Planning Education and Research* 16:92–102.

Kasarda, John. 1978. "Urbanization, Community and the Metropolitan Problem." In David Street (ed.), *The Handbook of Contemporary Urban Life*. San Francisco: Jossey-Bass, pp. 27–57.

Kaufman, George, and Kenneth Rosen. 1981. *The Property Tax Revolt: The Case of Proposition 13*. Cambridge, MA: Ballinger.

KCAL. 1993. "Los Angeles Mayoral Runoff, May 1993." Los Angeles: KCAL Television News.

Kearns, Kevin P. 1995. "Accountability and Entrepreneurial Public Management: The Case of the Orange County Investment Fund." *Public Budgeting and Finance* 15 (3):3–21.

Kling, Rob, Spencer Olin, and Mark Poster. 1991. *Postsuburban California: The Transformation of Orange County since World War II*. Berkeley: University of California Press.

Koehler, Cortius. 1983. *Managing California Counties*. Sacramento: California State Association of Counties.

Ladd, Helen, and Julie Wilson. 1982. "Why Voters Support Tax Limitations: Evidence from Massachusetts Proposition 2½." *National Tax Journal* 35:121–148.

Laffer, Arthur, and Jan P. Seymour. 1979. *The Economics of the Tax Revolt: A Reader.* New York: Harcourt Brace Jovanovich.

Lazarovici, Laureen. 1995. "Counties in Crisis." *California Journal* 26 (11):32–34.

Leeson, Nick. 1996. *Rogue Trader.* Boston: Little, Brown.

Legislative Analyst. 1993a. *Common Cents: Background Material on State and Local Government Finances.* Sacramento: State of California.

———. 1993b. *1993–1994 Budget: Perspectives and Issues.* Sacramento: State of California.

———. 1994. *Focus: Budget 1994.* Sacramento: State of California.

———. 1995a. *Cal Guide: A Profile of State Programs.* Sacramento: State of California.

———. 1995b. *Los Angeles County's Fiscal Problems.* Sacramento: State of California.

———. 1995c. *A Review of the Orange County Recovery Plan as Proposed August 22, 1995.* Sacramento: State of California.

———. 1996a. *Cal Facts: California's Economy and Budget in Perspective.* Sacramento: State of California.

———. 1996b. *Understanding Proposition 218.* Sacramento: State of California.

Lewis, Carol. 1996. "The Bond Market and Bankruptcy: A Civic Perspective." *Municipal Finance Journal* 17:51–80.

Lewis, Paul. 1996. *Shaping Suburbia: How Political Institutions Organize Urban Development.* Pittsburgh: University of Pittsburgh Press.

Liebschutz, Sarah. 1991. *Bargaining under Federalism: Contemporary New York.* Albany: State University of New York Press.

Lipset, Seymour, and William Schneider. 1983. *The Confidence Gap.* New York: Free Press.

Lo, Clarence. 1990. *Small Property versus Big Government: Social Origins of the Property Tax Revolt.* Berkeley: University of California Press.

Logan, John, and Harvey Molotch. 1987. *Urban Fortunes: The Political Economy of Place.* Berkeley: University of California Press.

Logan, John, and Mark Schneider. 1981. "The Stratification of Metropolitan Suburbs: 1950 to 1970." *American Sociological Review* 46:175–186.

———. 1982. "Governmental Organization and City-Suburb Income Inequality, 1970–1980." *Urban Affairs Quarterly* 17:303–318.

Los Angeles Times Orange County Edition. 1994a. "Tustin Pulls Its Money out of County Portfolio." April 14, p. B-1.

———. 1994b. "OC Treasurer Thrust into Spotlight over Risk Claims." April 30, p. A-1.

———. 1994c. "OC Treasury Turmoil Puts Officials on Alert." May 5, p. B-1.

———. 1994d. "Treasury Candidate Reiterates Concerns." May 13, p. B-2.

———. 1994e. "Treasurer Candidate Says County Portfolio Value Down." June 1, p. B-7.

———. 1995a. "Bankruptcy Saga." June 18, p. A-26.

———. 1995b. "Orange County to Recover Money Held by Brokerages." November 11, p. A-1.

———. 1995c. "Orange County Budget Puzzle Tough to Crack." March 5, p. A-1.

———. 1995d. "Popejoy Calls for 1,040 Layoffs." March 8, p. A-1.

———. 1995e. "OCTA May Offer Loan to Tide the County Over." January 10, p. A-1.

———. 1995f. "Orange County Plans to Lay off 400 Workers." January 11, p. A-1.

———. 1995g. "Council, School Leaders Hit Divide on Measure R." May 28, p. A-1.

———. 1996a. "Its Overdue Debt Paid, Orange County Exits Bankruptcy." June 13, p. A-1.

———. 1996b. "Orange County Sues Five Firms in Its Bid to Recover Investment Losses." June 12, p. A-1.

———. 1996c. "Misconduct Charges against Stanton and Steiner Dismissed." November 27, p. A-1.

———. 1996d. "SEC to Charge Merrill Lynch over Bonds." September 20, p. D-5.

———. 1996e. "County CEO Unveils Reorganization Plan." November 15, p. A-1.

———. 1996f. "O.C. Bankruptcy All but Over." June 6, p. A-1.

———. 1996g. "Citron Sentenced to a Year in Jail and $100,000 Fine." November 20, p. A-1.

———. 1996h. "Charter Campaign Instantly in Full Swing." November 30, p. B-6.

———. 1997a. "Orange County Investment Pools Draw Top Rating." March 2, p. D-1.

———. 1997b. "Trial of Raabe, Ex–Citron Aide, to Begin Today." March 24, p. A-1.

———. 1997c. "Raabe Guilty in Bankruptcy Case." May 3, p. A-1.

———. 1997d. "220 Positions Eliminated in County Reorganization." May 17, p. A-1.

———. 1997e. "Skimming Scheme was Raabe's, Citron Testifies." April 1, p. A-1.

———. 1997f. "O.C. Debt has Big Projects on Indefinite Hold." April 22, p. A-1.

———. 1997g. "Three Years After the Fall." December 6, p. A-1.

Masotti, Louis, and Jeffrey Hadden. 1973. *The Urbanization of the Suburbs.* Beverly Hills: Sage.

———. 1974. *Suburbia in Transition.* New York: New Viewpoints.

McClelland, Peter, and Alan L. Magdovitz. 1981. *Crisis in the Making: The Political Economy of New York State since 1945.* New York: Cambridge University Press.

McConnell, Malcolm. 1987. *Challenger: A Major Malfunction.* New York: Doubleday.

Merrill Lynch. 1995. "Setting the Record Straight: The Facts on the Orange County Bankruptcy." October. New York: Merrill Lynch.

———. 1997. "Merrill Lynch Agrees to Civil Settlement with the Orange County District Attorney." June 19. New York: Merrill Lynch.

Michelson, William. 1976. *Man and His Urban Environment*. Reading, MA: Addison Wesley.

Miller, Gary. 1981. *Cities by Contract*. Cambridge, MA: MIT Press.

Miller, Merton and Lexicon, Inc. 1996. "The Orange County Bankruptcy and Its Aftermath: Some New Evidence." April 25. Chicago: Miller, Merton and Lexicon, Inc.

Misczynski, Dean. 1984. "Perspectives on State and Local Finance. Senate Office of Research, January." Sacramento: State of California.

Moorlach, John. 1996. "Orange County Investment Pool Then and Now: Under New Management." January 31. Santa Ana, CA: Orange County Treasurer–Tax Collector.

Neiman, Max. 1980. "Zoning Policy, Income Clustering and Suburban Change." *Social Science Quarterly* 61:666–675.

New York Times. 1994a. "In Rare Move, California County Files for Bankruptcy Protection." December 7, p. A-1.

———. 1994b. "New Finger-Pointing in Orange County." December 10, p. A-1.

———. 1994c. "Risk Is Cited in Six More California Counties." December 22, p. A-1.

———. 1994d. "The Search for Municipal Cowboys." December 22, p. C-1.

———. 1995a. "A Bankruptcy Peculiar to California." January 6, p. A-1.

———. 1995b. "Bankrupt Orange County Sues Peat Marwick for $3 Billion." December 21, p. C-6.

———. 1995c. "Gov. Wilson's Veto Deals Setback to Orange County." August 3, p. A-1.

———. 1995d. "Orange County Adopts Plan to Get out of Bankruptcy." December 22, p. A-1.

———. 1995e. "Orange County Poor Are Feeling Much of the Pain." December 5, p. A-1.

———. 1996. "Leaving Bankruptcy, Orange County Sues for Damages." June 12, p. C-3.

Office of Senate Floor Analysis. 1995. "1995. Digest of Significant Legislation: Orange County/Los Angeles County Recovery Legislation." Sacramento, CA: State of California.

Office of the Treasurer–Tax Collector. 1991. "Annual 1990-1991 Financial Statement." August 28. Santa Ana, CA: County of Orange.

Office of the Treasurer–Tax Collector. 1993. "Annual 1992–1993 Financial Statement." September 10. Santa Ana, CA: County of Orange.

Orange County Business Council. 1995. "Report from the Orange County Business Council Restructuring Task Force." August 7. Irvine, CA: Orange County Business Council.

Orange County Grand Jury. 1995a. "Orange County Grand Jury Report, November 15, 1995." Santa Ana, CA: County of Orange.

————. 1995b. "Orange County Grand Jury Report, November 6, 1995." Santa Ana, CA: County of Orange.

Orange County Investment Pool. 1995a. "Orange County Investment Pool Bankruptcy: Update." January 11. Santa Ana, CA: Orange County Investment Pool.

————. 1995b. "Orange County Investment Pool Bankruptcy: Update." January 20. Santa Ana, CA: Orange County Investment Pool.

————. 1995c. "Orange County Investment Pool Bankruptcy: Update." April 12. Santa Ana, CA: Orange County Investment Pool.

————. 1995d. "Orange County Investment Pool Bankruptcy: Update." August 9. Santa Ana, CA: Orange County Investment Pool.

Orange County Register. 1995a. "A County in Bankruptcy: Report to the Taxpayers, First Quarter." March 12, special section.

————. "Chronology: A County in Bankruptcy." September 3, p. G-2.

————. 1996a. "Orange County: Southern California's Wealthiest Market." November.

————. 1996b. "Bankruptcy Is over, Challenges Remain." June 13, p. A-1.

————. 1996c. "Suit Targets Orange County over Bankruptcy Diversions." December 19, p. A-1.

————. 1996d. "Supervisors Inclined to Rein in CEO." December 20, p. A-1.

————. 1997. "Citron Will Swap Jail for Clerical Duties." January 10, p. A-1.

Orange County Registrar of Voters. 1991. "Final Vote, May 1991 Special Election." Santa Ana, CA: County of Orange.

————. 1994. "Final Vote, June 1994 Primary." Santa Ana, CA: County of Orange.

————. 1995. "Final Vote, June 1994 Special Election." Santa Ana, CA: County of Orange.

————. 1996a. "Final Vote, March 1996 Primary." Santa Ana, CA: County of Orange.

————. 1996b. "Final Vote, November 1996 General Election." Santa Ana, CA: County of Orange.

Ostrom, Elinor. 1983. "The Social Stratification–Government Inequality Thesis Explored." *Urban Affairs Quarterly* 19:91–112.

Ostrom, Elinor, and Robert Parks. 1973. "Suburban Police Departments: Too Many and Too Small?" In Louis Masotti and Jeffrey Hadden (eds.), *The Urbanization of the Suburbs.* Beverly Hills: Sage, pp. 367–402.

O'Sullivan, Arthur, Terri Sexton, and Steven Sheffrin. 1995. *Property Taxes and the Tax Revolt: The Legacy of Proposition 13.* New York: Cambridge University Press.

Palen, John. 1992. *The Urban World.* New York: McGraw-Hill.

————. 1995. *The Suburbs.* New York: McGraw-Hill.

Paterno, Susan. 1995. "When the Watchdogs Don't Bark." *American Journalism Review* 17:22–29.

Petersen, John E. 1995. "Municipal Bond Market: The Post–Orange County Era." *Governing* November, pp. 77–87.

Peterson, Paul. 1981. *City Limits.* Chicago: University of Chicago Press.

Pisarki, Alan. 1987. *Commuting in America: A National Report on Commuting Patterns and Trends*. Westport, CT: Eno Foundation.

Poole, Robert. 1995. "Rescuing Orange County." Policy Study no. 186. Los Angeles: Reason Foundation.

Popenoe, David. 1985. *Private Pleasure, Public Plight: American Metropolitan Community Life*. New Brunswick, NJ: Transaction Press.

Presidential Commission on the Space Shuttle *Challenger* Accident. 1986. *Report to the President, Volume I*. Washington, DC: U.S. Government Printing Office.

Rawnsley, Judith. 1995. *Total Risk: Nick Leeson and the Fall of Barings Bank*. New York: HarperCollins.

Raymond, Valerie. 1988. *Surviving Proposition 13: Fiscal Crisis in California Counties*. Berkeley, CA: Institute of Governmental Studies.

Reed, Deborah, Melissa Glenn Haber, and Laura Mameesh. 1996. *The Distribution of Income in California*. San Francisco: Public Policy Institute of California.

Romero, Philip, and Andrew Chang. 1994. "Shifting the Costs of a Failed Federal Policy: The Net Fiscal Impact of Illegal Immigrants in California." Sacramento: State of California, Governor's Office of Planning and Research.

Saltzstein, Alan. 1996. "Los Angeles: Politics without Governance." In H. V. Savitch and Ronald K. Vogel (eds.), *Regional Politics: America in a Post-City Age*. Thousand Oaks, CA: Sage, pp. 51–71.

San Francisco Chronicle. 1992. "Sacramento in Review." September 21, p. A-17.

———. 1995. "The Mayor's Race Benchmark Survey, August 1995, Final Report." San Francisco: San Francisco Chronicle.

———. 1996. "San Francisco November Election, October 1996, Final Report." San Francisco: San Francisco Chronicle.

Schlay, Ann, and Peter Rossi. 1981. "Putting Policies into Urban Ecology: Estimating Net Effects of Zoning." In Terry Clark and Lorna Ferguson (eds.), *Urban Policy Analysis*. Beverly Hills: Sage, pp. 257–286.

Schneider, Mark. 1989. *The Competitive City: The Political Economy of Suburbia*. Pittsburgh: University of Pittsburgh Press.

Schneider, Mark, and John Logan. 1981. "Fiscal Implications of Class Segregation: Inequalities in the Distribution of Public Goods and Services in Suburban Municipalities." *Urban Affairs Quarterly* 17:23–36.

———. 1982. "The Effects of Local Government Finances on Community Growth Rates: A Test of the Tiebout Model." *Urban Affairs Quarterly* 18:91–105.

Schneider, Mark, Paul Teske, and Michael Mintrom. 1995. *Public Entrepreneurs: Agents for Change in American Government*. Princeton, NJ: Princeton University Press.

Schneider, William. 1991. "Rule Suburbia: America in the 1990s." *National Journal* 39:2335–2336.

Schwadron, Terry, and Paul Richter. 1984. *California and the American Tax Revolt*. Berkeley: University of California Press.

Scott, Steve. 1995a. "Allen Wins, Willie Grins." California Journal
    26 (7):14–15.
———. 1995b. "Changing of the Right Guard." California Journal
    26 (10): 8–12.
Sears, David O., and Jack Citrin. 1982. Tax Revolt: Something for Nothing
    in California. Cambridge, MA: Harvard University Press.
Secretary of State. 1972. Statement of the Vote, November 1972. Sacramento:
    State of California.
———. 1978. Statement of the Vote, June 1978. Sacramento: State of
    California.
———. 1979. Statement of the Vote, November 1979. Sacramento: State of
    California.
———. 1980. Statement of the Vote, November 1980. Sacramento: State of
    California.
———. 1984. Statement of the Vote, November 1984. Sacramento: State of
    California.
———. 1988. Statement of the Vote, November 1988. Sacramento: State of
    California.
———. 1990. Statement of the Vote, November 1990. Sacramento: State of
    California.
———. 1992. Statement of the Vote, November 1992. Sacramento: State of
    California.
———. 1993. Statement of the Vote, November 1993. Sacramento: State of
    California.
———. 1994. Statement of the Vote, November 1994. Sacramento: State of
    California.
———. 1996. Statement of the Vote, November 1996. Sacramento: State of
    California.
Senate Special Committee on Local Government Investments. 1994.
    "Hearing, Monday, December 19." Sacramento: State of California.
———. 1995a. "Hearing, Tuesday, January 17." Sacramento: State of
    California.
———. 1995b. "Hearing, Friday, March 3." Sacramento: State of California.
———. 1995c. "Hearing, Friday, March 23." Sacramento: State of
    California.
———. 1995d. "Hearing, Friday, May 16." Sacramento: State of California.
———. 1995e. "Hearing, Friday, August 22." Sacramento: State of
    California.
Shefter, Martin. 1985. Political Crisis, Fiscal Crisis: The Collapse and Revival
    of New York City. New York: Basic Books.
Shields, Regis. 1995. "Investment Pitfalls: Five Simple Rules to Keep You out
    of the News." California County, July/August, pp. 30–31.
Sinnreich, Masha. 1980. New York: World City. Cambridge, MA:
    Oelgeschlager, Gunn and Hain.
Stahura, John. 1986. "Suburban Development, Black Suburbanization and
    the Civil Rights Movement since World War II." American Sociological
    Review 51:131–144.

Stanton, Roger. 1995. "Memo on the Subject: The Restructuring of Orange
County Government." January 2. Santa Ana, CA: County of Orange.

State Controller. 1978. *Financial Transactions Concerning Counties of
California, Annual Report 1977–1978*. Sacramento: State of California.

———. 1990. *Financial Transactions Concerning Counties of California,
Annual Report 1989–1990*. Sacramento: State of California.

———. 1991. *Financial Transactions Concerning Counties of California,
Annual Report 1990–1991*. Sacramento: State of California.

———. 1992a. *Financial Transactions Concerning School Districts of
California, Annual Report 1991–1992*. Sacramento: State of California.

———. 1992b. *Financial Transactions Concerning Special Districts of
California, Annual Report 1991–1992*. Sacramento: State of California.

———. 1992c. *Financial Transactions Concerning Counties of California,
Annual Report 1991–1992*. Sacramento: State of California.

———. 1993. *Financial Transactions Concerning Counties of California,
Annual Report 1992–1993*. Sacramento: State of California.

———. 1994. *Financial Transactions Concerning Counties of California,
Annual Report 1993–1994*. Sacramento: State of California.

State Senate. 1989. *Your Guide to Open Meetings: The Ralph M. Brown Act*.
Sacramento: State of California.

———. 1995. "Background Paper for the Hearing of the Senate Special
Committee on Local Government Investments, January 17." Sacramento:
State of California.

State Treasurer. 1995. *Task Force on Local and State Investment Practices:
Recommendations and Analysis*. Sacramento: State of California.

Stein, Robert. 1990. *Urban Alternatives*. Pittsburgh: University of Pittsburgh
Press.

Steinberg, James, David Lyon, and Mary Vaiana. 1992. *Urban America: Policy
Choices for Los Angeles and the Nation*. Santa Monica, CA: RAND.

Teaford, Jon C. 1997. *Post-Suburbia: Government and Politics in the Edge
Cities*. Baltimore: Johns Hopkins University Press.

Teitz, Michael. 1996. American Planning in the 1990s: Evolution, Debate and
Challenge." *Urban Studies* 33:649–671.

Tiebout, Charles. 1956. "A Pure Theory of Local Expenditures." *Journal of
Political Economy* 64:416–424.

Times Orange County Poll. 1989. "Ethics and Values." January. Costa Mesa,
CA: *Los Angeles Times* Orange County Edition.

———. 1992. "June Primary." May. Costa Mesa, CA: *Los Angeles Times*
Orange County Edition.

———. 1994a. "June Primary." May. Costa Mesa, CA: *Los Angeles Times*
Orange County Edition.

———. 1994b. "November Election." October. Costa Mesa, CA: *Los
Angeles Times* Orange County Edition.

———. 1994c. "Orange County Bankruptcy Poll." December. Costa Mesa,
CA: *Los Angeles Times* Orange County Edition.

———. 1995a. "Orange County Poor." September. Costa Mesa, CA: *Los
Angeles Times* Orange County Edition.

———. 1995b. "Orange County Bankruptcy Poll II: Coping with Crisis."
    January. Costa Mesa, CA: *Los Angeles Times* Orange County Edition.
———. 1995c. "Orange County Bankruptcy Poll III: Measure R Benchmark
    Survey." April. Costa Mesa, CA: *Los Angeles Times* Orange County
    Edition.
———. 1995d. "Measure R Pre-election Survey." June. Costa Mesa, CA:
    Los Angeles Times Orange County Edition.
———. 1996a. "Orange County Primary, Final Report." March. Costa Mesa,
    CA: *Los Angeles Times* Orange County Edition.
———. 1996b. "November Election, Final Report." October. Costa Mesa,
    CA: *Los Angeles Times* Orange County Edition.
Tuchman, Barbara W. 1984. *The March of Folly*. New York: Alfred A. Knopf.
United Way of Orange County. 1996. "United Way Forms $450,000
    Emergency Loan Consortium with Orange County Business Leaders to
    Help Charities." January 12. Irvine, CA: United Way of Orange County.
U.S. Bureau of the Census. 1951. *Census of Population, 1950*. Washington,
    DC: U.S. Government Printing Office.
———. 1961. *Census of Population, 1960*. Washington, DC: U.S.
    Government Printing Office.
———. 1977. *County and City Data Book, 1975*. Washington, DC: U.S.
    Government Printing Office.
———. 1987. "Patterns of Metropolitan Area and County Growth, 1980 to
    1987." *Current Population Reports*, series P-25, no. 139.
———. 1994. *County and City Data Book, 1994*. Washington, DC: U.S.
    Government Printing Office.
Wall Street Journal. 1995. "Orange County Names Chief to Cut Costs."
    February 13, p. B-5.
———. 1997. "Orange County Sells Bonds in an Unusual Transaction."
    January 15, p. C-1.
Weiher, Gregory. 1991. *The Fractured Metropolis: Political Fragmentation
    and Metropolitan Segregation*. Albany: State University of New York
    Press.
Zhang, Peter. 1995. *Barings Bankruptcy and Financial Derivatives*.
    Singapore: World Scientific.
Zimmer, Basil. 1976. "Suburbia and the Changing Political Structure." In
    Barry Schwartz (ed.), *The Changing Face of the Suburbs*. Chicago:
    University of Chicago Press, pp. 165–202.

Index

Mark Baldassare is a Senior
Fellow at the Public Policy
Institute of California in San
Francisco. He is founder and
Director of the Orange County
Annual Survey at the University
of California, Irvine, and the au-
thor of numerous books in urban
politics. Photo by Felipe Vasquez.